Escaping Nazi Europe

This book chronicles the escapes attempted by Belgian soldiers and civilians from Nazi-occupied Europe during the Second World War. Insofar as is practical, the authors have tried to let the subjects speak for themselves by making extensive use of their testimonies preserved in archives in Belgium and the United Kingdom.

The book begins with the stories of soldiers who managed to evade capture in the summer of 1940 and returned home, and the few that decided to continue the fight and joined the Allied forces in the United Kingdom. It also includes the prisoners of war who managed to escape from camps or *Arbeitskommando* inside the Reich and provides a detailed analysis of their narratives: their motivation for going on the run, their choices on when and how to travel, and the many obstacles they encountered along the way. Most escapees were content to return home, with some then joining resistance organisations, but a small minority were committed to joining the Allies, and further chapters recount their attempts to reach Spain and Switzerland, and the additional problems they encountered in those neutral states.

Final chapters reflect on the penalties inflicted on prisoners of war who were recaptured and on the escapees' struggle for recognition in the post-war world.

Bernard Wilkin (b. 1982) is Senior Researcher at the State Archives of Belgium. He has published several books and articles on the history of war in Belgium and France, including *Aerial Propaganda and the Wartime Occupation of France*, *French Soldiers' Morale in the Phoney War* (with Maude Williams) and *Fighting for Napoleon* (with René Wilkin).

Bob Moore (b. 1954) is Emeritus Professor of European History at the University of Sheffield. He has published extensively on the history of Western Europe in the mid-twentieth century, including in this context *The British Empire and Its Italian Prisoners of War 1940–1947* (with Kent Fedorowich, 2003), *Prisoners of War, Prisoners of Peace* (edited with Barbara Hately, 2005) and *Prisoners of War: Europe 1939–1956* (2022).

Routledge Studies in Second World War History

The Second World War remains today the most seismic political event of the past hundred years, an unimaginable upheaval that impacted upon every country on earth and is fully ingrained in the consciousness of the world's citizens. Traditional narratives of the conflict are entrenched to such a degree that new research takes on an ever important role in helping us make sense of World War II. Aiming to bring to light the results of new archival research and exploring notions of memory, propaganda, genocide, empire and culture, Routledge Studies in Second World War History sheds new light on the events and legacy of global war.

Recent titles in this series

Politics of Death
The Cult of Nazi Martyrs, 1920-1939
Jesús Casquete

Emotions in Yiddish Ghetto Diaries
Encountering Persecutors and Questioning Humanity
Amy Simon

The Allied Bombing of Central Italy
The Restoration of the Nile Mosaic and Sanctuary of Fortuna at Palestrina
Teresa Fava Thomas

Warlord Hitler
With Reference to the Campaign in Southern Russia in 1942
Alan Donohue

Escaping Nazi Europe
Understanding the Experiences of Belgian Soldiers and Civilians
in World War II
Bernard Wilkin and Bob Moore

For more information about this series, please visit: https://www.routledge.com/
Routledge-Studies-in-Second-World-War-History/book-series/WWII

Escaping Nazi Europe
Understanding the Experiences of Belgian Soldiers and Civilians in World War II

Bernard Wilkin and Bob Moore

LONDON AND NEW YORK

First published 2024
by Routledge
4 Park Square, Milton Park, Abingdon, Oxon OX14 4RN

and by Routledge
605 Third Avenue, New York, NY 10158

Routledge is an imprint of the Taylor & Francis Group, an informa business

British Library Cataloguing-in-Publication Data
A catalogue record for this book is available from the British Library

Library of Congress Cataloging-in-Publication Data
Names: Wilkin, Bernard, author. | Moore, Bob, 1954- author.
Title: Escaping Nazi Europe : understanding the experiences of Belgian soldiers and civilians in World War II / Bernard Wilkin and Bob Moore.
Description: New York : Routledge, 2024. | Series: Routledge studies in Second World War history | Includes bibliographical references and index.
Identifiers: LCCN 2023028940 (print) | LCCN 2023028941 (ebook) | ISBN 9780367136420 (hardback) | ISBN 9781032621104 (paperback) | ISBN 9780429027697 (ebook)
Subjects: LCSH: World War, 1939–1945—Personal narratives, Belgian. | Prisoner-of-war escapes—Belgium—History. | Escaped prisoners of war—Belgium—Biography. | Prisoners of war—Belgium—Biography. | Soldiers—Belgium—Biography. | Belgium. Armée—History—20th century. | Belgium—History—German occupation, 1940–1945.
Classification: LCC D805.B4 W55 2024 (print) | LCC D805.B4 (ebook) | DDC 940.54/720922—dc23/eng/20230909
LC record available at https://lccn.loc.gov/2023028940
LC ebook record available at https://lccn.loc.gov/2023028941

ISBN: 9780367136420 (hbk)
ISBN: 9781032621104 (pbk)
ISBN: 9780429027697 (ebk)

DOI: 10.4324/9780429027697

Typeset in TimesNewRoman
by codeMantra

Contents

Acknowledgements

This book is based primarily on the post-war testimonies of Belgian prisoners of war and civilians who attempted to escape from captivity in Nazi-occupied Europe. These were collected by both the Belgian and British governments. From 1944, the Belgian authorities compiled the stories primarily to award the Escapees' Cross to those who had fled the occupied territories to carry on the fight against Germany and her allies or had escaped from Stalags and Oflags. The British authorities' primary motivations were to unmask enemy agents masquerading as escapers or evaders at the time of their arrival in the United Kingdom during the war, and then in trying to understand and subsequently honour the escape networks that helped Allied servicemen inside occupied territories and in the neutral European states. Most of these latter testimonies are held in files from various record groups at the National Archives at Kew in London.

In compiling this book, Bob Moore would like to thank Frank Caestecker (Ghent), Barbara Hately (Sheffield) and Elizabeth Moore for their help in researching and revising the manuscript as well as acknowledging the help of fellowships from both the Lichtenberg-Kolleg in Göttingen and the Zentrum für Holocaust-Studien at the Institut für Zeitgeschichte in Munich. The authors also owe a debt of gratitude to Lynda Depienne for permission to quote from family papers that describe her father's escape from German captivity and his sojourn in the Soviet Union. Bernard Wilkin is grateful to the staff from the Archives de l'État (Liège and Brussels branches), especially Antoine Bonnivert, Sébastien Dubois and Michel Trigalet, the CEGES/SOMA and Pierre Lierneux from the Musée de la Guerre in Brussels.

Introduction

During the Second World War up to 6 million soldiers, sailors and aircrew were captured by German forces and became prisoners of war inside the Third Reich. By far the largest contingent came from the 5.8 million members of the Red Army taken during the war on the Eastern Front, although more than half died in the early stages of captivity. In addition, there were 1.8 million Frenchmen surrendered by their leaders in June 1940 and more than 1 million Italian military personnel interned after the armistice with the Allies in September 1943. While these three groups formed the bulk of the prisoner population – and of the labour force deployed in the German war economy – other occupied countries were also represented, including Belgium. On the outbreak of war on 10 May 1940 the Belgian armed forces numbered some 650,000 men and approximately 50,000 were taken prisoner during the eighteen-day campaign that followed.[1] A further 150,000 were rounded up by the victorious German forces inside Belgium and a further 25,000 formally handed over after the Franco-German armistice in June.[2] Remarkably, the remaining 425,000 servicemen, either in Belgium or in France, seem to have been able to return home without being formally demobilised.[3] Most of the 225,000 prisoners of war were initially taken to camps in Germany, but the Flemish elements were soon released on Hitler's direct order, leaving only around 100,000 Walloon (French-speaking) prisoners. Their numbers would be reduced over time by medical and other repatriations and by escapes, so that by 1942 German figures indicated only around 70,000 were still held in Oflags and Stalags across the Reich.[4]

In many respects, their experiences in four years of captivity paralleled those of their more numerous French counterparts – of life in camps and then being allocated to *Arbeitskommando* for work outside in the German war economy. While diaries, memoirs and autobiographies have chronicled their existence as prisoners, this book concentrates primarily on the small minority of soldiers and civilians who, for a variety of reasons, refused to accept their situation and attempted to evade capture or escape from captivity after the Belgian surrender on 29 May 1940. For some serving soldiers it was just a question of returning home, while for others it was a deliberate attempt to continue the armed struggle against the Axis by finding ways of joining the Allies. Their numbers were augmented by Belgian civilians who wanted to join the fight, including younger men who had reached military age and demobilised soldiers who found the occupation of their country increasingly

DOI: 10.4324/9780429027697-1

intolerable. To their number could be added the fugitive Jews and political enemies of the Nazis who fled their country, but while their trajectories were often similar, their stories were primarily about finding safety from persecution rather than continuing the struggle against the Axis.

Estimating the numbers of escapers and evaders is fraught with difficulties. In his extensive study, Georges Hautecler has identified 768 successful wartime escapes from German Oflags and Stalags, where the prisoners either made it home to Belgium or managed to join Allied forces. This represents approximately 1% of the Belgian servicemen in captivity, but there is no indication of how many other attempts ended in failure, so there is no statistical measure of the propensity of Belgian soldiers to escape. As a comparison, the available French War Ministry statistics list 55,700 successful escapes by its imprisoned servicemen, while the Veteran's Ministry has a higher total of more than 70,000 among the 1.6 million prisoners transferred to the Reich (4.37%).[5] However, there were only 31,248 medals awarded to escapers where the criteria were weighted very much towards those who had subsequently participated in resistance activity, but also included escapes from guarded camps inside France and those who could prove at least two unsuccessful attempts. Comparison is therefore difficult, and this is also true of the civilian elements. While we have knowledge of the civilians who successfully escaped from occupied Belgium and joined the Allied forces, the number who tried and failed remains unclear.

This book chronicles a multiplicity of escapes and evasions attempted by Belgians, both military and civilian, during the Second World War. Their country's surrender left many servicemen in a quandary. Some had already been taken prisoner during the eighteen-day campaign and shipped to Germany, but many others were still in the field. Theoretically they were also prisoners, but many appear to have been able to effectively demobilise themselves and return to their homes, with very little subsequent effort being made by the occupying power to find them. Others had greater problems, being stationed alongside the French and British forces that continued the campaign against the Wehrmacht onslaught. Although mandated to lay down their arms, they had choices to make about whether to return home when circumstances permitted or go into exile. While most chose the former option and many were caught by German checkpoints after the French armistice, a significant number also managed to evade these controls and returned home unnoticed. All of these were essentially evasions as the men concerned, although formally surrendered by their commander-in-chief, had never been taken prisoner by the enemy. Only a small minority of Belgian servicemen decided not to return home in 1940, but to continue to fight – usually by making their way to North Africa or the United Kingdom. These 'evaders of the first hour' had many different motivations for their decisions and many different experiences in fleeing France in the weeks and months after May 1940. The soldiers who did manage to reach England were rapidly subsumed into the nascent Belgian fighting force being established there, while the seamen and aircrew, being smaller in number, were incorporated into the Royal Navy or into the Royal Air Force, where they eventually formed designated Belgian Squadrons.

The chaotic weeks after the Belgian surrender, and that of neighbouring France some three weeks later, meant that only a minority of Belgian servicemen, perhaps 225,000 in total, became prisoners of war and were taken to camps in Germany. Their numbers were soon reduced even further when Hitler, for political and racial reasons, decided to free all the Flemish- and German-speaking Belgians in captivity, leaving only the francophone element. This was clearly a reworking of the *Flamenpolitik* carried out with mixed results by the German Imperial state in the First World War, but meant that the narratives of escape from the Third Reich were almost exclusively those of the Walloons. Like their much more numerous French counterparts, the captured Belgian soldiers were initially concentrated in large prisoner-of-war camps, but soon their usefulness as a labour force saw them deployed into so-called *Arbeitskommando*. These could be small groups or large contingents of 500 men or more that were allocated to farms, factories, workshops and construction sites. Here they became the responsibility of their employers, and conditions varied enormously.

Most of the evidence on escapes and evasions is heavily skewed towards those who were successful and lived to recount their experiences later. Their journeys involved absconding from camps or workplaces often in the Eastern *Gaue* (regional districts) of the Reich and then finding ways and means to travel westwards towards their homelands. Despite the many controls it seems that the railways often presented the most attractive option for moving quickly across the country. Many stories talk of travelling by passenger train and being able to mix in seamlessly with the huge numbers of foreign forced and volunteer labourers traversing the Reich. Long distances could be covered on single trains, although it seemed well known that border crossings would need to be negotiated differently, and usually on foot. Conversely, goods trains were seldom subject to searches at the border and could also be used successfully, especially if the destination was known in advance, but the unknown factor in all this was how long a journey might take.

For nearly all the Belgians in German captivity, the logical choice was to travel westwards, but there were exceptions. Some prisoners were held in camps close to the border with the Soviet Union – either in East Prussia or in the newly acquired Warthegau and Danzig-West Prussia. While the USSR remained neutral, it represented an escape route that was much shorter than the journey westwards. This choice was made by a small number of Frenchmen and at least two Belgians, one of whom left us a detailed account of his experiences. Crossing the frontier had specific problems, but once inside the USSR, fugitives could not survive unaided for long. Their fate was to end up in the hands of the NKVD and be treated as potential spies and/or Nazi agents. Interned for months with other suspects of many nationalities, both military and civilian, freedom came only when the Soviet Union was attacked and entered the war on the side of the Allies.

For some of those who escaped, reaching Belgium was an end in itself – returning to home, family and loved ones – but for others it represented only a beginning. All escapees had to live clandestinely, and this led appreciable numbers to continue the fight in some form of resistance activity in their respective localities. Others saw travelling westwards merely as a way-station to joining the Allied cause again by finding their way to unoccupied countries and from there to the United Kingdom. In this regard there were two rational choices, either Switzerland or Spain, although both borders were known to be difficult to cross. Those who succeeded were likely to be interned, and passage out of the country could be equally difficult. Not all of this was known at the time, but Spain was always to have been a more popular choice.

The stories of Belgians attempting to travel to Spain involve both escaped servicemen and civilians eager to enlist and join the fight. In this, they were joined by escaping British Commonwealth and later United States prisoners and aircrew attempting to find their way back to the United Kingdom. Under international law, escapees should have been permitted to carry on their journeys once in neutral states, but civilian and military evaders ran the risk of being sent back to their country of origin or handed over to their pursuers. Travelling across France also had its difficulties, although francophone Belgians had some distinct linguistic advantages in negotiating this part of the journey. But the main issue was crossing the border into Spain. There were the railway links, but these were heavily policed by both sides and were seldom used. Another possibility was by boat westwards from the French coast into Spanish ports, but the most popular route was on foot over the Pyrenees.

Escapes into Spain were sometimes made by individuals using their initiative and finding local expertise when and where they needed it. However, they were probably a minority as over time, specialist networks were created to help them and other escaping Allied servicemen. Some of the most famous escape lines such as *Comète* and *Sabot* were Belgian initiatives, whereas others were creations of the British and Belgian secret services – using the cloak of their diplomatic status to engage in espionage, but also to expedite the journeys of valuable aircrew and other military fugitives back to the United Kingdom. This required a careful balancing act vis-à-vis the Spanish authorities to ensure that those interned could be freed and then sent on their way. Others who had managed to evade capture could be smuggled into Portugal and evacuated by boat or, if they were considered particularly important, by aeroplane. Gibraltar was also used as a haven, but entry was difficult because the border was closed and accessible only by diplomats.

While joining the Allied cause against the Axis was the primary objective for most Belgians attempting to escape from occupied Europe, some at least found refuge from internment by joining the French Foreign Legion and serving in North Africa. This could involve being deployed in colonial policing but later also included fighting the Germans as the Tunisian campaign reached its peak. A few became prisoners of war of the Germans and were initially transferred to Italian custody before being taken to Germany in late 1943. Other evaders used North Africa as a staging post from southern France but ended up being trapped there, either interned by the Vichy French authorities or being unable to travel further.

One last, but equally important, part of the story of Belgian escapers and evaders is what happened to those who tried to escape and failed. In this regard, Belgian prisoners in German camps were treated similarly to their French counterparts, where serial recidivists were sent to specific camps in the East that were much more primitive and brutal than anything experienced in the conventional camp system. This resulted in a number of deaths and some men suffering permanent incapacity, but stays in these camps were limited both by circumstances and by Red Cross intervention. Nevertheless, this much harsher regime made clear the German stricture that 'escaping was no longer a sport'. If the captured servicemen could rely on their captors' broad adherence to the Geneva Convention and the oversight of the International Committee of the Red Cross, no such protection existed for the civilian evaders who tried to make their way out of occupied Belgium. They were unprotected by international conventions and were subject to imprisonment and even execution if they were caught. This was indeed the price of failure.

For most Belgian narratives of escape, the story ends with the Allied liberation of their country and a return home, but these fail to encompass the struggles for the post-war remembrance and recognition of the men who had attempted to flee from German-occupied Europe. Toward the end of the conflict, the Belgian government created a specific distinction between those who had escaped German camps and those who had left occupied Belgium. The imposition of unrealistic criteria to qualify for an award meant that several escapees remained unrecognised, and these men saw this as unwarranted discrimination – a feeling made worse with the government's decision to close down the body in charge of awarding the Escapees' Cross in 1954. For decades after the war, former escapees fought for better benefits

Figure 0.1 The Escapees' Cross, obverse (Private collection of the author)

Figure 0.2 The Escapees' Cross, reverse (Private collection of the author)

and a dedicated status. The limited number of survivors (referred to as évadés in the Belgian literature) meant that their cause was largely ignored in the press and parliament, and they therefore failed to attract much attention in the political world. Progress was made only in the 1970s when an escapee's status was finally agreed, but the attribution of the Escapees' Cross remained a point of frustration until 1994, when the Defence Minister finally agreed to hand a few medals to the last survivors.

These veterans also fought a battle to preserve the memory of their actions. There had been an organisation to represent escapees from the First World War since 1928, and the *Union nationale des Évadés de Guerre* (UNEG) was unified with escapees from the Second World War specifically to honour those who had refused to remain idle, and to tell their stories. Apart from representing the escapees to the authorities and pressing for awards and recognition, the organisation also launched various initiatives during the decades after the war, such as newspapers, ceremonies and competitions. These did have some positive effects and there was a gradual recognition of the specific histories of the escapees and evaders, but as UNEG membership inevitably dwindled over time, its influence reduced until it was finally wound up around 2009.

The history of the Belgian armed forces during the Second World War has not been a major topic for historians, and this is especially true of those who became prisoners of war. While there are a number of published memoirs, most have remained in manuscript form in libraries and archives.[6] The most comprehensive studies of Belgian captivity were written by E. Gillet in a series of articles in *Revue belge d'histoire militaire* between 1987 and 1990 and by Maurice de Wilde in a chapter for the third volume of *België in de Tweede Wereldoorlog*.[7] Unlike the British and American escapees from Nazi Germany whose experiences have been extensively chronicled and formed the subject matter for innumerable feature films, their Belgian counterparts have been largely ignored both by their countrymen and by the wider world. There are only a few published individual narratives and only one major collection of stories that give anything like a comprehensive picture of the Belgians' experiences of escape and evasion.[8]

The archival sources used in this book are as diverse as the stories they tell, ranging from MI9 escape and evasion reports collected by British interrogators during the war, through Belgian military, judicial and post-war award records, to the later autobiographical publications of both evaders and escapers. Of paramount importance were the archives of the Escapees' Cross board, held at the *Archives générales du Royaume* in Brussels. Escapees were systematically interviewed during or soon after the war in order to analyse and corroborate their stories with German sources or official documents. The archives of the main escapees' association, UNEG, were also crucial to this study. The veterans left individual interviews about their war service as well as documentation on their post-war activism and tributes. Various files of deceased Belgians killed while serving in the Allied armies after having escaped to Britain or Africa were also identified in the State Archives of Liège. Wherever possible, the authors have tried to use the words of the men themselves, either in direct quotations or paraphrased, to present their version of events as they understood and recounted them.

Notes

1 Rüdiger Overmans, 'Die Kriegsgefangenpolitik des Deutschen Reiches 1939 bis 1945', in: Jörg Echternkamp (ed.), *Das Deutsche Reich und der Zweite Weltkrieg Vol. 9/2 Die Deutsche Kriegsgesellschaft 1939–1945: Ausbeutung, Deutungen, Ausgrenzung*, (München: Deutsche Verlags-Anstalt, 2005), p. 776.

2 E. Gillet, 'Histoire des sous-officiers et soldats belges prisonniers de guerre, 1940–1945', in: *Revue belge d'histoire militaire*, Vol. 28, No. 1 (1989), p. 51.

3 Werner Warmbrunn, *The German Occupation of Belgium 1940–1944*, (New York: Peter Lang, 1993), p. 187 and Overmans, 'Die Kriegsgefangenpolitik', p. 776.

4 Overmans, 'Die Kriegsgefangenpolitik', p. 777. Bob Moore, *Prisoners of War: Europe 1939–1956*, (Oxford: Oxford University Press, 2022), pp. 100–103.

5 Musée Royal de l'Armée belge (MRAB), Fonds Georges Hautecler, 59/39, Statistiques d'évasion.

6 Most of these are held in the archives of CEGES/SOMA, Brussels.

7 E. Gillet, 'Histoire des sous-officiers et soldats belges prisonniers de guerre, 1940–1945', in: *Revue belge d'histoire militaire*, Vol. 27, Nos. 3 and 5 (1987–1988), Vol. 28, Nos. 1–5 (1989–1990). Maurice de Wilde, 'De Belgische Krijgsgevangen', in: Paul Louyet (ed.), *België in de Tweede Wereldoorlog, Vol. 3 De Nieuwe Orde*, (Kapellen: DNB/Peckmans, 1982).

8 Doc Adam, *S'évader mort ou vif,* (Brussels: Collet, 1986). Roger Jacquemin, *Le chemin de Londres : une évasion vécue,* (Brussels: La Renaissance du Livre, 1945). Georges Hautecler, *Évasions réussies,* (Liège: Soledi, 1966). Gustave Rens, Guy Weber and Willy Deheusch (eds), *Évasions de guerre, 1940–1945,* (Braine l'Alleud: Éditions J.-M. Collet, 1995) and Georges Hautecler, 'Statistiques au sujet des évasions réussies de prisonniers de guerre belges en 1940–1945', in: *Revue belge d'histoire militaire,* Vol. 19, No. 8 (1972).

1 The Belgian Armed Forces 1918–1940

The Experience of the First World War

To understand the motivations and trajectories of Belgian escapers and evaders in the Second World War, it is important to place them in a broader context. Their country had been invaded and all but overrun a little more than two decades earlier, and the memories of that conflict and the sufferings it inflicted on the population were still very evident in 1940. The army of 1914 had remained in the field and with few reserves had adopted a defensive strategy until the final stages of the campaign. Many civilian lives had been lost and there had been substantial economic damage inflicted on the economy. There were also practical legacies. The war forced changes to the country's military organisation, albeit some of these were more nominal than real. Changes in the country's international position as well as conflicts over military spending in the crisis years of the 1930s meant that much of its defence capability remained unmodernised and heavily reliant on outside help. Nor had the external threat lessened the strife between the two major linguistic groups, the Flemish in the north and west of the country and the Walloon French in the south and east.

The Belgian armed forces came out of the First World War with a reputation for dogged resistance in having held the initial German advance for two weeks in 1914 by using the fortresses in the eastern part of the country, and later by defending a small salient of their country between Nieuwpoort and Ypres from German occupation for the duration of the conflict. An army that had numbered 117,000 men in 1914 had grown to 166,000 by May 1918, with 141,974 having combatant status. With most of the country in German hands, recruitment was severely hampered but overall, some 320,000 served at some time and in some capacity during the conflict. They included 70,000 conscripts, mainly from the Belgian diaspora augmented by a further 50,000 volunteers, many of whom had fled the country on the outbreak of war or who had subsequently escaped via the neutral Netherlands.[1] Surprisingly, nearly all these volunteers seem to have come from the towns and cities as 'the peasant population proved immune to patriotic idealism'.[2] At the behest of their commander-in-chief, King Albert I, Belgian forces had not been used offensively for most of the war but did participate in the final Allied campaigns between September and November 1918 that presaged the armistice. Despite this, their losses were still substantial with approximately 40,000 dead (12.5%) and a

DOI: 10.4324/9780429027697-2

further 77,422 wounded.[3] Belgian soldiers were also twice as likely to succumb to illness than their Allied counterparts. This may have been a consequence of their spending much longer in frontline duty than British and French soldiers, who were regularly rotated and who had the possibility of being allowed home on leave. The Belgians' tenacity in holding onto a small area of their country served to create the image of a heroic army defending its homeland. This became an integral part of the country's subsequent wartime narrative but was also evident in the international recognition afforded to 'plucky little Belgium' and the welcome given to the many civilian refugees who fled the country – both to belligerent Britain and France but also to the neutral Netherlands.[4]

The first weeks of the invasion had seen huge numbers of Belgian civilians trying to leave the country, either southwards into France in advance of the Germans, or northwards into the Netherlands. This latter escape route allowed between 800,000 and 900,000 people to escape the fighting in the summer of 1914, although a year later most had returned home, leaving perhaps 50,000–100,000 as more or less permanent refugees.[5] Flight from occupied territory was to remain a possibility until the Germans constructed an electric fence along the whole frontier, but even this was not a complete deterrent, and the fence subsequently claimed the lives of as many as 3,000 people.[6]

The invasion and occupation of most of Belgium in August 1914 had seen German troops commit widespread atrocities against Belgian civilians as well as damage to property, most notably the widespread destruction of Leuven and the burning of its university library. Some territories in the East were annexed to Germany and the provinces of East and West Flanders remained a military zone, while the rump of the country became a General Government, although the whole country remained under martial law. Many industrial and manufacturing enterprises closed as a result of being cut off from necessary raw materials – rendering their workforces unemployed. Those industries that continued were often subject to go-slows by the workforce, a form of passive opposition that even the introduction of German overseers failed to remedy. Much agricultural production was sent to Germany as were manufactured goods, leaving shortages in the domestic economy. The overwhelming impression is one of economic, political and social stagnation as institutions shut down of their own accord and political parties ceased to function.

It became apparent that Berlin did not really have any plans for an occupied Belgium save that it should be permanently politically disengaged from France. This might involve some form of annexation or merely an administration that encouraged the country to rebuild within its changed situation. As we have seen, internal regeneration was a failure and by 1916 it had been decided to exploit the linguistic divisions within the country and encourage Flemish separatism. This resulted in a new-found German dynamism, pushing *Flamenpolitik* in the north and *Wallonenpolitik* in the south. The Flemish community received a Flemish-speaking university in Ghent and an activist parliament named the Council of Flanders – an attempt to harness the country's pre-war linguistic conflicts. The creation of this institution triggered indignation at home and abroad but was partly successful and played a role in continuing post-war political divisions. The separation became a major topic of propaganda and was continuously developed by German-financed newspapers such as *De Vlaamsche Stem*. Activism was also encouraged in the south through pro-Walloon journals with differing political slants, but these failed to trigger much enthusiasm.[7] The German *Flamenpolitik*, which was grounded in a cultural pan-Germanism but driven by a desire to drive a wedge between the Flemish and Walloon populations, had few practical results inside the country but did lead to the segregation and better treatment of Flemish activists among the prisoners in camps at Göttingen and Giessen in an attempt to further exploit the linguistic conflicts among the Belgians. This included encouraging a newspaper, *Onze Taal*, which was widely circulated.[8] Unfortunately for the Germans, this change in policy took place at much the same time as more coercive measures were introduced against the Belgian people. For example, the opening of the university in Ghent coincided with the first workers being conscripted for labour inside Germany. Thus, while Flemish nationalism was being courted, the country was simultaneously being stripped of its machinery, goods and workers and the Germans had 'reverted to brute force' in order to achieve their objectives.[9]

The stories surrounding Belgian military resistance need some qualification. The country's neutrality had left it ill-prepared for a military conflict. Conscription had only been introduced in 1909 and planned reforms had barely begun when war broke out in 1914.[10] As a result, the army had few modern weapons and both officers and men were not yet fully trained. This was compounded by ongoing disagreements between King Albert and his chief minister, Charles de Broqueville, both on strategy and on the structure of the supreme command, which meant that there were no clear plans in place even when the army was mobilised to meet the threat of invasion on 31 July. That said, when the threat became a reality, there was remarkable unity on all sides of the political spectrum, and mobilisation was orderly and satisfactory.[11] While the defence of Liège in delaying the German advance and the role of Belgian forces in holding the Yser Front in 1914 created an image of heroic defence and of providing time for the French and British forces to move northwards to confront the enemy, other commentators have pointed out that the German planning for the military defeat and occupation of Belgium was more or less carried out on schedule.[12] Indeed, while there were isolated successes, the real story of the campaign was one of almost consistent retreat. The bulk of the army defending Brussels was withdrawn to Antwerp on 20 August, almost before it was engaged, and then by-passed as the Germans swung southwards to confront the advancing French. Only when their advance had been halted at the Marne did the Germans mount an assault on Antwerp, and the city fell on 10 October. Some troops had already been withdrawn, but some 35,000 Belgian servicemen were cut off by the German advance and fled northwards to be interned by the Dutch authorities for the remainder of the war.[13]

The remains of the army, led personally by the King, now no more than 60,000 strong, took up positions behind the river Yser and then withstood an eight-day German offensive that ended only when the Belgians opened the sluices at Nieuwpoort and flooded the Yser valley. With the immediate threat averted, the Belgians continued to hold a small strip of their country between the sea and the British positions around Ypres until 1918. King Albert took the view that as Belgium remained a neutral state, its troops should only be used to further Belgian interests. He thus refused to engage with the offensive actions carried out by Anglo-French forces during the war. In fact, this was a policy born of necessity as he had neither the manpower nor the resources to mount a sustained campaign despite the recruitment campaigns that slowly increased the number of soldiers under his command.

In general terms, the soldiers were not particularly well supplied or well looked after. Life in the trenches was hard, and with little scope for leave, the men spent much more time at the front than their British or French counterparts. Poor health and higher levels of illness resulted, including approximately 7,000 deaths from typhus alone during the course of the war.[14] Belgian authorities were very slow in providing appropriate welfare, educational and leisure activities for their soldiers. Prior to 1917, most of what was available came from private (and usually Catholic) charitable sources. Information about conditions at home was scarce, and the limited and sporadic communication soldiers might have with their families relied on mails being smuggled across the Dutch frontier or on aeroplanes dropping propaganda newspapers written by Belgian, British and French propagandists.[15] The composition of military units was much more cosmopolitan than in other armies, where certain occupations were exempted from military service as being essential to the war effort. With no such restriction in place, there was a much greater social mix with much larger numbers of industrial workers among the Belgian armed forces, making up 60% of infantry units where farmers and agricultural workers comprised just 25% and the remainder being those in trade and commerce.[16]

Far more important in this context was the ongoing tension between the many Flemish-speaking soldiers and their French-speaking superiors. Although a country of several different tongues, French was the language of the elites and of governance and used almost exclusively in the armed forces for issuing orders, official publications and instruction manuals. The history of discrimination shown against Flemish speakers by their overwhelmingly French-speaking officers (even if they were themselves Flemish) inevitably exacerbated tensions between the two major linguistic groups, and this was exploited by Flemish nationalist elements that established a secret movement within the armed forces, the so-called *Frontbeweging*, which lobbied for more linguistic rights for Dutch speakers. Reputedly attracting approximately 5,000 members and frustrated by a lack of progress, the movement prompted a series of demonstrations and riots in the rear zone in 1917 and 1918 where red flags were also in evidence. Its cause was bolstered by rumours that the number of Flemish casualties (70% of the dead between 1915 and 1918) was considerably greater than the 55% of the population they represented.[17] This was taken up by two of seven deserters from the Belgian army who, as late as August 1918, were used by the German propaganda mill to expound the evils of Belgian militarism. Their theme was taken up by other publications that talked of Flemish blood being considered cheap and of a plot by the (Walloon) Belgian elites to exterminate the entire people.[18] The Flemish elements in the army were portrayed as victims of hatred from their own side and as being sacrificed for the interests of the Entente Powers.[19]

Despite the German propaganda and the incidences of internal subversion, there were none of the mutinies or outbreaks of serious disobedience experienced by the French. Militant Flemish nationalists were either imprisoned or fled, and the ordinary Flemish soldiers continued to obey the commands of their superiors. Thus, the Belgian High Command was able to curb any incipient problems with only minimal concessions, for example by instituting a (very simple) Dutch language test for all officers and having official texts translated into Dutch. Many other promised reforms were quietly forgotten once the war was over, and even those made in the pre-war period were often delayed. Thus, for example, a law of 1913 had sanctioned a school for Flemish junior officers, but five years later it had still not been created.[20]

The First World War has been characterised as the country's 'finest hour' and reinforced a 'strong sense of Belgian nationhood', with King Albert elevated to 'almost universal veneration'.[21] The ceremony held on 24 July 1919 during which French President Raymond Poincaré, together with King Albert and several high-ranking officers, awarded the Legion of Honour to the city of Liège, epitomised the level of pride reached after the First World War. Much-needed social reforms were also discussed after the conflict. The introduction of universal male suffrage in 1918 and concessions to Flemish interests altered the political landscape, with interwar governments being coalitions of Catholics, Socialists and Liberals from both linguistic groups. Nevertheless, the country failed to find an alternative to the nineteenth-century domination of the francophone bourgeoisie, and nowhere was this more apparent than in the armed forces, which remained a stronghold of conservative values.[22]

During the conflict, Belgium had 40,500 soldiers and 730 officers taken prisoner by the Germans, of whom around 2,000 died in captivity.[23] In general, detention in Germany was precarious. Despite the signing of the Hague Convention in 1907, Germany had made no special provision for housing captives. Belgian soldiers were poorly fed, even if that did not differ from the German population. Prisoner exchanges were planned but nations were hostile to the idea of sending back able-bodied men who could return to combat or contribute to the war effort.[24] The Belgians were usually held alongside other nationalities and were often included in French negotiations to improve conditions. Walloon soldiers also benefited and contributed to francophone newspapers and cultural events inside prisoner-of-war camps. Spain acted as the protecting power for Belgian interests in Germany but had no access to prisoners retained in Belgium. The Belgian government also arranged for additional parcels to be sent to its soldiers via the neutral Netherlands – something that was of vital importance as conditions inside Germany worsened in the latter stages of the war.

A few Belgian soldiers escaped from Germany during the First World War. The lack of study and the absence of a specific medal to reward that deed mean that it is impossible to know precisely how many tried to leave captivity or reach Belgium between 1914 and 1918. An association of former escapees, the *Union nationale des Évadés de Guerre* (UNEG), was formed after the conflict but failed to attract the public eye. Its archives indicate that it had over a hundred members, but membership was voluntary and involved a subscription, which means that there were certainly more escapees.[25] The armistice in November 1918 did not entirely end the suffering of those who had been prisoners of the Germans. The King had expressed a certain amount of sympathy for their plight, noting that 'the return of war prisoners, internees and Belgian refugees from foreign lands, should be organised in the best possible way. They should be welcomed with solemnity and, as soon as they are back in Belgium, they should enjoy as much comfort as possible and moral assistance'. In reality, they were greeted with suspicion by a worn-out civilian population. Between December 1918 and January 1919, more than 40,000 Belgian prisoners of war were repatriated by train. Others were freed by their captors and found their way back to Belgium on their own. By the end of January 1919, only those unfit to travel remained in Germany, alongside a handful who had decided to settle there permanently. The prisoners who came back to Belgium were given a month's leave, fifty francs and a few additional clothes. Civilian prisoners were awarded 150 francs. In the years that followed, former prisoners of war were forced to fight an uphill battle to have their status and their suffering recognised by the Government.[26] After the Second World War, former captives of 14–18 were still waiting for medal committees to approve their distinctions.

Between the Wars

After 1919, Belgium continued its alliance with France and Britain, but its armed forces remained unmodernised and there was no investment in either tanks or aircraft. The country's defensive strategy continued to be vested in fortifications around Liège and Antwerp, even though these had proved ineffective in the previous war. A few voices tried, without success, to oppose the policies adopted by the armed forces. Willy Coppens de Houthulst, the leading Belgian aviation ace during the First World War, wrote several articles in the press.

> Belgium has enjoyed eighty-four years of peace during which four generations were used to the idea of being left alone and being strong economically. Despite 1914, when the resistance of our Army was the only reason we did not lose our independence and our freedom, the new generation is tempted to not pay the insurance premium, always more expensive, in the shape of an army and an aviation corps.[27]

The army was also gradually reduced in size, from twelve divisions in 1923 to a mere four by 1926.[28] Apart from a small core of career officers, most of its manpower came from conscripts, who served full-time for only thirteen months before joining the reserve. In response to Hitler's appointment as Chancellor of Germany in 1933, plans were enacted to reinforce the fortresses close to the German frontier – Eben-Emael, Namur and Liège – but, like most other western European states, the long-term effects of economic depression made defence spending politically unpopular and a low priority.[29]

Franco-Belgian military co-operation on defence was compromised when Belgium returned to its neutral status in 1936. The circumstances surrounding this change of course were complex. The military agreement signed with France in 1920 had never been popular, especially in Flemish circles where any element of French influence was seen as anathema, but even the High Command was worried about excessive dependence on a neighbour who was always likely to put her own interests first.[30] Unguarded and tactless statements by French generals only served to raise concerns that France might use Belgium as a jumping-off point for an attack on Germany, and her system of alliances merely increased the likelihood of such an eventuality. While the decision to decouple Belgium from its French alliance was taken the day before the German reoccupation of the Rhineland, the outcome of the crisis demonstrated very clearly that France was unwilling or unable to fight even when its own interests were threatened and that Britain was still averse to any continental commitment.[31] Although aware that any real military threat was likely to come from Germany rather than from France, the Belgians ostentatiously maintained their new policy of neutrality – fearing that any lapses would provoke German anger externally and Flemish anger internally. While the emergence of an increasingly radical crypto-fascist Flemish nationalist movement (*Vlaams Nationaal Verbond*, VNV) led by Staf de Clerq on one side of the linguistic divide and an equally rightist Rexist Movement led by Léon Degrelle on the other gave the impression of a deeply divided country, there had been very little real opposition to the country's neutrality from any quarter before the outbreak of war. The portrayal of neutrality as a truly national policy had created a political consensus that allowed the government to increase its defensive measures – for example, by extending the period of conscription to seventeen months in December 1936. This was one section of a wider Military Law that also involved military purchases, anti-aircraft defences and fortifications. The Law gained the largest parliamentary majorities ever for a government defence bill with support from both sides of the linguistic divide and across a spectrum of political interests, [32] but, as was to become apparent, many deficiencies remained when war broke out in September 1939 and the Belgian armed forces were mobilised once again.

Belgian resolve continued to be tested, even after the outbreak of a European war in September 1939 and perhaps most notably in November 1939 and January 1940 when there was strong evidence of an imminent invasion. On the latter occasion, a German aircraft had crash-landed on Belgian soil which contained two German officers carrying detailed plans for an invasion of western Europe.[33] Questions of exactly how Belgian neutrality was to be interpreted in these circumstances created practical and constitutional rifts between King Leopold III and his government led by Hubert Pierlot, with the King ostensibly acting outside his powers by using personal contacts to negotiate with the major Allied powers. The conduct of secret military consultations with the Netherlands, France and Britain presented a substantial danger to Belgian professions of neutrality, while their outcome merely confirmed that the various national defence plans – where they existed at all – were completely incompatible.[34] Official policy remained unchanged. Neutrality was to be observed and the country would be defended against invasion from any foreign country. This 'armed independence' was not just Leopold's policy, but one that was enthusiastically supported by the Belgian parliament and the people. The fact that, despite the linguistic and political fissures in Belgian society, mobilisation had taken place with 'devoted unanimity' was testament to this widespread acquiescence to the value of neutrality. It also meant that Leopold could continue to resist attempts by the major powers to alter his stance to the point where, even after the German incursions into neutral Denmark and Norway, on 17 April 1940 the Belgian Senate voted overwhelmingly in favour of continuing the country's independence.[35]

The Eighteen-Day Campaign

The international crisis of the late 1930s had allowed the Belgian military to begin preparations to defend the country's neutrality. The standing army had 4,800 officers, 19,000 non-commissioned officers (NCOs) and professional soldiers as well as a strength of 47,000 conscripts at any given moment, a core that would be augmented by 20,000 reserve officers and a further 550,000 men to be recalled in the event of a full mobilisation.[36] On paper this was impressive given a total population of around 8 million people, but there were some major weaknesses. Leave and demobilisation for economic reasons, primarily to mining and agriculture, reduced the numbers considerably. Thirty thousand conscripts considered 'unsuitable', presumably for medical or political reasons, were also discarded, as were 10,000 fathers of large families.[37] Like their neighbours to the south, Belgian military planning had not really changed since 1914 and was almost entirely predicated on a defensive strategy, with huge amounts of money being outlaid on static fortifications.[38] This meant that spending elsewhere was compromised. In 1940 the Belgian Army had only eight tanks and 200 light armoured vehicles, but these, along with the 184 airworthy aeroplanes, contained many examples that could best be described as 'museum pieces'.[39] Moreover, the country had few anti-aircraft guns to combat the possibility of air attacks, and its field artillery was still predominantly horse drawn. Morale among the troops was poor and exacerbated by winter manoeuvres conducted against both potential enemies as well as long periods of enforced inactivity. To this could be added the increasingly radical stance of the VNV in distributing nationalist propaganda to Flemish soldiers – a tactic that prompted demonstrations within individual Flemish infantry units in late 1939 and again in January 1940.[40] On the eve of war, Staf de Clerq and the leader of the Verdinaso (a fascist political movement active in Belgium), Joris van Severen, urged their supporters not to fight or to desert, although it is unclear how many soldiers took this to heart or acted on it.[41] Choosing concrete over mobility was to have a hugely detrimental effect on the country's ability to defend its territory against a much better-equipped enemy. The Belgian armed forces, not unlike France, had forgotten the hard-learned lessons of mobility that had proved so successful during the Allied counter-offensive of 1918.

When the country was attacked on 10 May 1940, the Belgian armed forces were still underprepared. Leave concessions meant that many units were under strength by as much as 15%, there were shortages of ammunition for both infantrymen and machine-gunners, and other materials were also in short supply. Discipline and morale were poor in many units and communication problems between francophone officers and Flemish soldiers remained an issue. The plan to defend near the frontier was rapidly undermined when the fort at Eben-Emael was overrun by German commandos on the first day, probably the biggest humiliation inflicted on the nation in this early phase of the war. The forces defending the bridges over the Albert Canal were similarly outflanked by glider-borne troops and attacked from the rear. As a result, two German panzer divisions were able to cross intact bridges before any reinforcements could be called up.[42] Elsewhere to the south, demolitions were more successful and the German advance was slowed by several hours. The *Chasseurs ardennais* in that area fought tenaciously, for example around Bodange and Strainchamps, but those who survived became some of the earliest Belgian prisoners of war.[43]

A meeting between the military leaders of Belgium (Leopold III and General Raoul Van Overstraeten), France (Daladier, generals Georges, Billotte and Champon) and the British Expeditionary Force (General Pownall and Brigadier Swayne) at the Château Casteau north-east of Mons served to coordinate the operations of all three forces under the overall command of General Billotte, but by that stage the Germans had already successfully crossed the Meuse.[44] Although the following days saw some actions that slowed or stopped the German advance, the dangers of a breakthrough in the sectors held by the Second and Ninth French Armies and the possibilities of German forces attacking from the Netherlands necessitated the evacuation of the so-called Koningshooikt–Wavre (K–W) or Dijle Line, which ran from Antwerp in the north to Wavre in the south. The potential loss of the country's two largest cities inevitably sapped troop morale as they engaged in a series of night retreats to the west between 16 and 19 May.[45]

The Belgian cabinet convened at Breendonk on 16 May made plain the pessimism of the King and his generals about the war situation.[46] Belgian forces were still intact but in almost constant retreat. Van Overstraeten recorded a conversation with Lieutenant-General Alphonse Verstraete on 18 May where the latter spoke of his troops being tired and enervated, of exhaustion and of officers sending reports of panic and claims that their lines of concrete shelters were untenable.[47] A day later, he noted one unit having 'a complete lack of military spirit and discipline'.[48] German radio propaganda was now being directed to Belgian forces in the field, with Flemish troops being encouraged to surrender as the sooner the war was over, the better it would be for them, while the francophones were being told that they were merely sacrificing themselves for English and French capitalists.[49]

By 21 May, the Germans had reached the French coast at Abbeville, thus cutting off the Allied armies in the north. At this stage, a proposed meeting of the military commanders at Ypres almost descended into farce as attendees came and went without all of them sitting down together at one time. The upshot was that the Belgians were asked to extend their line in the north to relieve elements of the British Expeditionary Force for an attack in the south and to retreat behind the river Yser, which would give them a more defensible line. Further complications arose when General Billotte was killed in a car crash after leaving the meeting and before he could transmit the decisions made to his commanders. He was not replaced until four days later. The following day, the Belgians extended their line as planned but retreated only as far as the river Lys, this being considered the best option by the Chief of Staff, Major-General François Michiels. At this stage, morale among the majority of the Belgian troops was still being maintained, but a German attack on 23 May, while stoutly resisted, did result in the loss of Ghent with the capture of between 8,000 and 9,500 prisoners. The following day, two German armies, comprising twelve divisions, attacked the two Belgian divisions around Courtrai with the latter suffering heavy casualties. Ground was lost when at least one Flemish unit broke and abandoned the line. While this was recouped the following day, it was clear that Belgian forces were starting to crumble. There were reports of widespread surrenders in other sectors, for example the 4th Infantry Division, which had been poorly equipped and badly mauled in the opening days of the campaign, gave up more or less *en masse* at Meigem. Made up largely of Flemish units, this division had been identified as problematic in the months before the war had begun, with reports of nonchalance on the part of the officers and indiscipline among the men. A toxic mixture of poor leadership, poor morale and disaffection caused by Flemish nationalist propaganda probably all played a role here.[50] By this stage, there was political chaos with Leopold looking for a way to surrender, while his government under Pierlot was determined to continue the fight, in exile if necessary. On 27 May it became clear that Belgian military resistance was no longer viable. While the troops continued to fight doggedly, they were running out of reserves and ammunition – spiking their guns when all their rounds had been exhausted. The King's forces' behaviour under fire has been described as 'less than glorious' by some,[51] but given that its much more powerful ally to the south suffered from the same malaise, the fact that the Belgians managed to stay in the field for eighteen days, and considerably longer than their Dutch neighbours to the north, says something about their abilities and the tenacity of their campaign.[52]

Around 12.30pm on 27 May, King Leopold III telegraphed the British General Lord Gort (Commander of the British Expeditionary Force) and informed him that Belgian forces confronting the German advance were losing heart, and after four days continuous fighting with no respite from heavy bombardment, they would soon be unable to continue the fight. By 4pm, after reports of three German breakthroughs in the Belgian lines, the High Command advised that further organised resistance was impossible and, in order to prevent a complete collapse, the King sent an envoy to the Germans to ask for an armistice.[53] By this time, the bulk of the Belgian forces, together with the British Expeditionary Force, French units and a colossal number of refugees, were penned into a small salient of Belgian territory close to the Channel coast after being surrounded by the German advance.

Despatched immediately to negotiate with the enemy, the Deputy Chief of the General Staff, Major-General Jules Derousseaux, returned at 10pm the same evening bringing with him the German demand for unconditional surrender. This was agreed by the King and the Chief of the General Staff, and fighting stopped at 4am on the following day, although some units deployed in the Roulers–Ypres section of the front were unaware of the ceasefire and continued their resistance for a further two hours.[54] The written Protocol was signed by Derousseaux and General Walther von Reichenau (Commander in Chief of the Sixth Army) and included in its provisions was the stipulation that 'the Belgian Army shall unconditionally lay down its arms at once and shall from that time onwards regard itself as prisoner of war'. An additional protocol noted that 'as a mark of honourable surrender, the Officers of the Belgian Army shall retain their weapons'.

The King's final proclamation to the army from his headquarters was sent the same day:

> Officers, Non-Commissioned Officers, and Men:
>
> Plunged unexpectedly into a war of unparalleled violence, you have fought courageously to defend your homeland step by step.
>
> Exhausted by an uninterrupted struggle against an enemy very much superior in numbers and in material, we have been forced to surrender.
>
> History will relate that the Army did its duty to the full, Our Honour is safe.
>
> This violent fighting, these sleepless nights, cannot have been in vain. I enjoin you not to be disheartened, but to bear yourselves with dignity. Let your attitude and your discipline continue to win you the esteem of the foreigner.
>
> I shall not leave you in our misfortune, and I shall watch over your future and that of your families.
>
> Tomorrow we will set to work with the firm intention of raising our country from its ruins.
>
> Leopold[55]

This rather anodyne explanation for the end of Belgian resistance masked the true extent of the Belgian defeat. The country's forces had been driven back by the German onslaught and suffered grievous casualties, with approximately 50,000 men being taken prisoner in the course of the fighting as successive German breakthroughs weakened their lines, and poor communications between the Allied armies hindered proper coordination.[56] The events of the last week in May 1940 provide stark testimony to Leopold's demoralisation and his desire to end what he perceived as further unnecessary casualties in a losing cause. Having signally failed to match his father Albert's role during the Great War in maintaining resistance on Belgian soil in the face of German aggression, Leopold also insisted that he would share the fate of his army and allow himself to become a captive.[57]

His explanation for his actions to King George VI spoke of being better able to ameliorate the 'hardships of foreign occupation' and preventing his countrymen from being associated with any action 'against the countries which have attempted to help Belgium in her plight'.[58] In spite of protests from his ministers and advice from his allies, Leopold refused to change his mind about becoming a prisoner of the Germans, erroneously assuming that he would somehow have the ability to influence policies under a foreign occupation. Both his decisions to surrender and to remain in Belgium as an imprisoned head of state were to have important ramifications for his soldiers, both in captivity and fighting alongside the Allies for the remainder of the war.

While Leopold's actions had been widely approved inside the country, the French Prime Minister, Paul Reynaud, lost no time in condemning the Belgian Army and its surrender for the lost campaign in Flanders and attacked Leopold as a traitor for having surrendered without warning those who had come to his country's aid. His words led to verbal and sometimes physical attacks on Belgian refugees in France. The exiled Prime Minister, Hubert Pierlot, attempted to remedy the situation with a condemnation of the King's actions and a renewed commitment to help the Allied cause.[59] While this helped to deflect anger away from the Belgians in exile, it served to heap all the responsibility onto Leopold as the author of the Allied collapse.

If the French response was vitriolic, then the British reaction was only marginally less extreme. Lord Gort had been incensed to be told about the Belgian request for an armistice only a few hours before it took effect. Leopold had a staunch advocate in Admiral Sir Roger Keyes, who had been appointed British liaison officer on 10 May 1940. As the MP for Portsmouth North, Keyes was able to defend the King's actions in parliament, suggesting that the French had scapegoated him to cover their own responsibility for Allied military failure. There were suggestions that the French were so worried about his speech that they asked for its press coverage to be minimised, but the impact of his rhetoric seems to be contradicted by the comments of Sir Alexander Cadogan, who described him as 'stupid, sentimental and quite inarticulate'.[60] While Churchill had been unwilling to publicly condemn Leopold's actions on 28 May, by 4 June his concerns about Allied co-operation and the need to support France led to a substantial change of tone. In a statement to the House of Commons, he spoke of Leopold and his government having severed themselves from the Allies who had saved them in the previous war. Had they not taken refuge in a 'fatal neutrality', the French and British Armies might have saved not only Belgium, but Poland as well.

> He and his brave, efficient Army, nearly half a million strong, guarded our eastern flank and thus kept open our only line of retreat to the sea. Suddenly, without prior consultation, with the least possible notice, without the advice of his Ministers and upon his own personal act, he [...] surrendered his Army and exposed our whole flank and means of retreat. I asked the House a week ago to suspend its judgement because the facts were not clear, but I do not feel that any reason now exists why we should not form our own opinions on this pitiful episode.[61]

In fact, British indignation merely cloaked their own evacuation plans that had been in place since 25 May when Gort had decided to withdraw his forces to the coast.[62]

The Chaos of Surrender

Some of these consequences of Leopold's decision were immediately evident. Under the terms of the surrender, all Belgian combatants had become *de jure* captives

Figure 1.1 Belgian soldiers surrendering (@CEGESOMA/Archives de l'État en Belgique)

of the Germans.[63] Although men captured early in the conflict had often already been taken to Germany, the surrender left many still on Belgian soil and another 200,000 further south in France.[64] They were supposedly meant to lay down their arms, raise white flags and wait for further instructions. This was difficult enough in Belgium itself, with many men separated from their units, but even more problematic for those in France who were still supposedly operating alongside French and British forces.[65] Their situation was an impossible one, and it was only with the fall of France some three weeks later that these men also became *de facto* prisoners of war.[66]

With their political and military leadership hopelessly divided and with little or no actual power to influence events, the Belgian soldiers not actually in German hands when the armistice came into force had to make their own minds up about what to do next. The desire just to return home seems to have been uppermost in determining the actions of most Belgian servicemen; prompted by individual decisions, the advice or attitudes of commanding officers or by the orders of the Germans themselves.[67] For their part, the German authorities attempted to impose some control on the chaos after 28 May by setting up control posts along the rivers Lys and Escaut to intercept returning Belgian soldiers and place them in holding centres, with officers being separated out and sent directly to Germany.

Nevertheless, many columns of soldiers and convoys of trucks managed to avoid these controls and returned home, as did others who managed to engineer their escape from German custody. Herman Bodson probably reflected the views of many Belgian soldiers. He was a sergeant attached to the Belgian Medical Corps, having been a scientist before the war. With his unit in France at the time of the armistice, the Germans were keen for these medical specialists to return to Brussels. While some staff were reluctant,

> many of the troops were willing to go home. I sided with the men, feeling I could be of more use at home than wasting time in a friendly but foreign land. There was nothing I could do in France, artificially divided and politically disrupted. At home I had friends, a nation – at least united, although small and not free.[68]

The Belgian government made some attempts to recruit and regroup Belgian forces in France in the first two weeks of June 1940, but the collapsing French war effort encouraged Foreign Minister Paul-Henri Spaak to ask for British ships to evacuate 35,000 soldiers. However, Churchill's agreement on 17 June came too late and the overwhelming majority were swept up as the war ended some three days later.[69] This included remnants of the Belgian armed forces who had been trapped by the French armistice, and, in the case of the 7th Infantry Division, left behind when the British evacuated their forces from Brest and Saint-Nazaire. These military repatriations that began in July meant that many soldiers were effectively handed over directly to the Germans. Armand Ghiot was among the men trapped with their units in France after the Belgian capitulation. He described in his memoirs the mindset of those who had nowhere to go:

> We left from Lunel on 29 August 1940 in a column of 177 vehicles (cars, trucks and motorbikes) after having stopped at Pont-Saint-Esprit, Tournon, Saint-Étienne, the following day we reached Paray-le-Monial, next to the demarcation line. Not knowing what would happen to us, I left a box in a shop (which I recovered in 1945) in the village. Then, we decided with a few friends to buy ourselves an extraordinary meal (for the time), we ate an omelette with herbs, bread and a bottle of white wine. Then, a little bit worried about the following day, we went to sleep. Was luck on our side? According to some, such as Minister of Defence General Denis we were authorised to go back home to Belgium as free men. During a meeting the previous day, a German officer might have promised the column commander that we would not be bothered and that we could go home to Belgium.[70]

Far from being allowed to return to his native Brabant, Ghiot was taken into captivity and sent eastwards with his comrades.

Of the 650,000 men in the Belgian army in May 1940, perhaps 425,000 (65%) of them were able to return home without being formally demobilised and by avoiding German attempts to imprison them.[71] This rather haphazard outcome came as a result of different interpretations given to the orders issued by the responsible German military commander von Reichenau and the mixed messages from the King and General Van Overstraeten in the hours and days following the surrender.[72] Thus, in the final analysis only around 225,000 Belgian servicemen were taken as prisoners of war to Germany.[73]

Notes

1 Tom Simoens, 'Belgian Soldiers', in: Ute Daniel, Peter Gatrell, Oliver Janz, Heather Jones, Jennifer Keene, Alan Kramer and Bill Nasson (eds), *1914–1918 International Encyclopedia Online.* https://encyclopedia.1914-1918-online.net/article/belgian_soldiers [1 August 2023].

2 E.H. Kossmann, *The Low Countries 1780–1940,* (Oxford: Clarendon, 1978), p. 524 cites Henri Pirenne, *La Belgique et la Guerre mondiale,* (Paris: Publications de la Dotation Carnegie pour la Paix Internationale, Section d'Économie et d'Histoire, 1928), p. 53 and Robert Devleeshouwer, *Les Belges et le danger de guerre,* (Louvain/Paris: Nauwelaerts, 1958), p. 277.

3 Rémy Porte, 'Armée belge', in: François Cochet and Rémy Porte (eds), *Dictionnaire de la Grande Guerre 1914–1918,* (Paris: Robert Laffont, 2008), p. 124.

4 Michael Amara, 'Les grands défis de la propaganda belge durant la Première Guerre mondiale', in: Bénédicte Rochet and Axel Tixhon, *La Petite Belgique dans la Grande Guerre : une icône, des images,* (Namur: Presses universitaires de Namur, 2012), pp. 21–35.

5 C(ornelis) Smit, *Nederland in de Eerste Wereldoorlog (1899–1919), Tweede Deel: 1914–1917,* (Groningen: Wolters Noordhoff, 1972), pp. 174–175.

6 Maartje Abbenhuis, *The Art of Staying Neutral: The Netherlands in the First World War, 1914–1918,* (Amsterdam: Amsterdam University Press, 2006), pp. 164–169.

7 Sophie de Schaepdrijver, 'Occupation, Propaganda and the Idea of Belgium', in: Aviel Roshwald and Richard Stites (eds), *European Culture in the Great War,* (Cambridge: Cambridge University Press, 1999), pp. 267–294.

8 Kenneth Steuer, 'German Propaganda and POWs during World War 1', in: Troy Paddock (ed.), *Propaganda and World War One,* (Leiden/Boston: Brill, 2011), p. 169.

9 Kossmann, *The Low Countries,* p. 527.

10 Kossmann, *The Low Countries,* p. 519.

11 Kossmann, *The Low Countries,* pp. 519–520.

12 Hew Strachan, *The First World War: Volume I: To Arms,* (Oxford: Oxford University Press, 2001), pp. 208–212, 216. Clayton Donnell, *Breaking the Fortress Line 1914,* (Barnsley: Pen and Sword, 2013), pp. 196–200.

13 Kossmann, *The Low Countries,* p. 522.

14 Michel Dumoulin, *L'entrée dans le XXe siècle. Nouvelle histoire de Belgique,* (Brussels: Le Cri, 2010), p. 138.

15 Bernard Wilkin, *Aerial Propaganda and the Wartime Occupation of France, 1914–1918,* (London: Routledge, 2017).

16 Tom Simoens, 'Belgian Soldiers'. https://encyclopedia.1914-1918-online.net/article/belgian_soldiers [1 August 2023].

17 This remains a tendentious issue. See, Luc De Vos and Hans Keymeulen, 'Een definitieve afrekening met de 80%-mythe?' Het Belgisch Leger (1914–1918) en de sociale en numerieke taalverhoudingen onder de gesneuvelden van lagere rang', in: *Belgisch Tijdschrift voor Militaire Geschiedenis,* XXVII/8, December (1988), pp. 81–104; XXVIII/1, March (1989), pp. 589–612 and XXVIII/2, June (1989), pp. 1–37 and Sophie de Schaepdrijver, *La Belgique et la Première Guerre mondiale,* (Brussels: Peter Lang, 2006), pp. 194–202.

18 Bruno Yammine, *Fake News in oorlogstijd. Duitse mediamanipulatie en de Flamenpolitik (1914–1915)*, (Leuven: Leuven University Press, 2021), p. 311.
19 Yammine, *Fake News*, p. 312.
20 Yammine, *Fake News*, p. 311.
21 Martin Conway, *Collaboration in Belgium. Léon Degrelle and the Rexist Movement, 1940–1944*, (New Haven CT: Yale, 1993), pp. 6–7.
22 Conway, *Collaboration in Belgium*, p. 6. Els Witte and Jan Craeybeckx, *La Belgique politique de 1830 à nos jours : les tensions d'une démocratie bourgeoise*, (Antwerp: Labor–Nathan, 1985), pp. 151–154.
23 Karolien Cool, *Het Leven van de Vlaamse krijgsgevangenen in Duitsland in de Eerste Wereldoorlog*, (Brussels: Algemeen Rijksarchief, 2002).
24 Jean-Jacques Becker, *Dictionnaire de la Grande Guerre*, (France: André Versailles, 2008), p. 181.
25 Archives de l'État en Belgique, CEGES/SOMA, Archives de l'Union nationale des Évadés de Guerre (UNEG).
26 Michael Amara, 'Le retour en Belgique en 1918–1919', in: Pierre Lierneux and Natasja Peeters (eds), *Au-delà de la Grande Guerre : la Belgique 1918–1928*, (Tielt: Racine, 2018), pp. 55–60.
27 Willy Coppens de Houthulst, *Hélices en croix*, (Genève: Éditions du Rhône, 1945), p. 54.
28 *Histoire de l'armée belge : tome 2 de 1920 à nos jours*, (Brussels: Centre de documentation historique des forces armées, 1988), pp. 23–35.
29 Albert Crahay, *L'Armée belge entre les deux guerres*, (Brussels: Louis Musin, 1978), pp. 205–214.
30 Brian Bond, *France and Belgium, 1939–1940*, (London: Davis Poynter, 1975), p. 23 and Witte and Craeybeckx, *La Belgique politique de 1830 à nos jours*, pp. 167–173.
31 Bond, *France and Belgium*, pp. 23–24 and Michael Smith, 'Britain and Belgium in the Nineteen Thirties', in: *Belgique 1940 : une société en crise, un pays en guerre*, (Brussels: Centre de Recherches et d'Études Historiques de la Seconde Guerre Mondiale, 1993), pp. 85–111.
32 Roger Keyes, *Outrageous Fortune: The Tragedy of Leopold III of the Belgians 1901–1941*, (London: Secker and Warburg, 1984), p. 63.
33 Alain Colignon, 'Belgium: Fragile Neutrality, Solid Neutralism', in: Neville Wylie (ed.), *European Neutrals and Non-Belligerents during the Second World War*, (Cambridge: Cambridge University Press, 2002), p. 112. See also, Jean Vanwelkenhuyzen, *Neutralité armée. La politique militaire de la Belgique pendant la 'Drôle de guerre'*, (Brussels: Renaissance du Livre, 1979). Keyes, *Outrageous Fortune*, pp. 133–135.
34 Kossmann, *The Low Countries*, p. 591.
35 Keyes, *Outrageous Fortune*, p. 159.
36 Jonathan Epstein, *Belgium's Dilemma: The Formation of the Belgian Defense Policy, 1932–1940*, (Leiden: Brill, 2014), p. 236. Colignon, 'Belgium', p. 113.
37 Colignon, 'Belgium', pp. 113–114.
38 Crahay, *L'Armée belge entre les deux guerres*, pp. 205–214.
39 Colignon, 'Belgium', p. 114. Epstein, *Belgium's Dilemma*, p. 236 estimates that 118 combat aircraft were usable, but only twenty-four British-built Hawker Hurricanes were modern, and these were all destroyed on the ground on 10 May.
40 Epstein, *Belgium's Dilemma*, pp. 236–237. Edmond de Fabribeckers, *La campagne de l'Armée belge en 1940*, (Brussels: Rossel, 1978), p. 62.
41 De Fabribeckers, *La Campagne,* p. 62.
42 Lionel F. Ellis, *The War in France and Flanders 1939–1940*, (London: HMSO, 1953), p. 40. Epstein, *Belgium's Dilemma*, p. 240.
43 Georges Hautecler, *Het Gevecht te Bodange, 10 mei 1940*, (Brussels: Ministerie van Landsverdediging, Generale Staf-Landmacht, Algemene Directie Inlichtingen, Cijferschrift en Geschiedenis, Krijgskundige Sectie, 1955); René Autphenne, *Les Chasseurs*

ardennais à Bodange, (Bruxelles: Office du Livre, n.d.) and Epstein, *Belgium's Dilemma*, p. 241.

44 Ellis, *The War in France and Flanders*, pp. 42–43.

45 Epstein, *Belgium's Dilemma*, pp. 244–245.

46 Jean Vanwelkenhuyzen and Jacques Dumont, *1940 : le grand exode*, (Brussels: RTBF éditions, 1983), p. 52.

47 Raoul Van Overstraeten, *Albert I – Leopold III : vingt ans de politique militaire belge 1920–1940*, (Bruges: Desclée de Brouwer, 1948), p. 633.

48 Van Overstraeten, *Albert I – Leopold III*, p. 635.

49 Van Overstraeten, *Albert I – Leopold III*, p. 638. Epstein, *Belgium's Dilemma*, p. 248.

50 Epstein, *Belgium's Dilemma*, pp. 251–252. See also Jacques Wullus-Rudiger, *La Défense de la Belgique en 1940*, (Villeneuve-sur-Lot: Alfred Bador, 1940), p. 281.

51 Colignon, 'Belgium', p. 114.

52 Epstein, *Belgium's Dilemma*, p. 236.

53 Belgian Ministry of Foreign Affairs (BMFA), *Belgium: The Official Account of What Happened, 1939–1940*, (London: Evans Brothers, 1941), pp. 49–50; Jean-François Verbruggen, 'Le Grand Quartier Général belge et la bataille de la Lys (15–28 mai 1940)', in: *Revue du Nord*, No. 209 (1971), pp. 239–245, here, p. 244.

54 BMFA, *Belgium*, p. 50.

55 BMFA, *Belgium*, p. 51.

56 Robert W. Allen, *Churchill's Guests: Britain and the Belgian Exiles during World War II*, (Westport CT: Praeger, 2003), pp. 10–12.

57 Conway, *Collaboration in Belgium*, p. 22.

58 Allen, *Churchill's Guests*, p. 13 cites PREM4/24/4 Leopold III to George VI, 25 May 1940.

59 Allen, *Churchill's Guests*, pp. 14–15.

60 David Dilks (ed.), *The Diaries of Sir Alexander Cadogan, 1938–1945*, (London: Cassell, 1971), p. 291, diary entry for 28 May 1940.

61 Winston Churchill, House of Commons Debate 04 June 1940, vol. 361, cc. 789. Similar sentiments were expressed in the House of Lords by Viscount Caldecote, House of Lords Debate 04 June 1940, vol. 116, cc. 455–462.

62 Keyes, *Outrageous Fortune*, p. 305.

63 Gillet, 'Histoire', *RBHM*, Vol. 27, No. 3, pp. 229, 245.

64 Jean Jamart, *L'armée belge de France en 1940*, (Bastogne: Schmitz, 1994), p. 331.

65 Gillet, 'Histoire', *RBHM*, Vol. 27, No. 3, p. 231 notes that while the French were happy to incorporate the Belgians into their ranks, the British were universally hostile to any mixing.

66 Gillet, 'Histoire', *RBHM*, Vol. 27, No. 3, pp. 229–230.

67 Gillet, 'Histoire', *RBHM*, Vol. 27, No. 3, p. 234.

68 Herman Bodson, *Agent for the Resistance. A Belgian Saboteur in World War II*, (College Station TX: Texas A&M University Press, 1994), p. 48.

69 Allen, *Churchill's Guests*, p. 16.

70 Bernard Wilkin (ed.), *Correspondance du brigadier Armand Ghiot : prisonnier de guerre belge au Stalag IIB, 1940–1945*, (Brussels: Archives Générales du Royaume, 2018), p. 28.

71 Warmbrunn, *The German Occupation of Belgium*, p. 187. Overmans, 'Die Kriegsgefangenenpolitik', p. 776.

72 De Wilde, 'De Belgische Krijgsgevangenen', p. 102.

73 Gillet, 'Histoire', *RBHM*, Vol. 28, No. 1, p. 49.

2 Evaders of the First Hour

Heading Home

To all intents and purposes, King Leopold became the lightning conductor for Allied frustration at the Belgian surrender, although antipathy towards the Belgians who had fled to France, including as many as 150,000 servicemen, and those who had found their way to the United Kingdom, continued to be manifest. The military chaos was mirrored by indecision among the politicians about the best course of action. With their country being overrun, the cabinet headed by Hubert Pierlot had moved to Bordeaux. Although Foreign Minister Paul-Henri Spaak had personally favoured moving the government-in-exile to London, he had been outvoted by his cabinet colleagues. Subsequently, the government pursued something of a bifurcated policy. The Minister for the Colonies, Albert de Vleeschauwer, had already been appointed as Administrator-General for the Congo and Ruanda-Urundi and had left for neutral Portugal to ensure the continued independence of the colonies and their *de facto* co-operation with the British war effort. The Minister for Public Health, Marcel-Henri Jaspar, had also left Bordeaux for Britain, albeit without the knowledge or sanction of his colleagues, and had issued a call for continued resistance on 23 June.[1] This prompted his immediate dismissal, but indicated the stark divisions within the government-in-exile on their future policy. Jaspar feared that Pierlot might surrender and to forestall this, he announced a Belgian government in London with Camille Huysmans and other notables who had found their way to the British capital.

Pierlot's government was focused largely on the welfare and repatriation of the 2 million or so Belgian nationals inside France, a process that had largely been completed by October of that year.[2] Beyond that, his regime exercised no real power from its base in Bordeaux and became something of an embarrassment to the Vichy government headed by Marshal Pétain. On 16 September, it received a letter from the French leader that effectively ordered its dissolution as, under pressure from the Germans, all diplomatic missions representing countries occupied by the Reich were to be shut down.[3] Only when their hand was forced was some unity restored to Belgian politics. De Vleeschauwer had arrived in London on 5 July, the same day that Jaspar had made his announcement. The British had refused to recognise Jaspar's initiative, but de Vleeschauwer was a serving minister in the government

DOI: 10.4324/9780429027697-3

and was joined by Camille Gutt, the Minister of Finance, who had made his own way to London. These men formed the so-called 'Government of Two', which was transformed into the 'Government of Four' when Pierlot and Spaak belatedly arrived in London on 22 October, having been detained for some time in Francoist Spain. Recognised by the British as the legitimate representatives of the Belgian state, these men then formed the basis for the government-in-exile, based in Eaton Square in London.

Given the indecision, lack of unity and mixed messages coming from the politicians and the King, it is hardly surprising that the ordinary soldiers still in the field, either in Belgium or in France, were left in limbo. How much they knew about what was going on is open to question, but memories of the previous conflict would doubtless also have played a role in their decisions. As we have seen, a substantial cohort of serving soldiers, although technically rendered as prisoners of war by the armistice, were able to avoid internment by the Germans – effectively demobilising themselves and disappearing back into civilian life. The desire just to return home seems to have been uppermost in determining the actions of most Belgian servicemen; prompted by individual decisions, the advice or attitudes of commanding officers or by the orders of the Germans themselves. The German commanders had attempted to impose some control on the chaos after 28 May by setting up control posts along the rivers Lys and Escaut to intercept returnees and place them in holding centres, with officers being separated out and sent directly to Germany. Nevertheless, many columns of soldiers and convoys of trucks managed to avoid these controls altogether, as did others who managed to engineer their escape from German custody. Although never recognised as such, this was evasion on a massive scale, involving tens if not hundreds of thousands of men. The fact that little subsequent effort was made to track them down may have been partly a political German decision not to inflame opinion in the newly occupied territories, but also a function of the sheer numbers of French prisoners already in their hands.

In every respect, the Belgian soldiers who had fallen into German hands before the armistice or who were effectively handed over by their officers were the unlucky ones. Already in captivity and rapidly being transported into Germany, a small number became the first escapees. Indeed, the first such documented escapes happened at the end of May and at the beginning of June 1940, while Belgian soldiers were being dispatched to Germany. Willy Van Raerndonck, a non-commissioned officer in an anti-aircraft unit, managed to leave a column of prisoners on 28 May 1940, the same day he had been caught by the enemy. His escape was witnessed by a friend:

> Both of us were corporals with a C40 cannon still fighting on 28 May at 7 in the morning, [and] unaware of the capitulation. [...] I invited him to leave the column, which looked impossible and dangerous. I insisted and, after a lengthy hesitation, he jumped to the side out of the column, crossing the empty space on the left side of the road, under the nose of our German guards, and sneaked through the crowd toward the Café Sport. He only left

there when the column had passed (we were headed for the fort of Wilryck)[4] and jumped on tram number 5 which stopped not far from his home, close to the Palace of Justice.[5]

Jean Delepeleere was captured on 25 May 1940 and brought as a prisoner of war by train to Germany. At the border between Belgium and the Reich, he jumped from the train and, although fired on by the guards, managed to walk back to Brussels.[6] Likewise, two other soldiers escaped a column of prisoners in May 1940. They remembered the scene in a post-war book:

> "I really want to escape our guardians," said Jules. "When you think about it, they are not very numerous and I'll be damned if we cannot manage to escape. What do you think brother?" – "I have been thinking about it for a while, let us try our luck at the first opportunity. So to hell with the conse- quences! The first thing to do, slow down so we are at the back of the column. You should lace your shoes; go to the side and let the others go. I will come with you." One of the guards came across immediately and forced the two soldiers, with his rifle butt, to go back in the column. They had, however, dropped back considerably and were now on the right side of the road near the ditch. At this moment, the head of the column was slowed down and this messed up the rear. [...] – "This is it," said Jacques. They dived, head first, in the ditch fortunately full of grass. A few metres separated them from the column. They crawled in the vegetation. It seems that the Huns did not notice them and the gap left by the two men was quickly filled by others who tried to cover for them.[7]

These two were by no means the only ones who managed to escape from the columns heading eastwards into captivity, but such enterprise still required ap- propriate circumstances, nerve and a good deal of luck to succeed. Some lives were doubtless lost in other attempts given the propensity of German guards to shoot at anyone who stepped out of line. For the most part, those fleeing German captivity in this early phase of the occupation were more concerned with staying in their homeland than in continuing the fight elsewhere, but a very small minor- ity among the Belgian forces scattered across western Europe were minded to do more.

Refuge in the United Kingdom: The Belgian Army

Only a small number of Belgian servicemen found their way to Britain. Reportedly 163 men had been evacuated from the beaches at Dunkirk or had come via ports in France. They included Lieutenant Richard Smekens, Pierre Lefevre and thirty- three other Belgian soldiers who had refused to abandon the struggle despite the King's surrender and had been temporarily attached to the First Company of the 92nd Engineer Battalion of the French 2nd North African Infantry Division.[8] Sev- eral of them had been seriously wounded, but they were evacuated from Dunkirk and disarmed when they arrived in Folkestone. His group was soon joined by Major Emile Cambier and about twenty *Chasseurs ardennais* who had come via the same route.[9]

Others came from Ostend and Nieuwpoort, including some officers who had been attached to British units as the defence of France collapsed, such as Hector Laureys (alias Mac), who had waded out into the sea as part of a human chain to be picked up by a torpedo boat and taken to Ramsgate.[10] As with the French troops evacuated with the British forces, a proportion of the Belgians, comprising sixty officers and 490 men, were returned almost immediately to France to continue the struggle. This was also the case of Lieutenant Gaston Dieu, the commander of the 34th battery of the 2nd regiment of DTCA (*Défense Terrestre Contre Aéronefs*; anti-aviation ground defence), who fought in Belgium until 28 May before leaving with a group of officers and NCOs toward Nieuwpoort and De Panne. From there, he walked towards Dunkirk and embarked on the French ship *Cyclone* to Dover, which he reached on 31 May 1940. By 3 June 1940, he was back on French soil to carry on the fight, but he and others would soon be caught up in the chaos following the French armistice some two weeks later.[11]

Captain Georges Truffaut had a different escape from Belgium.[12] Still with his unit on 27 May 1940 in Eeghem near Tielt, he fled toward Ruddervoorde, where he heard the next day that the country had surrendered. Truffaut jumped in a car and drove to Nieuwpoort and then De Panne, where he reached the French border. The French refused to let him enter the country and even insulted him for being a traitor. Back in Nieuwpoort, Truffaut managed to find a small boat with an engine. Making progress towards Dunkirk, he and seven others were picked up by a British warship and brought to Dover. Searched at gunpoint, he received an icy welcome.[13] At this stage, the reputation of the Belgians in the eyes of the Allies could not have sunk much lower. Belgians arriving from Dunkirk were disarmed by the British on arrival as their country's forces had capitulated. Churchill's statements on the 'pitiful' betrayal of the Allied cause had reverberations in British society, with reports of Belgian civilians being harassed in London and even their war wounded being given short shrift by nurses.[14] As one escapee was to observe: 'To opt for Britain in the summer of 1940 supposed a good deal of courage, clear-sightedness or naivety'.[15]

If the evacuations from the Dunkirk beaches had provided a limited means of escape for Belgian personnel, others found alternative routes. From 17 June 1940, the day Pétain famously announced the French capitulation on radio, the south of France became a viable escape path for a little more than a week. The Wehrmacht was not yet occupying the ports of Bayonne, La Rochelle or Bordeaux, and the French authorities were indifferent to those trying to reach Britain or North Africa. Several Polish and Czech soldiers used these roads to flee Nazi occupation and carry on the fight. A few Belgians did the same. After his icy welcome at Dover, Georges Truffaut had returned to France almost immediately to continue the fight but was caught by the French armistice. Making his way to Bayonne, he was taken on board a cargo vessel as a stoker and left the port on 27 June, just before the Germans arrived. Sailing via Gibraltar and Casablanca, he reached Liverpool on

17 July. He made himself useful to the Allied cause by alerting London to the existence of the gold reserves of the Banque Nationale de Belgique held in the Belgian Congo and was sent there by Camille Gutt to secure the necessary paperwork. Opposed to the policies of the government-in-exile, he confined himself to his military role but was accidentally killed during a grenade-throwing exercise in Hereford on 3 April 1942.

Another evader was Jacques Wanty, who provided a much more detailed account of his journey.

I had myself, with the Centre d'instruction des sous-lieutenants d'artillerie [Artillery Second Lieutenants Training Centre, CISLA], been evacuated to Limoux, in Aude. The CISLA numbered about eight hundred men, including three hundred students and officers from the Military School, four hundred to five hundred horses and a large amount of artillery equipment. Some of my classmates from the 97th class and I had been contemplating the possibility of a French capitulation for a week, when it was announced on June 17 by the quivering voice of Marshal Pétain. Six of us had mutually pledged not to give up and to join England or North Africa if the struggle continued there. With Britain immediately proclaiming that she would not capitulate, we reaffirmed our resolve and prepared to depart.

From the evening of June 17, the Belgian military authorities on whom we depended made known the attitude they were adopting and from which they no longer departed. It could be summed up as follows: "The duty of each and everyone lies in strict discipline. No one has the right of individual initiative. The only tolerable course of action is to await the directives of the chiefs and to yield to it without reserve and without discussion."

Our military hierarchy deployed enormous efforts to inspire the whole CISLA with a spirit of surrender and to fight any individual initiatives of dissidence, which it seemed to fear much more than it had feared defeat. The intellectual baggage of our leaders, at least at the upper echelons, seemed limited to a literal and passive adherence to military regulations. Since none of them foresaw the conjunction of military defeat and political collapse that we were experiencing, they found themselves completely helpless in a situation that was beyond them and for which nothing had prepared them. They stuck to a simple idea: everyone should stay together and wait for orders. From whom? It didn't matter, while waiting for those of the Germans.

Pressure that amounted to blackmail was exerted on the CISLA students in two ways. First, formal discipline was invoked; a reassuring and proven concept. More subtly, we were begged not to perjure our oath to the king, an argument that touched many of us. But the six members of our group (Guy de Patoul, Marcel Haes, Robert Hynderick de Theulegoet, Pierre Neuray, André van Vyve, Jacques Wanty) did not believe that loyalty to the king could consist in surrender to the aggressor and to Nazism. They did not believe that an action of individual resistance constituted disobedience to the Constitution and the laws of the Belgian people. [...]

Six of us left from Limoux to Bayonne in the morning of 19 June, in a big taxi requisitioned the previous day. We had fake papers, mission orders lacking any credibility but stamped with the real seal of the CISLA, which we had stolen. We were in uniforms, GP pistols by the side, carrying light luggage. [...][16] Our taxi took two days to make Limoux to Bayonne, a bit more than 400 kilometres, with a stop at Lourdes. While we were leaving Limoux, a check was happening on the road, by order of the Belgian authorities. Our fake military orders were inspected thirteen times, always successfully, by French gendarmes who cared for nothing and were demotivated. The city of Bayonne was flooded by refugees from everywhere. They were all around in the streets and the squares and sitting in all public offices. We had noticed the importance of the military commander in charge of the port. We decided to ask for his help. This commander was a French Colonel of the Engineers. He was charming and encouraging, saying "I am happy to help young comrades and let them do what I cannot for myself. Congratulations and good luck." He wrote on our identity cards the magical words "going to England" and applied his seal and signed. Moreover, he told us about the presence of a Belgian ship that had arrived from Argentina in the Adour estuary, a few kilometres from Bayonne, that it was the Leopold II, belonging to (Armement) Deppe Shipping Company.[17] We went there without delay. About a hundred people, politicians, state servants, Belgian trade union members, were already embarked. Ten private cars were also on the deck [...][18]

Wanty was suitably sceptical about many of his fellow passengers, suggesting that they were just fleeing to save themselves, but was far more positive about one member of the 'Nomenklatura', namely Camille Huysmans, the Mayor of Antwerp and President of the Chamber of Deputies, whom he described as combative. Aside from the politicians, the passengers included around sixty Polish soldiers with their weapons and some Czech and British civilians, together with three other Belgian servicemen. Lunden and De Vuyst were airmen and Terlinden a reservist from the Lancers. They had fled from Dunkirk and acquired a machine gun from a wrecked German aeroplane along with a quantity of ammunition.

There were also some eccentric elements to this story. A Director-General from the Ministry of Justice disguised as a sailor had taken up station at the head of the gangplank to control the potential passengers, whose numbers on the quay were beginning to swell, and managed to get rid of as many as possible. Fearful of his own safety, he offered his car, 'a superb Packard', to the harbour pilot in a successful attempt to persuade him to let the ship leave early. The ship finally set sail on the afternoon of Friday 21 June with four hundred souls on board but, as Wanty noted, "We could have easily carried three to four times as many". His view of the civilian 'Nomenklatura' was not improved when, on the first morning of the voyage, a delegation came to ask the Belgians and the Poles in uniform to "kindly keep away from the railings, lest a German submarine take [them] for a troop transport". However, he also noted that a violent storm which arose on the second evening put these delightful people out of action for the duration of the voyage. Arriving in Falmouth after two days and nights at sea, and unlike some of their compatriots arriving elsewhere, they were given a charming welcome (*l'accueil charmant*) and with no apparent screening. After one night in a transit camp, they were taken by train to Tenby.[19]

Wanty and his colleagues were not the only defectors from CISLA. At least two others from the same cohort also managed to escape. Henri Marchal and Adolphe Meny headed for Bordeaux on a motorcycle and also found their way to the United Kingdom, to be reunited with their comrades. All were reported as deserters by their commanding officers and their conduct subsequently 'investigated', albeit *in absentia*.

With some persuasion from the Belgian Embassy in London, the British authorities had decided that Belgian military personnel and civilians of military age should be collected in one place. This was initially Haverfordwest and then Tenby on the South Wales coast, where the Atlantic Hotel became the headquarters of the *Camp Militaire de Regroupement Belge*.[20] By the end of July there were sixty-nine officers and 369 men assembled there, but they remained confused by the policy pursued by the King on the one hand, and the ambivalent attitude adopted by Pierlot's Cabinet on the other. Neither appeared to be wholeheartedly supporting the British cause against the German invaders. Indeed, British reticence about the status and commitment of the Belgians on their soil meant that the early arrivals were taken to Wales under guard.[21] The Belgians' own disaffection was heightened by political uncertainty, the unreliability of their officers and shortages of supplies, and by August 1940 it was noted that only 124 of the 300 men at Tenby wanted to continue fighting. They were initially attached to the Royal Army as a combat unit, while the remainder were sent to pioneer companies or factories.[22]

This state of affairs was gradually remedied by their commander, Lieutenant-General Chevalier Victor van Strijdonck de Burkel. He had come to Britain on 15 May as part of a commission to purchase horses for the Belgian army but had been trapped there by the surrender.[23] Strijdonck is credited with improving both the conditions and morale of his men, and also relations with the local civilian population to the point where his men were trusted to be deployed on coastal patrol duties from 28 September onwards. He also managed to persuade some doubters among the officers that they could still be loyal to Leopold III while supporting the Allied cause.[24] This was also aided by the arrival in London of Pierlot and Spaak to join Gutt and de Vleeschauwer to form the nucleus of a proper government-in-exile.[25]

Conditions for those in Tenby continued to improve in the later part of 1940, with the First Belgian Fusilier Battalion being formed in October under the command of Major Charles Cumont.[26] This introduced a training regime and a restoration of military discipline; drunkenness was curbed and Strijdonck insisted that the men learn English. By the end of the year, the Battalion had grown to 823 men and the Pierlot government, now established in London, decided to conscript all Belgian males in Britain between the ages of 18 and 45 and coupled this with the registration of Belgians living in other Allied countries. The Battalion received its own standard from Pierlot on 15 February 1941 as a permanent unit, and a second Battalion was formed at Great Malvern on 1 July 1942, led by Major William Grisar with Captain Jean Bloch as his second in command.[27] Both these men were trained reservists with Grisar having been an Antwerp shipowner before the war.[28] All four officers appear to have escaped through France and made their way to Britain.

By this stage, the Belgian armed forces in the United Kingdom numbered more than 1,600, including more than 200 from North America, and their command structure was revised with Strijdonck becoming Inspector-General of Belgian Ground and Air Forces in Great Britain, while command of the Land Forces was handed to Lieutenant-General Raoul Daufresne de la Chevalerie, who had been commander of the 17th Division before being captured. Rapidly released by the Germans, he had subsequently escaped to Britain where his rank and seniority demanded that he be given a prominent position. However, his tenure in command lasted only three months, primarily because his own conservative, monarchist leanings and antipathy towards the Belgian government-in-exile served to encourage similar sentiments among other pro-monarchists within the officer corps.[29] He was sarcastically remembered by one of his successors as follows:

> One day I met the reserve lieutenant-general to whom the command of the little army had been entrusted. In 1914 he had been a cavalry officer, but at his request he was transferred to the infantry. He had fought there with honour. In 1918 he left the army to practise his talents as a *salonjonker* in a more profitable business. He left the service as captain and during the twenty years of peace he received promotions that would not have come to him even as an active soldier. He owed this, so they said, to the protection of a very high-ranking friend. During the mobilisation of 1939, he had been given the command of a division of the second reserve with the rank of Major-General. He had arrived in Great Britain in a spectacular way, after an easy trip from Marseille to London via the United States, and this in luxury class. The general had introduced Sunday tea parties and Wednesday lunch parties in the mess. He had arranged, with subsidies from the Ministry, a small salon with pink seats and divans. There he received the most beautiful girls from the company. He was elegant, embellished, very sporty and well 'preserved' despite his sixty years of age, and they whispered that he still achieved admirable scores with the ladies.[30]

It was thus not only the British Royal Army that had to deal with Colonel Blimp as the Belgians also had their share of poor-quality and dilettante officers, who ultimately needed to be purged if their armed forces were to move forward.[31] The problem was in finding suitable replacements from the self-selecting sample of officers who had found their way to Britain. In some respects, the Belgian government-in-exile was handed a golden opportunity in December 1941 when Leopold III married Lilian Baels, the Flemish daughter of the pre-war Governor of West Flanders. This lowered his prestige even amongst his own supporters as his deceased wife, Astrid, who had died in a car accident in 1935, had been extremely popular. Moreover, the wedding took place with great pomp and splendour – which rather undermined his image of sharing the fate of his soldiers as a prisoner of war – and in the presence of many uniformed members of the occupying power. This was to have a profound effect on the entire Belgian officer corps, both in captivity and in exile.

The scandal surrounding the royal marriage allowed for stronger action to be taken against monarchist sentiments among the officer corps, and the removal of Daufresne provided the opportunity to divide his office into two, to be staffed by majors. One of his replacements was Jean-Baptiste Piron, who had been captured by the Germans in May 1940 and interned at Maria-ter-Heide in the Netherlands but had escaped. In April 1941 he had left Belgium and made his way via Marseilles and Spain to Gibraltar from where he was able to sail to the United Kingdom, arriving in Greenock on 6 January 1942. Once appointed, he oversaw major organisational changes to the Belgian forces in Britain whereby he took charge of Group I (Carmarthen), which contained the main combat units, while Group II (Leamington Spa) was the recruitment and training depot. The latter was used to sideline officers with royalist sympathies and keep them away from frontline units and from the headquarters in London. Belgian units were increasingly attached to British units and benefited from increased training opportunities. Ultimately, the bulk of Group I formed the basis for the Piron Brigade, which followed the Normandy landings and was later to play a symbolic role in the liberation of Brussels on 4 September 1944.[32]

The Seafarers

Unlike their land army counterparts, the Belgian naval personnel and civilian mariners who escaped to Britain were a prized resource and almost immediately incorporated into the British Royal Navy (RN) or the Merchant Navy. Victor Billet, who had been an officer on a mail ship, was the first Belgian to be awarded a British commission as a lieutenant in the Royal Navy Volunteer Reserve on 10 October 1940. Less than two weeks later, he was in command of the first tranche of thirty Belgian trainees at HMS Royal Arthur at Ingoldmells, Skegness.[33] This had been made possible by the provisions of the Emergency Powers Act of 28 September 1939 that allowed aliens to join the British armed forces, and they were formally incorporated into the Royal Navy as the RN Section Belge on 3 April 1941.[34] Some of these men had already seen active service and been honoured by their hosts, for example Leading Seaman Georges Ragaert, who had been the master of the trawler Lydie Suzanne, a fishing boat that had escaped to Dieppe and then to Ramsgate before making four return trips during the evacuation from Dunkirk. Ragaert was awarded a Distinguished Service Cross by King George VI on 18 November 1941 for his heroic actions.[35]

Large numbers of Belgian fishing boats seem to have escaped the clutches of the Germans, with 122 recorded as continuing their activities from British ports while 119 were taken into service by the Admiralty.[36] The men of the RN Section Belge were a mixture of military and civilian personnel who were trained and then used by the Admiralty in a wide range of roles including minesweeping, boom and barrage balloon defences, and coastal patrols in home waters using their own boats. Their existence was also important in allowing British seafarers to be freed up for service elsewhere. They were also deployed as individuals or as whole crews on specific RN vessels, such as the corvettes Godetia and Buttercup, which were used as convoy escorts during the war of the Atlantic and later played a role in the Normandy landings.[37] A somewhat different trajectory was that of Joris van Lierde, who was 39 years old when the war broke out and in France. After the surrender, he attempted to enter Spain but was *refoulé* (forcibly sent back) by the Spanish authorities. A second attempt in 1941 saw him successfully cross the frontier near Lourdes, but like many others he was soon arrested, and he then spent a fortnight in the prison at Pamplona before being taken to the internment camp at Miranda de Ebro. Released after three months, he made his way to England via Gibraltar and enlisted in the Section Belge. Although he lost the sight in one eye during shooting practice, he nonetheless served with distinction on convoy escorts across the Atlantic and to Russia, reaching the rank of quartermaster and being awarded the Atlantic Star.

The Belgian Air Force and its Pilots

Some of the first aviators to reach Britain came via France. Captain De Soomer and Major Renson, both Belgian pilots, reached London through Dunkirk during the evacuation of May–June 1940.

> They reached Dunkirk during the night, an awful night of nightmares. They wandered everywhere looking for the British HQ in the streets while the houses were burning with a deafening sound. Soldiers stopped them, interrogated them, then reluctantly released them. English, French, then again an English patrol, then a French one, and this lasted until 4 in the morning on the 1st of June. Ammunition depots burned. German shells exploded everywhere. Thick black smoke rose from the fires of the fuel tanks in the destroyed city. They walked close to the walls, took over shared cars, walked on bricks, weapons, luggage, instinctively keeping their heads down each time the German artillery fired or bombs were heard. Through the fire, the columns advanced in good order, resigned, toward the port or the beaches where long lines of trucks drove to the sea or improvised quays. Ships embarked again and again, sailing away and coming back to take more soldiers. Finally, De Soomer and Renson joined a line headed toward a ship. They breathed a sigh of relief: this time, they were on the right path for England.[38]

Recruitment of Belgian Air Force personnel into the Royal Air Force seems to have occurred almost by chance when RAF Squadron Leader Michael Lister Robinson met five Belgian Air Force escapees on a train taking them to the Belgian military depot at Tenby in July 1940. Having been impressed by the Belgian airmen who had helped him escape from France the previous month, and the calibre of the men he had encountered, he requested their inclusion when given command of 609 Squadron after it was moved to Biggin Hill in February 1941. Although it sustained heavy losses during the Battle of Britain, the squadron was augmented

Figure 2.1 Giovanni Dieu, a Belgian pilot who escaped from France to Britain and fought during the battle of Britain (@ Battle of Britain London Monument)

by aircrew from France, Poland, the United States and the Dominions as well as its Belgian recruits. In November of that year, the Belgians formed their own 350 Squadron, with eighteen Spitfires and more than two dozen pilots.[39] By March 1942, the squadron was led by Squadron Leader Désiré Guillaume.

A second Belgian RAF unit, 349 Squadron, was formed in Ikeja in Nigeria in November 1942 but made up from pilots recruited in the Congo and trained in South Africa flying Tomahawk aircraft. Their deployment in West Africa became irrelevant when neighbouring French colonies fell out of Vichy control, and the squadron was moved to RAF Wittering in June 1943 and equipped with Spitfires.[40] Here its commanding officer was Squadron Leader Comte Ivan du Monceau de Bergendal, who had enrolled at the Belgian military academy in November 1936 and, after being commissioned as a second lieutenant in the cavalry, volunteered for pilot training and was evacuated to France after the German invasion and from there to Oujda in Morocco. Having decided to continue the struggle, he travelled with some fifty like-minded other Belgian aviators on the SS David Livingstone from Casablanca to Britain.[41] In February 1941 he became a Pilot Officer and was posted to 609 Squadron.[42] Seeing action in that unit and later in 350 Squadron, he was eventually promoted to lead 349 Squadron on 8 June 1943. His main task then was to make the unit operational as quickly as possible. From 13 August, his command was used for only defensive duties, but by October it was carrying out sorties over occupied France.[43] After leading 110 missions, he was appointed to a staff position within the Inspectorate of the Belgian Air Force and was awarded the Distinguished Flying Cross (DFC). His subsequent wartime military career took him to Canada and the United States.[44]

Roger Malengrau was a qualified pilot whose unit was also evacuated to France during the German invasion, but he was able to escape directly to Britain on the passenger ship SS Apapa from Port-Vendres in southern France during the narrow window around the time of the French armistice.[45] Transferred initially to the Belgian depot at Tenby, he was soon one of the twenty-nine Belgian aircrew brought into the RAF. Eventually attached to 609 Squadron, he was hit and had to make a forced landing on 11 July 1941. Subsequently, he was promoted to Flight Lieutenant and became the commanding officer of 349 Squadron while it was still in Nigeria.[46]

Henry Gonay was a trainee pilot whose unit had been in France, but after the armistice he and three colleagues managed to make their way to Bayonne where they embarked for Britain on the SS Koningin Emma.[47] On arrival, he seems to have enlisted directly with the RAF and was promoted to Pilot Officer on 12 July 1940. Thereafter he served in several RAF Squadrons, including 350 as a flight commander. He was shot down and killed during a patrol over Jersey on 14 June 1944 and was posthumously awarded a DFC. The citation noted that he had completed 138 operational sorties and displayed outstanding ability, courage and determination.[48] Other future pilots found other ways to escape from France. Paul Evrard found himself in Saint-Jean-de-Luz and was able to smuggle himself on board a Polish troopship. Joining the Belgian forces in Britain, he volunteered for pilot training and was killed on 4 November 1943 while attached to the Air Sea Rescue service.[49]

One of the Belgian airmen was something of a serial escaper/evader. Baron Jean Michel P.M.G. de Sélys Longchamps had been an officer in the armoured *1er Régiment des Guides* before being one of the Belgians evacuated from Dunkirk. However, he returned to France almost immediately but when France sued for an armistice, he found his way to Gibraltar via Marseilles. There he joined a group of Belgian pilots trying to reach England but was apprehended and imprisoned in a POW camp near Montpellier. Escaping again, he was able to reach Spain and arrived in England, where he immediately volunteered for pilot training by the Royal Air Force, forging his papers as, at 28 years old, he was too old to be considered. On completion of his training, he was posted to 609 Squadron on 30 September 1941 to fly Hawker Typhoons. On 20 January 1943 and acting without orders, he peeled off from his mission attacking rail traffic in Belgium and mounted a lone attack on the Gestapo Headquarters at 453 Avenue Louise in Brussels, which led to at least four deaths and five serious injuries. The official reaction to his actions was contradictory, with demotion to Pilot Officer for his insubordination but also an award of the DFC.[50] He was later killed when his plane crashed on landing at RAF

Manston after a sortie over Ostend. A plaque on the wall of the former Gestapo building and a nearby bust of de Sélys Longchamps commemorate his actions.

Not all the Belgian servicemen who escaped to Britain in the summer of 1940 were keen to (re)join their country's armed forces in exile. Perhaps the most famous example is that of Albert-Marie Guérisse, who had been a doctor with a cavalry regiment during the eighteen-day campaign and had then found his way to Gibraltar. There he met Claude-André Péri, a French naval sub-lieutenant who had more or less commandeered a French cargo vessel Le-Rhin on its way from Marseilles to Morocco and had brought it to the British naval base. Eventually the vessel sailed to Britain for a refit where Péri, who subsequently changed his name to Langlais, opted to join the Royal Navy rather than the Gaullist Free French and his ship was recommissioned as HMS Fidelity.[51] Guérisse was unimpressed by the Belgian political set-up in London and unwilling to resume his vocation as a doctor, so he joined Fidelity's crew and was commissioned into the Royal Navy as a lieutenant-commander. Refitted by the British as an armed merchantman/special service vessel in June 1940, its French origins made it ideal for clandestine operations such as putting agents ashore in occupied territory. On a mission on 26 April 1941 to collect a group of Polish evaders from Cerbère on the coast near Perpignan, Guérisse commanded the fishing boat used to pick them up, but attracted the attention of gendarmes in the harbour and was eventually captured.[52] Rather than admit his true identity, he used his alias of Patrick Albert O'Leary, an evading Canadian airman, to explain his less-than-perfect English and disguise his role with SOE.[53] Interned by the Vichy authorities at Saint-Hippolyte-du-Fort near Nîmes, he was soon able to escape and it was in this guise that he later ran an escape network that came to bear his name as the 'Pat' line and was credited with moving more than 600 people to safety, including volunteers for the Free French and Belgian forces.[54] He was arrested in a Toulouse café on 2 March 1943 but survived Gestapo torture and incarceration in Neue Bremm (Saarbrücken), Mauthausen, Natzweiler-Struthof and finally Dachau until its liberation in 1945. He went on to have a successful career in the post-war Belgian Armed Forces, serving in Korea and heading the army's medical services before his retirement in 1970.[55] Langlais and his crew, including virtually the only woman on active service afloat with the Royal Navy, First Officer Madeleine Barclay (Bayard), were not so fortunate as the ship was torpedoed and sunk by U-435 with few survivors off the Azores on 30 December 1942.[56]

The Belgian servicemen and civilians who fled to the United Kingdom in the first days and weeks after the fall of their country were relatively few in number, and their routes involved negotiating the English Channel or travelling via France and Spain. While the soldiers took time to reorganise and come to terms with their new situation, the sailors and airmen were highly prized for their skills and rapidly incorporated into fighting units. Ultimately, they were all engaged in the war against Germany and served with distinction in a number of theatres before Belgian RAF and Section Belge corvettes were directly involved in D-Day operations, while the Piron Brigade arrived somewhat later but was included, for sound political reasons, among the Allied forces that entered Brussels on 3 September 1944.

Notes

1 Luc de Vos, 'The Reconstruction of Belgian Military Forces in Britain, 1940–1945', in: Martin Conway and José Gotovitch (eds), *Europe in Exile. European Exile Communities in Britain, 1940–45*, (Oxford: Berghahn, 2001), p. 83; Allen, *Churchill's Guests*, p. 18.

2 Robert W. Allen Jr., 'Britain Revives the Belgian Army, 1940–45', in: *Journal of Strategic Studies*, Vol. 21, No. 4 (1998), p. 79 and Simon Catros and Bernard Wilkin, 'Sur les chemins de l'exode : les réfugiés belges dans l'Eure, 1940', in: *Histoire, économie & société : époques moderne et contemporaine*, 41st year, n° 1 (2022), pp. 57–73.

3 Jacques Wullus-Rudiger, *La Belgique et la crise européenne, 1914–1945*. Vol. II : 1940–1945, (Paris: Berger-Levrault, 1945), p. 37.

4 Now a suburb of Antwerp.

5 Archives Générales du Royaume (AGR), Ministre de la justice : dossiers relatifs à l'octroi de la Croix des Évadés, 1940–1945, file 3390: Willy Van Raerndonck.

6 AGR, Ministre de la justice : dossiers relatifs à l'octroi de la Croix des Évadés, 1940–1945, file 535: Jean Delepeleere.

7 Vic Bodson, *La Croix des évadés*, (Harlue: De la terre à la plume, 1987), pp. 161–162.

8 Rens et al. (eds), Évasions, p. 22.

9 De Vos, 'The Reconstruction', p. 82.

10 Rens et al. (eds), Évasions, p. 22.

11 Rens et al. (eds), Évasions, p. 33.

12 Georges Truffaut was a well-known politician before the war and as a reservist, resumed his commission in the army in September 1939.

13 Rens et al. (eds), Évasions, pp. 44–46.

14 Allen, 'Britain Revives the Belgian Army', p. 80.

15 De Vos, 'The Reconstruction', p. 83.

16 These were Browning GP-35 (Grand Puissance) pistols developed originally for the French army in the interwar period.

17 The Leopold II went into Allied service but was sunk by a mine of Lowestoft on 23 December 1941, carrying a cargo of wood pulp from Canada to London.

18 Rens et al., Évasions, pp. 39–40. Le récit de Jacques Wanty, http://www.francaislibres. net/pages/page.php?id=236 [24 January 2023]. De Vos, 'The Reconstruction', p. 84 cites Jacques Wanty, *Combattre avec la Brigade Piron*, (Bruxelles: Collet, 1985).

19 Rens et al., Évasions, pp. 39–40. Le récit de Jacques Wanty, http://www.francaislibres. net/pages/page.php?id=236 [24 January 2023].

20 De Vos, 'The Reconstruction', p. 84.

21 Allen, *Churchill's Guests*, p. 48.

22 Luc De Vos, 'The Reconstruction', p. 84; Allen, *Churchill's Guests*, p. 48; Allen, 'Britain Revives the Belgian Army', p. 81.

23 De Vos, 'The Reconstruction', p. 81.

24 Allen, *Churchill's Guests*, pp. 48–49.

25 Allen, 'Britain Revives the Belgian Army', p. 82.

26 De Vos, 'The Reconstruction', pp. 85, 87.

27 Allen, 'Britain Revives the Belgian Army', p. 83; Allen, *Churchill's Guests*, p. 49.

28 The National Archives (TNA) WO208/3675/5. Grisar had escaped from Belgium in December 1941 and arrived in Britain on 20 March 1942.

29 Allen, 'Britain Revives the Belgian Army', p. 86.

30 Jean-Baptiste Piron, *Souvenirs 1913–1945*, (Brussels: La Renaissance du Livre, 1969).

31 Colonel Blimp was a character created by cartoonist David Low and first appeared in the *London Evening Standard* in April 1934. Blimp was pompous, irascible, jingoistic and stereotypically British, as well as, by extension, militarily incompetent.

32 Allen, 'Britain Revives the Belgian Army', p. 91.

33 The Royal Navy "Section Belge", http://www.be4046.eu/RNSB.htm [17 January 2019]. Billet was later reported missing in action during the Allied raid on Dieppe on 19 August 1942. HMS Royal Arthur was a shore establishment (land-based training facility). It later moved to Corsham in Wiltshire.

34 Allen, *Churchill's Guests*, pp. 46–47.

35 The Royal Navy "Section Belge", http://www.be4046.eu/RNSB1.htm; Les amis de la section Marine du Musée royal de l'Armée et d'Histoire militaire, http://www.marine-mra-klm.be/georges_ragaert__dsc__1920___2008__848.htm [both 17 January 2019]. Three other Belgians were also honoured in this way, namely Henri Teugels (Captain), Georges Timmermans (Commodore) and Carolus Bauwens (Soldier). W. Gardner (ed.), *The Evacuation from Dunkirk: 'Operation Dynamo', 26 May–June 1940*, (London: Frank Cass, 2000), p. 157 credits the Lydie Suzanne (Z50) as having rescued 416 ser-vicemen from the Dunkirk beaches. Ragaert stayed in Britain after the war and worked as a window cleaner in south-west London, married a British woman and became a naturalised British subject on 27 January 1953. *London Gazette*, 10 March 1953, p. 1380.

36 A.J. Beirens, 'Vissen in bezette wateren', in: *Vlucht naar Penzance*, (Puurs: Uninbook, 2010). This chapter records 369 of 507 fishing boats that left their home ports before or as the occupation began.

37 For example, the patrol vessels HMS Phrontis, HMS Raetea, HMS Electra II, HMS Sheldon (all former trawlers), HMS Kernot (the former Belgian patrol boat P-16) and two newly built corvettes, HMS Buttercup and HMS Godetia. Belgians also manned six ships of the 112th and 118th Minesweeper Flotilla, based at Harwich. Allen, *Churchill's Guests*, p. 138. See, for example, De Vos, 'The Reconstruction', p. 86; Johnny Geldof, *Royal Navy Section Belge in Focus 1940–1945*, (Heule: Verraes, 2002); Frank Decat, *De Belgen in Engeland 40/45: de Belgian strijdkrachten in Groot-Brittannië tijdens WOII*, (Tielt: Lannoo, 2007); Allen, *Churchill's Guests*, pp. 137–138, 149.

38 Rens et al. (eds), *Évasions*, p. 32.

39 Allen, *Churchill's Guests*, p. 125.

40 Allen, *Churchill's Guests*, p. 125.

41 Jean-Pierre Decock, 'Ivan du Monceau de Bergendal', in: *De Vieilles Tiges van de Bel-gische luchtvaart. Gedenkboek van de Belgische luchtvaart*, pp. 1–4, 8.

42 Decock, 'Ivan du Monceau de Bergendal', p. 4.

43 Decock, 'Ivan du Monceau de Bergendal', p. 10.

44 Decock, 'Ivan du Monceau de Bergendal', p. 11.

45 The SS Apapa operated between Liverpool and West Africa but was diverted into the Mediterranean to collect Allied troops. These included numbers of Polish servicemen. The ship left Port-Vendres on 17 June and travelled via Gibraltar before arriving in Liv-erpool on 7 July. The ship was subsequently sunk by a German bomber on 15 November 1940.

46 Roger Malengrau, http://www.vieillestiges.be/nl/bio/16 [18 January 2019].

47 The passenger ship SS Koningin Emma had escaped to Britain in May 1940 and was requisitioned by the Ministry of War Transport as a troopship. After returning French soldiers to the port of Brest, she was ordered to Bayonne to evacuate Allied civilians and military personnel. She arrived on 20 June and embarked 1,482 people. Later converted as an armed assault vessel, she was returned to her civilian owners in 1946.

48 Henry Gonay, http://www.vieillestiges.be/nl/bio/13 [18 January 2019].

49 Paul J.N. Evard, http://www.vieillestiges.be/nl/bio/11 [18 January 2019].

50 Allen, *Churchill's Guests*, p. 127.

51 Brooks Richards, *Secret Flotillas, Volume 2, Clandestine Sea Operations in the Mediterranean, North Africa and the Adriatic, 1940–1944*, (London: Frank Cass, 2004), p. 16.

52 See, Marcel Jullian, *H.M.S. Fidelity: bateau mystère; souvenirs recueillis auprès de Pat O'Leary*, (Paris: Amiot-Dumont, 1956).

53 Richards, *Secret Flotillas*, p. 18.
54 M.R.D. Foot and J.M. Langley, *MI9 Escape and Evasion 1939–1945*, (London: Bodley Head, 1979), pp. 74–75. Graham Pitchfork (ed.), *Escape from Germany. True Stories of Escapes in WWII*, (London: National Archives, 2009), p. 14. Claire Andrieu, *When Men Fell from the Sky. Civilians and Downed Airmen in Second World War Europe*, (Cambridge: Cambridge University Press, 2023), pp. 144–146, 180.
55 See, Vincent Brome, *The Way Back*, (London: Cassell, 1957).
56 Edward Marriott, *Claude and Madeleine: A True Story of War, Espionage and Passion*, (London: Picador, 2005).

3 The Belgian Armed Forces in Captivity

Imprisoned in Germany

The men captured during the eighteen-day campaign were rapidly transported away from the fighting and far into German territory, usually in goods or cattle wagons, ending up in East Prussia or the newly annexed regions of Posen and West Prussia in camps previously used to house Polish prisoners.[1] On arrival, they were placed in barracks or in tents, the latter being possible because it was still high summer. Others were evacuated along the Rhine on barges via the Netherlands to camps in western Germany.[2] The logistics involved were probably conditioned by the transport available to the Wehrmacht and the space in its existing prisoner-of-war camps. Subsequent Belgian accounts made much of the 'inhuman' conditions experienced by these captured soldiers and the alleged numerous German breaches of the Geneva Convention, with captives being deprived of food and water for long periods and transported for days in cattle wagons and coal ships.[3] At the time, these events were considered extreme but were more the result of the Wehrmacht's inability to cope with its military successes rather than part of a deliberate policy. However, there were certainly cases where prisoners lost their lives in transit, for example when a barge transporting prisoners *en route* for Germany hit a mine near Willemstad in the Netherlands, killing 166 men and injuring a further 276.[4]

The ultimate fate of Belgian prisoners was very much tied up with German plans for the future of the Low Countries. In a reprise of occupation policies from the First World War, Berlin resorted to a revised form of the *Flamenpolitik* that involved favouring the Flemish elements within Belgian society at the expense of the Walloon French.[5] In 1914–1918, this had produced mixed results in encouraging Flemish support for German interests, not least because of the inherent contradictions involved. For example, the opening of a highly controversial German-sponsored Flemish university in Ghent in 1916 took place in the same week that the first forced labourers were deported from the city. Likewise, attempts to propagandise Flemish prisoners of war fell on stony ground to the point where its chief proponents were described as commanders without an army.[6] While never a coherent German political policy in the First World War, *Flamenpolitik* nonetheless exacerbated the linguistic divisions within the country, and these formed the basis for Hitler's more concerted and more overtly racially based favouring of Flemish interests in occupied Belgium after May 1940.[7]

DOI: 10.4324/9780429027697-4

From the outset, German forces in the field were ordered to segregate Flemish and Walloon prisoners immediately they were captured, and this was reinforced by further directives after the Belgian surrender on 28 May – with the Flemish elements being released and the Walloon elements retained with a view to being taken to the Reich as a labour force.[8] A far-reaching Führer decree of 5 June dictated that the German-speaking inhabitants of Eupen, Malmedy and Moresnet should all be released, as well as all Flemish prisoners currently interned except for those who were career soldiers.[9] In addition, French speakers were also to be liberated according to a strict set of priorities which ran from doctors and veterinarians at the top, through policemen and employees of public utilities, to miners and workers with specialised skills.[10] Those released were required to report to the police in their home towns and to return to their former workplaces. All military equipment and clothing were to be handed in to the police on or before 18 June 1940.[11]

Flemish soldiers who had already found themselves in German camps were given privileged treatment by their captors and their first repatriations took place as early as July 1940 from Stalag XII-A (Nuremberg) and Stalag XII-B (Metz), but these presaged a much more comprehensive screening of all Belgian prisoners held in other camps. Over the following seven months, August 1940–February 1941, incomplete Red Cross figures show that at least 105,833 Flemish soldiers were returned from captivity.[12] Among them were 1,997 officers and 3,024 'others', a category that included civilians, customs officials, policemen, doctors and priests. Given that these figures only related to repatriations through Antwerp, it has been estimated that the total number of Flemish speakers returned home in this period may have been around 140,000.[13]

The process of identifying the Flemish elements relied almost exclusively on linguistic competence. There were instances where those involved in the screening were able to get additional francophones onto the repatriation lists without the responsible Germans noticing, while others were coached by comrades to pass as Flemish speakers.[14] Although the desire to escape captivity and return home was pre-eminent among most prisoners, there were exceptions. For example, one francophone officer who originated from Ghent in Flanders and who was bilingual refused to pass himself off as Flemish.[15] His reward for adhering to his principles was to spend the next five years in an Oflag. It was also reported that around fifty Flemish speakers remained in Stalag I-A (Stablack) throughout the war and refused to be returned home, out of a sense of camaraderie and patriotism.[16] Soldiers from Brussels and Brabant were in an ambiguous position. The bilingual province gave some the opportunity to pass as Flemish. Brigadier Armand Ghiot, from the French-speaking part of Brabant, although perfectly fluent in Flemish, also refused to use his language skills to return to Belgium and remained a captive of the Reich for five years. A different example was that of a native of Charleroi who was violently anti-Flemish but knew enough of the language to pass the relevant tests – but thought long and hard before doing so. In this case, his principles were overridden by his desire to be reunited with his family.[17] It was also the case that the screening process never reached all the Belgian prisoners, so for example the Flemish speakers in Stalag VIII-C (Sagan) were never reviewed by the commissions.[18]

By the end of 1940, German statistics suggested that most of the 100,000 ordinary Belgian soldiers still in captivity were employed either in agriculture (60%) or industry (40%). On 21 March 1941, the Belgian authorities enumerated 123,789 (overwhelmingly francophone) Belgians still in German hands, while German statistics for June of that year gave only 82,136 and 5,459 officers. These discrepancies are difficult to reconcile as there were further untabulated repatriations on the grounds of ill health, and an even smaller number of notified escapes during this period.[19] What is clear is that by the summer of 1942, the number in captivity had fallen to around 70,000, and this continued to be reduced by repatriations of the sick, further escapes and deaths in captivity during the remaining years of the war. At the liberation there were 4,008 officers and 67,591 men in German hands, their numbers having been augmented by some former soldiers who had been re-interned as dangerous after the Allies had landed in north-west Europe.[20]

Table 3.1 Distribution of Belgian Prisoners of War by Military District in 1944

Camp	Prisoners	Percentage
I-A Stablack	6,300	10.01
II-A Neubrandenburg	4,485	7.13
II-B Hammerstein	4,595	7.30
II-C Greifswald	5,525	8.78
IV-A Elsterhorst	1,975	3.14
V-A Ludwigsburg	340	0.54
V-B Villingen	1,525	2.42
VI-A Hemer/Iserlohn	1,385	2.20
VI-D Dortmund	1,990	3.16
VI-F Bocholt	738	1.17
VI-J Krefeld	585	0.93
VIII-A Görlitz	4,330	6.88
VIII-C Sagan	775	1.23
IX-A Ziegenhain	815	1.29
IX-C Bad Sulza	635	1.01
X-A Schleswig	3,070	4.88
X-B Sandbostel	1,725	2.74
X-C Nienburg/Weser	2,425	3.85
XII-A Limburg a/d Lahn	515	0.82
XII-D Trier	162	0.26
XII-F Forbach	305	0.48
XIII-A Sulzbach	1,750	2.78
XIII-B Weiden	1,785	2.84
XIII-C Hammelburg	4,620	7.34
XIII-D Nuremberg/Langw.	1,175	1.87
XVII-A Kaisersteinbruch	785	1.25
XVII-B Krems-Gneixendorf	2,900	4.61
XX-B Marienburg	425	0.68
Stalag 398 Pupping/Linz	940	1.49
Oflag II-A Prenzlau	2,600	4.13
Oflag X-D Fischbek	1,755	2.79
Total	62,935	100.00

Rather than being kept together as one national group, the Belgians could be found in most German *Wehrkreise* (military districts) and in a variety of camps and *Kommandos*, with no apparent rationale for their distribution save their usefulness for the German war effort and perhaps a policy of moving them as far away from home as possible.[21] This may help to explain their concentration in the districts I and II in the north-east of the country, namely East Prussia and Mecklenburg/Pomerania and in Austria. The table below shows their distribution in the last stages of the war.

Prisoners as Labour

As they were primarily seen as a source of labour for the Third Reich, the Belgians' employment was dictated in much the same way as their more numerous French counterparts, so that most found themselves allocated to *Arbeitskommando* which, while nominally attached to a Stalag, could be some considerable distance away. It was also not unusual for a soldier to be redeployed from one *Arbeitskommando* to another after a matter of weeks or months. This meant that the totals given for prisoners in camps were only nominal and failed to reflect their widespread geographical distribution or their deployment in many sectors of the German war economy.

Figure 3.1 Three Belgian soldiers from Stalag II-B in July 1941 (Private collection of the author)

Deployment in agriculture across the Reich often entailed *Kommandos* being subdivided, with many sent to specific villages where they were allocated to the local farmers according to need. This often began with their being held at a central point and then distributed each day, but over time it became more common for the men to be accommodated on the farms where they worked – usually in barns or outhouses. One prisoner described the initial allocations as being like a livestock market, with the strongest being chosen first.[22] This sensation was also described by Armand Ghiot, who wrote the following:

> After breakfast, we are taken by truck. After a while, we are offloaded in a village. It is near a lake. It seems that there is a Flak training camp nearby. [...] We are exhibited as if at a livestock market. Our potential employers are gathered and look at us, trying to estimate how much workload we can provide. I am led by a farmer to a farm only a few hundred metres from our campsite. A very small farm, a horse, four cows and as many pigs will be my daily work.[23]

Kommandos could also be established for industrial enterprises, and there were many recorded examples where deployments were made in apparent contravention of the Geneva Convention, most notably to armament factories or to coal, salt or lead mines where conditions were notoriously dangerous.[24] Those with specific skills were increasingly sent in small groups to work for private employers as so-called *kommandos artisanaux*. As the situation for the Germans deteriorated, skilled Belgian prisoners were also drafted into specialist units as glaziers, roofers and builders, who were housed permanently close to the urban areas being targeted by British and American bombing.[25] Many well-known German industrial combines also used captured soldiers as workers. For example, almost 2,000 French-speaking Belgian prisoners of war were sent to the Opel works at Rüsselsheim between September and November 1941. These men were paid less than the German employees and were required to do more. They were usually accommodated in separate barracks. Earlier German reports from 1940–1941 indicated that Belgian soldiers worked well, but it seems that quality declined in the following years owing to poor wages, less than average food and a lack of consideration.[26] Prisoners of war were also required to clear the streets of damaged German cities, a dangerous task made more difficult by the lack of supplies.[27]

It is also clear that prisoners were often moved around. For example, one soldier had been sent initially to Stalag XIII-D (Nuremberg-Langwasser) and then to an *Arbeitskommando* near the Grafenwöhr military base. In August 1941 he was moved to a farm near Obersdorf run by a mother and daughter. This lasted for three months until November, when he was moved on to a porcelain factory. He worked here for a further three months before being transferred to Stalag XIII-B (Weiden), from where he was deployed to three more farms before finally ending up in the camp infirmary.[28] Another prisoner had also moved from industry to agriculture and back again, being employed successively on the *Reichsbahn* (national railway), in a sugar factory, at a boilerworks, in an aviation factory, as a woodcutter, on constructing breakwaters on the Baltic coast, in a savings bank and in a café, before finally being allocated to a small farm.[29] While the Germans made some initial attempts to segregate the *Kommandos* according to nationality, it was often the case that Belgians found themselves working alongside the French. This made linguistic sense, but as the war continued, many more units became mixed to include Poles, Russians, Yugoslavs, and later still Italians. Finally, there was also mixing of prisoners with forced and volunteer civilian labourers from across the occupied territories.[30]

Belgian prisoners were treated much the same as their French counterparts, not least because nearly all were themselves francophones, and were subject to the same propaganda initiatives. For example in the summer of 1942, an '*appel*' from Fritz Sauckel, the General Plenipotentiary for Labour Deployment from March of that year, clearly laid out the German position – that they were fighting for European civilisation and that their treatment would be dependent on their behaviour, but that those who refused to work would be punished by being sent to a camp in the occupied Eastern territories.[31] This mixture of carrot and stick continued through the war – and included attempts to have prisoners give up their prisoner status in exchange for better civilian conditions and to force NCOs to work. Whereas their French counterparts were positively encouraged to do this by the representatives of the Scapini Mission, the Belgians had no such prompting, and, with limited information, the vast majority decided not to give in to the Germans' blandishments. Their reasoning was largely pragmatic, seeing that a return to civilian status would lose them the rights to Red Cross parcels and also lose their families rights to payments while they remained in the armed forces. There was no guarantee that payments as civilian workers would cover these losses, and there was also the question of how they, as labourers volunteering to work in the German war economy, might be received as and when they returned home.[32] The group of Belgian prisoners most heavily targeted by the Germans as a potential labour force was the NCO who stood by their rights under the Geneva Convention not to work, but who were put under enormous pressure by their captors. Sent to Stalag 325 (Rawa Ruska) and Stalag 369 (Kobierzyn), they were subjected to extreme conditions. With no outside contact or advice, many nonetheless continued their refusal to co-operate throughout the war. Others who succumbed were given administrative tasks within camps, but the precise numbers in each category are unknown.[33]

Although it was imperative for Germany to use the prisoners of war to substitute for domestic labour conscripted into the armed forces and also to offset the costs of their captivity, this created a contradiction as it had the potential to create a much closer relationship with civilian populations than the government would have liked. Ideological, political and cultural values were all at stake here, and these debates were played out at national and local levels throughout the conflict. In essence, there was an ongoing tension between the need to exploit prisoner labour on the one hand, and to minimise contacts with civilians, especially female civilians on the other, and to prevent any racial mixing.[34] This had been an issue in the First World War, but was to be repeated in more extreme forms and on a much broader scale after 1940, not least because of the sheer numbers of captives involved.

Despite this, there is clear evidence that the Belgians engaged sexually or romantically with German women. The phenomenon is not always easy to document owing to the taboos of the era, but there are allusions in memoirs and surviving memorabilia, such as a picture given to prisoner Fernand Wilkin of a German woman on a farm with a declaration of love on the back, that hint at a widespread phenomenon.[35] The question of prisoners' social and sexual contact with German women and girls had been discussed by Himmler and Hitler as early as 10 September 1939, with the latter insisting that prisoners who had engaged in such intimate relations were to be shot and the woman or girl publicly disgraced by having her head shaved or being sent to a concentration camp. This Führer order was given substance early in 1940 when the OKW (*Oberkommando der Wehrmacht*, the German supreme military command) ordered that all Polish prisoners found to have committed such crimes were to be handed over to the local Gestapo offices and the RSHA (Reich Security Main Office) informed, in the knowledge that they would be subject to a minimum term of ten years' imprisonment and possibly the death penalty. By this stage, SD *Lageberichte* had reported the first prosecutions of women for having sexual relations with Poles, with one Grete Kask being given a six-year sentence.[36] All instances of Polish men having sexual relations with German women were reported direct to Himmler personally, who invariably insisted on a death sentence for the man concerned.[37] The only possible exceptions were if the Pole concerned was deemed suitable for Germanisation and was prepared to marry the woman involved, in which case he was gaoled until such time as his case could be dealt with.[38] If the result was positive, he was freed; if not, then the designated sentence was carried out.

Some of the early executions were carried out in public, but it seems that this was soon stopped. In the case of two Polish prisoners of war who had been found guilty of sexual relations with German women, the regulations permitted their public hanging, but it was decided to send them to a concentration camp for the sentences to be carried out, as otherwise 'great agitation would have resulted among the [local] Catholic population'.[39] The RSHA and the Nazi Party had pressed for the same penalties to be applied to workers and prisoners of war from western Europe, but this was overruled for fear of offending collaborationist governments and especially the Vichy regime in France.[40] While there was close control of communities by the Party as well as the Gestapo and the security apparatus from the very beginning of the war, the Nazis struggled to impose their brand of racial apartheid on the German people. The decrees and legislation of the first months were in large part a response to reported instances of fraternisation.[41] In Catholic areas of the Reich there was markedly more sympathy for coreligionists, Belgians included, with many examples of priests holding services and collections for them.[42] As would become evident for all the countries using prisoners as labour and confronting the problems of them coming into contact with civilians, the demonisation of the abstract enemy rapidly broke down when confronted with sociable and likeable individuals. In spite of all the prohibitions and restrictions, keeping the prisoners and increasing numbers of foreign civilians apart from the German public proved an impossibility – especially in rural areas where many farms were run entirely by women and where close co-operation was essential.[43] The Nazi District Leaders (*Kreisleiter*), who were responsible for monitoring behaviour and enforcing the legislation, were particularly encouraged to watch the wives of serving soldiers and their behaviour towards other German soldiers and foreign labourers. Statistics from *Landgericht Landshut* (Landshut District Court) emphasised the scale and extent of the problem in this rural area. In the course of a year, there had been a total of 122 cases brought against German women for having relationships with prisoners of war. More than half the women (54.9%) were from agricultural backgrounds, 18.8% were workers, 9.0% artisans, 5.7% officials and 11.5% traders.[44] While the courts continued to punish offenders, it did little to affect civilians' behaviour, as is evidenced by high-level complaints in 1944 that such illegal acts had increased in volume in spite of the draconian penalties which had 'not achieved an overwhelmingly successful result'.[45] There was also a strong public sense that the regime was employing a double standard throughout the war, as civilian men accused of relations with foreign women were usually just given a warning, and Wehrmacht soldiers were often seen openly consorting with French women on German soil, something that the High Command refused to censure.[46]

The Belgian Prisoner-of-War Regime

At home, and with the agreement of the German military command, the King was instrumental in creating an organisation to help career soldiers with pay, pensions and reintegration into civilian life. The *Office des Travaux de l'Armée Démobilisée* (Service to Oversee the Activities of the Demobilised Army, OTAD) was established on 31 August 1940 under the overall control of the Finance Ministry but was led by Général de brigade Maurice-Colombe-Louis Keyaerts, previously the commander of the 2nd *Chasseurs ardennais*, who was brought back from German captivity to fulfil this role. Although ostensibly an administrative and welfare organisation, it was also planned with a view to creating a focus for officers loyal to the Crown and to initiate the creation of a new defence force for the country.[47] Once again, the selection of officers to run OTAD and their negotiated release from camps in Germany created the same resentments that the ruling classes were once again favouring their own.[48] The organisation continued throughout the occupation, carrying out its role ostensibly in an a-political fashion by helping ex-servicemen to reintegrate into society and supporting them materially, but never compromised its neutrality by acting as a front for resistance. This aligned with King Leopold's view of the administration's role during the occupation, but there were also fears of reprisals if OTAD was associated with armed resistance, although there were examples where individuals did use the organisation as cover for clandestine activities. This strict neutrality meant that OTAD retained the confidence of the occupying power until January 1944 when Keyaerts and some of his fellow officers were arrested and re-interned in Germany. Ostensibly, the order had come from Berlin rather than from the Military Government in Brussels, but it represented a fear that such autonomous organisations might be a threat in the future. In fact, it seems that the precipitate action of the Germans produced exactly the result that they had feared, with officers associated with OTAD defecting into the ranks of the organised resistance.[49]

There was also the question of international protection for the Belgians held as prisoners in Germany. The United States was the protecting power for Belgium until the end of 1941, when the latter also became involved in the conflict.[50] Finding an appropriate replacement agency proved problematic; the Belgian Secretaries-General regarded appointing a new protecting power as a political act forbidden to them by the decree of 10 May 1940, while the Germans refused to recognise the Belgian government-in-exile as legitimate. Given this *impasse*, a new solution had to be found. General Keyaerts favoured an organisation embedded within OTAD, a solution that was finally approved by the OKW in June 1942 with the creation of the *Délégation du Service de liaison avec les prisonniers de guerre belges* (DSLP).

The organisation had its headquarters in Brussels, but its Berlin office was in the fashionable Hotel Adlon in Unter den Linden.[51] Led by Jacques Edmond Joseph, Count t'Serclaes de Wommersom, its role was to liaise with the German Foreign Office and with the *Allgemeine Abteilung für das Kriegsgefangenwesen* (General Department for the Prisoner of War) of the OKW to help maintain the morale and material well-being of the Belgian prisoners still in Germany. Its delegates visited camps where Belgian prisoners were held and compiled reports on their conditions, with a view to intervening where there were perceived deficiencies. Several commentators also pointed to an underlying motive in having the new organisation linked to the OTAD, and thus also to the King. This was to repair the damage done by the announcement of the King's second marriage to Liliane Baels at the end of 1941. This second marriage – kept secret for three months – came as a shock, and the reports of the lavish celebrations at the palace involving both Belgian and German officers led to portraits of the King being taken down from barrack walls and in some cases thrown out of windows in disgust.[52] It exposed the myth, once and for all, that he was also a prisoner and somehow suffering in the same way as his men in Germany.[53]

As far as Keyaerts was concerned, the DSLP was to concern itself solely with the morale and material conditions of all Belgian prisoners, but German agencies perceived it as the alternative to having a protecting power, and as a conduit for negotiating the wider use of prisoners within the war economy, along the same lines as the Scapini Mission for French soldiers.[54] However, the DSLP ostensibly stuck rigidly to its terms of reference, but had great difficulty in operating in the same manner as a protecting power, having none of the advantages of independent reporting or access to external channels of communication. Although the representatives of the DSLP in Berlin made contacts with other neutral states acting as protecting powers, and also with the International Committee of the Red Cross (ICRC) and YMCA, it kept the representatives of the Scapini Mission at arm's length, seeing them as being too close to the Germans in spite of their shared interests in prisoner welfare.[55] The DSLP also found that its activities were severely hampered by German restrictions on the use of trains and other forms of transport to visit the camps, but delegates were ultimately able to visit many of the 300+ locations where Belgian prisoners were held between June 1942 and November 1943. However, these visits had to be notified long in advance, giving camp commanders every opportunity to sort out any irregularities, and DSLP reports had to be vetted by a German officer who accompanied every camp visit and by the OKW, something that inevitably limited the questions that could be asked about living conditions and food. The reports were also filtered through the German Foreign Office as direct communication with Brussels was forbidden. To get round this, the delegates would have face-to-face meetings with General Keyaerts on their visits home, and in some cases even visit the families of particular prisoners.[56] In general terms, the DSLP had little success in negotiating with the Germans and many issues remained unresolved at the war's end, their sole victory being in facilitating the repatriation of conscripts who had six or more children, although even this was less generous than the terms afforded French prisoners who were liable for repatriation if they had four or more offspring.[57] Other requests for releases, on the grounds of age, or having been a prisoner in the Great War, fell on stony ground.[58] There was also little coordination between the DSLP and other organisations concerned with prisoner welfare, most notably the Belgian Red Cross and the *Secours d'Hiver*.

As with their French counterparts, conditions for the Belgians varied enormously between locations and over time, but the DSLP reports regularly spoke of shortages and deprivations of both food and clothing. *Kommandos* in rural areas tended to fare better when it came to food, as all manner of products could be scrounged from the locality. For example, Belgians attached to Stalag I-A (Stablack) were able to find potatoes, vegetables, eggs and poultry to augment their rations. A more surreal addition to their diet came in the winter of 1943, when an Indian elephant, *en route* to the Königsberg zoo, was unable to walk and was killed close to the camp. The camp canteen staff were thus able to butcher the carcass and add elephant to the prisoners' soup.[59]

Ameliorative aid to the prisoners was expedited by the Belgian Red Cross in the form of 12 million parcels provided by the *Office national de secours aux prisonniers de guerre*. This amounted to around 600 tonnes per month, including over 3 million kilos of sugar and 177 million cigarettes. The distribution system was reputedly not very efficient, and the Belgian government-in-exile took advantage of a private charitable organisation established in Lausanne by Edgard Biart, the 'Aide aux prisonniers et internes belges', which operated under the auspices of the ICRC and became incorporated into the Belgian Red Cross in 1940. The organisation reputedly sent 11.7 million kilos of aid to Belgians in captivity, including American and Canadian parcels, as well as many items of clothing all paid for by credits from the Belgian government-in-exile.[60] The Belgian Red Cross also supervised national charities, such as the *Secours d'Hiver*, dedicated to the relief of prisoners of war. It was led by Colonel Bastin until 1944 when he was replaced by Major André de Meeûs d'Argenteuil. The Belgian Red Cross was divided into three sections, which included the *Tricot du Prisonnier* (Knitting for Prisoners), supervised by Baroness Genevieve Rolin and tasked with providing clothes to the captives. Parcels were usually packed by women from the wealthier levels of society.[61] An American organisation 'Parcels for Belgian Prisoners' shipped in food and clothing, as well as aid emanating from other countries, including the Congo. Beyond this, there was a plethora of other bodies, either official, semi-official or private, that concerned themselves wholly or in part with the welfare of prisoners. Families also supplied tinned food, jam and other goods to their loved ones, playing an important role in keeping the Belgian prisoners healthy, but parcels were often delayed or disappeared. According to the Geneva Convention, a five-kilo parcel was allowed every two months and a one-kilo parcel every month.[62] Relatives were equally preoccupied by the intellectual well-being of the captives. Books and newspapers were habitually included, an important relief often shared among prisoners of various nationalities, especially the French and Belgians.[63] Parcels continued to be sent until Belgium was liberated by the Allies and communication with the camps in Germany ceased.[64]

German attempts to direct political propaganda at their francophone captives usually fell on stony ground and, if anything, reinforced national sentiments among the majority. *Le Trait d'Union* was distributed freely in the camps, but as one officer recorded, they were only kept as toilet paper or to light the stoves in the barracks.[65] Details of the war situation provided by the Germans outlining victories against the USSR were greeted with disbelief, especially in camps where the inmates had illicit access to a radio and therefore to BBC broadcasts as a counterweight.[66] Specific Belgian publications, mostly pro-German newspapers, were also circulated, for example *Volk en Staat* and *le Pays Réel*, and these had the advantage of containing some news about conditions at home. *Le Maréchal vous parle* was also in circulation, and although designed primarily for French prisoners, there were sometimes pages devoted to the Belgians. Francophone books were also made available, usually through the Red Cross or YMCA, although there was a long list of interdictions. Here again, the francophone Belgians benefited from the presence of their much more numerous French counterparts and had access to a much broader range of literature, as well as theatrical and musical entertainment, than might otherwise have been the case. However, although this provision was apparent in the major camps, it did not always filter down to the smaller *Kommandos*, where contact with printed material was often sporadic and by no means guaranteed.[67] Prisoners at Stalag XVII-B (Krems-Gneixendorf) and in some *Kommandos* reported rare visits to civilian cinemas and the organisation of football matches between different units stationed within marching distance, but these appear to have been the exception rather than the rule in the prisoners' everyday existence. At Stalag I-A (Stablack) there was a cinema within the camp which showed a certain number of feature films but also a constant diet of newsreels extolling the bravery of German soldiers in keeping Europe safe from Bolshevism.

While there were undoubted benefits from captivity alongside the French, relations were not always cordial. In some cases, there were animosities between the two national groups, with the French blaming the Belgians for having surrendered in May 1940. These frictions were exacerbated by the differential distribution of parcels, and in some instances, such as at *Kommando* 1227 attached to Stalag VIII-C (Sagan), the Belgians asked to be physically separated from the French.[68]

It was also argued that nationalist morale among the Belgians was much stronger than among the French, who were divided among themselves between convinced Pétainists and those who were inclined towards opposition and resistance.[69] This perception is reinforced by the lack of success experienced by recruiters for the *Légion Wallonie* (Walloon Legion) where volunteers from the camps and *Kommandos* were minimal. Only 136 men were persuaded and agreed to serve in the German army. Out of the 67 veterans of the *Légion Wallonie* interviewed by Jean-Marc Vanderlinden after the conflict, only one claimed that he had joined primarily to get out of a prisoner-of-war camp.[70]

Belgian Officers

The Belgian officers in German captivity were taken first to Oflag VI-A (Soest), but after Hitler's directive the majority of Flemish reserve officers were released in early June 1940, and only career officers were kept in captivity. Anyone identified as particularly *deutschfeindlich* (anti-German) was sent to *Sonderlager* (special camps) such as Colditz or Lübeck.[71] On 20 July, around 3,500 Flemish and French-speaking career officers were sent to Oflag III-B (Tibor), with 500 at Oflag VII-B (Eichstätt) and a similar number at Oflag IX-A (Rotenburg). By this stage, there was a widespread view that Germany had won the war and that they would soon be sent home. The apparent German preference for the Flemish elements provided a premium for being placed in that group, so that many francophone officers also tried to pass themselves off as Flemish, with varying degrees of success. However, the repatriations that did take place during the summer were largely composed of aristocratic and upper-class French-speaking artillery and intelligence officers, whose releases had been requested by the Belgian *Commissariat Général à la Restauration du Pays/Commissariaat-Generaal voor 's Lands Wederopbouw* (General Commission for National Reconstruction), ostensibly to expedite the decommissioning of the Maas Forts and the rebuilding of bridges.[72] This rationale was perceived as no more than an excuse and caused widespread resentment among the prisoners that the elite were once again looking after their own.

Reports from the DSLP suggested that opinions had been polarised between a group that were anti-royalist and republican and a group called *Les Servants du Roi*, which espoused a more authoritarian (and possibly military) regime led by the King.[73] By the summer of 1943, all of the latter had been gathered in a single camp, Oflag II-A (Prenzlau), but other fractures within the officer corps were also apparent, for example between the 'defeatism' of senior officers who had been there for some time and their more recently arrived junior colleagues. During the second half of 1940, Belgian officers in captivity had created groups and associations to while away the long hours of captivity. However, a specific group made up of extreme Flemish nationalists established the *Luitenant De Winde-Kring* (LDWK), named after the Flemish poet and nationalist soldier Juul de Winde, who had been instrumental in the creation of the cultural association *De Vlaamse Kring* in 1909 and who had been killed a few weeks before the end of the First World War in 1918. This group of pro-German Flemish officers and NCOs also sought to create a

Nieuwe Raad van Vlaanderen (New Flemish Council) as a means of engaging with the presumed Nazi new order in Europe.

The Flemish nationalists within the ranks of the career officers were of sufficient interest to the Germans that 121 were transferred to a special compound at Oflag III-A (Luckenwalde) on 12 December 1940. This also accommodated several other ethnic groups who regarded themselves as oppressed minorities in their own countries – including Bretons and some elements of the Irish. The new arrivals were apparently greeted by a German *Abwehr* officer who merely enquired if they had been deloused. Their living conditions were less than ideal, with indifferent food and shelter and temperatures as low as –20°C, suggesting that they were not considered a high priority.[74] Only thirty-five of these men were members of the LDWK, but they soon came to dominate the Belgian group, and, with the collusion of the Germans, those who stood out against them were removed. Their first leader, Lowie Reekmans, a moderate, socially conscious Flemish nationalist, was replaced at the beginning of 1941 by the far more radical Norbert Nierinck. Those not already part of the LDWK saw the writing on the wall and all had joined within a few days. They were joined on 25 January 1941 by the well-known Luitenant-Kolonel Adriaan Emiel Van Coppenolle, a hero of the First World War, as their senior officer. He was instrumental in dealing with disputes between the group about the politicisation and direction of the LDWK and was ultimately responsible for the removal of Neirinck and his replacement by Herman Verreydt. The latter again had opponents removed from the camp and returned to other Belgian camps where they were treated as traitors by their comrades and had to be segregated in a separate compound referred to as the 'lepers' island'.[75]

Van Coppenolle and Verreydt, although by no means of one mind, now controlled the direction of the LDWK and insisted on a new statute that was to be signed by each officer and linked Flemish nationalism explicitly to German *volkisch* ideology and a belief in a German victory as being the key to future Flemish autonomy. A total of 120 of 158 men in the camp at that time chose to sign, although whether this was out of conviction is open to debate. Conformity was the pragmatic option for men whose morale had been weakened by the defeatism of their senior officers and whose main hope was for a swift return home. At the end of May 1941, fourteen of them were selected to join the newly formed *Vlaamse Wacht* in their homeland. This was intended to form the core of a future defence force that would replace German troops garrisoning Belgium, suggesting that the Germans retained a greater confidence in the Flemish officer corps than in their French-speaking counterparts.[76] A matter of days later, the *Abwehr* officers involved showed their continuing commitment to the LDWK by inviting its leaders to a Flemish cultural exhibition in Berlin, wining and dining their guests at a restaurant owned by a Flemish nationalist who had been sentenced to death in his own country at the end of the First World War and who had chosen to stay in Germany.[77] Verreydt continued to screen new arrivals to the camp and used his influence with the *Abwehr* to insist on the removal of those whom he regarded as *deutschfeindlich* or unsympathetic to his leadership.[78]

Soon afterwards, Gérard Romsée, as Secretary-General of the Interior Ministry, made a request to the German military authorities for the return of 150 men from Luckenwalde to augment the strength of a reformed Belgian gendarmerie which, it was hoped, would act as an effective instrument to carry out German policies inside Belgium.[79] Van Coppenolle, who had originally been appointed as Police Commissioner for Antwerp, was instead appointed as head of the *Police Générale/ Algemene Rijkswachtpolitie* when he and 150 others were repatriated to Belgium on 5 August 1941.[80] After this, the remaining Belgians at Luckenwalde were sent back to the camps at Eichstätt and Rotenburg, and the *Abwehr* project came to an end. These two camps also produced their own autonomous study groups, for example the *Cercle de Rénovation Nationale* founded by Luitenant-Kolonel Emile Wanty in Rotenburg. Prompted by the concept of a new order in Europe and worried about the future of their country, its twenty or so members, which included both Flemish and Walloon officers, were more heavily influenced by the corporatist ideas of Mussolini and Salazar. Officers here also petitioned to join the Flemish Legion once the war against the Soviet Union had begun.[81] Whatever the German or Belgian intentions behind the repatriations, the subsequent careers of those sent home were by no means identical. While the majority found a home in the police or the *Vlaamse Wacht* and a few went to fight on the Eastern Front or volunteered to work in Germany, at least twenty-eight ultimately went underground and joined the resistance.[82] This suggests that the ideological views, even among those thought to be the most promising supporters of the new order, were far from uniform.

For most Belgian prisoners of war, staying in Germany was the more secure option until Allied bombing began to take its toll, and one where continuing service in the armed forces meant that families could be supported, even *in absentia*. Conversely, returning home in person would mean living illegally without valid papers, and there was no certainty about what would happen to those who were caught on the run. Clearly, these were the dominant sentiments among the Belgians who effectively sat out the war in German captivity. Belgium being a belligerent power during the First World War meant that Hitler's concession in liberating the Flemish-speaking elements within the armed forces has to be seen as an exception. While there was no question that French-speaking soldiers would be interned, freeing the Flemings was essentially a pragmatic step designed to rebuild the idea of a *Flamenpolitik* which had first been tried during the occupation of the country between 1914 and 1918. When it was first enacted, prisoner labour was not a priority for the Third Reich and so a linguistic differentiation could be carried out without damage to the German war effort.

Notes

1 This is for example the case of Armand Ghiot, whose letters were published. Wilkin (ed.), *Correspondance du brigadier Armand Ghiot*.
2 Gillet, 'Histoire', *RBHM*, Vol. 27, No. 5, pp. 362–363.
3 Gillet, 'Histoire', *RBHM,* Vol. 27, No. 5, pp. 365–366.
4 Gillet, 'Histoire', *RBHM*, Vol. 27, No. 5, p. 367.

5 Gillet, 'Histoire', *RBHM*, Vol. 28, No. 1, p. 49.
6 de Schaepdrijver, *La Belgique et la Première Guerre mondiale*, p. 163.
7 de Schaepdrijver, 'Occupation, Propaganda and the Idea of Belgium', pp. 281–294; Jay Howard Geller, 'The Role of Military Administration in German-occupied Belgium, 1940–1944', in: *Journal of Military History*, Vol. 63, No. 1 (1999), p. 106.
8 Wilfried Wagner, *Belgien in der deutschen Politik während des Zweiten Weltkrieges*, (Boppard am Rhein: Boldt Verlag, 1974), pp. 160–163; Charles Burdick and Hans-Adolf Jacobsen (eds), *The Halder War Diary 1939–1942*, (London: Greenhill, 1988), p. 170. Entry for 28 May 1940 reporting meeting between Hitler and Commander in Chief of the Army Walther von Brauchitsch. Conway, *Collaboration in Belgium*, p. 25; Warmbrunn, *The German Occupation of Belgium*, p. 186.
9 It should be noted that Belgian soldiers from the German-speaking part of the country were later enrolled in the German army and forced to fight. There are several cases of veterans of the eighteen-day campaign dying on the Eastern Front and elsewhere. See Archives de l'État à Liège, État-civil de Verviers, dossiers de soldats allemands décédés.
10 Michael Wiesner, "Wer die Macht hat, hat Recht". De Belgische krijgsgevangenen in Duitsland en de Conventie van Genève, 1940–1945, (Licentiate Thesis, KU Leuven, 2005), p. 35; Gillet, 'Histoire', *RBHM*, Vol. 27, No. 5, pp. 359, 371. There was also some considerable debate on how the distinctions were to be made; domicile, language and 'ethnicity' were all considered. Wagner, *Belgien*, pp. 160–163.
11 Overmans, 'Die Kriegsgefangenenpolitik', p. 776. Gillet, 'Histoire', *RBHM*, Vol. 27, No. 5, p. 373. Text of the relevant *Entlassungsschein* (discharge certificate).
12 'Les Prisonniers de Guerre Belges en 1940–1945', in: *Mensuel de l'Amicale des Anciens Prisonniers de Guerre de Stalag XIIIB (Weiden)*, n° 203, 1970. Gillet, 'Histoire', *RBHM*, Vol. 28, No. 1, p. 49 suggests that there were in total about 145,000 Flemish and 80,000 French prisoners in German hands.
13 'Les Prisonniers de Guerre Belges en 1940–1945'.
14 Gillet, 'Histoire', *RBHM*, Vol. 28, No. 1, p. 50.
15 Testimony of Georges Rovillard, Forchies-la-Marche, 22 August 2011, http://nouvellesduprogres.skynetblogs.be/archive/2011/12/09/sur-les-prisonniers-de-guerre-1940-1945-de-forchies.html [6 August 2015].
16 Gillet, 'Histoire', *RBHM*, Vol. 28, No. 1, p. 51.
17 Unnamed testimony, 28 December 2014, http://gege6220.skyrock.com/451931930-Les-prisonniers-de-guerre-belges.html [6 August 2015].
18 Gillet, 'Histoire', *RBHM*, Vol. 28, No. 1, p. 51.
19 Overmans, 'Die Kriegsgefangenenpolitik', p. 777 suggests there were around 13,000 repatriations on medical grounds and a further 1,000 escapes.
20 'Les Prisonniers de Guerre Belges en 1940–1945'.
21 Gillet, 'Histoire', *RBHM*, Vol. 28, No. 1, pp. 53–55.
22 Gillet, 'Histoire', *RBHM*, Vol. 28, No. 2, p. 126.
23 Wilkin (ed.), *Correspondance du brigadier Armand Ghiot*, p. 36.
24 Gillet, 'Histoire', *RBHM*, Vol. 28, No. 2, p. 129.
25 Gillet, 'Histoire', *RBHM*, Vol. 28, No. 1, p. 47, Vol. 28, No. 4, p. 308.
26 Reinhold Billstein, Karola Fings, Anita Kugler and Nicholas Lewis, *Working for the Enemy: Ford, the General Motors, and Forced Labor in Germany*, (New York: Berghahn Books, 2004), pp. 54, 69–71.
27 Harry Spiller, *Prisoners of Nazis: Accounts of American POWs in World War II*, (Jefferson NC and London: McFarland), p. 29.
28 'Lessiver en Captivité!', in: *Mensuel de l'Amicale des Anciens Prisonniers de Guerre de Stalag XIIIB (Weiden)*, n° 301, 1979. See also Reinhard Otto, *Wehrmacht, Gestapo und sowjetische Kriegsgefangene im deutschen Reichsgebiet 1941/42*, (München: Oldenbourg, 1998), p. 125.
29 Gillet, 'Histoire', *RBHM*, Vol. 28, No. 2, p. 131.

30 See, in this context, Rolf Schwarz and Gerhard Hoch (eds), *Verschleppt und Sklavenarbeit. Kriegsgefangene und Zwangsarbeiter in Schleswig-Holstein*, (Bremen: Geffken, 1985), pp. 149–191.

31 *Mensuel de l'Amicale des Anciens Prisonniers de Guerre de Stalag XIIIB (Weiden)*, n° 317, 1981.

32 Gillet, 'Histoire', *RBHM*, Vol. 28, No. 2, p. 125.

33 Gillet, 'Histoire', *RBHM*, Vol. 28, No. 2, pp. 133–134.

34 Robert Gellately, *The Gestapo and German Society: Enforcing Racial Policy, 1933–1945*, (Oxford: Clarendon, 1990), p. 216.

35 Fernand Wilkin was born on 21 August 1908 in Rechrival (province of Luxembourg). He was a conscript in the Belgian army when he was captured in May 1940.

36 *Meldungen aus dem Reich*, No. 44, 24 January 1940. Uli Herbert, *Hitler's Foreign Workers: Enforced Foreign Labour under the Third Reich*, (Cambridge: Cambridge University Press, 1997), p. 75. Gellately, *The Gestapo*, pp. 223, 233. Moore, *Prisoners of War*, p. 39.

37 Jill Stephenson, *Hitler's Home Front: Württemberg under the Nazis*, (London: Bloomsbury Academic, 2006), pp. 271–272, 279.

38 From 1942 onwards, Poles being investigated to see if they were regarded as *Volksdeutsche* were concentrated at SS-Sonderlager KZ Hinzert near Trier.

39 Gellately, *The Gestapo*, p. 235.

40 BA NS18/649 Memorandum from Martin Bormann 20 June 1940 demanding that French and British having relations with German women should be treated '*wie bei Polen*'. Peter Longerich (ed.), *Akten der Partei-Kanzlei der NSDAP. Rekonstruktion eines verlorengegangenen Bestandes. Regesten*, Vol. 4, (Munich: K.G. Saur und R. Oldenbourg, 1992), p. 43. Gellately, *The Gestapo*, pp. 232–233.

41 Gellately, *The Gestapo*, p. 226 cites Heinz Boberach (ed.), *Meldungen aus dem Reich: Die geheime Lageberichte des Sicherheitsdienst der SS 1938–1945*, (Herrsching, 1984), p. 528.

42 See for example, Meldungen aus dem Reich, No. 27, 11 December 1939, No. 47, 31 January 1940

43 Gisela Schwarze, *Gefangen in Münster: Kriegsgefangene, Zwangsarbeiter, Zwangsarbeiterinnen 1939 bis 1945*, (Essen: Klartext, 1999).

44 *SD-Berichte zu Inlandsfragen*, 10 June 1943, (Blaue Serie: Volkstum und Volksgesundheit).

45 Gellately, *The Gestapo*, p. 244.

46 Stephenson, *Hitler's Home Front*, pp. 280–281, 283.

47 Jan Velaerts and Herman van Goethals, *Leopold III: de koning, het land, de oorlog*, (Tielt: Lannoo, 2001), pp. 469–470, 708. Wiesner, "Wer die Macht hat, hat Recht", p. 21.

48 De Wilde, 'De Belgische Krijgsgevangenen', pp. 103–104.

49 Velaerts and van Goethals, *Leopold III*, p. 730.

50 Wiesner, "Wer die Macht hat, hat Recht", pp. 17–18.

51 Named after the Commander, Count de t'Serclaes de Wommersom.

52 De Wilde, 'De Belgische Krijgsgevangenen', pp. 119–120.

53 Eddy de Bruyne, 'Le recrutement dans les stalags et des oflags en faveur de la Légion Wallonie', in: *Histomag*, No. 92, July–October (2015), p. 64.

54 Gillet, 'Histoire', *RBHM*, Vol. 28, No. 2, pp. 136–137.

55 Gillet, 'Histoire', *RBHM*, Vol. 28, No. 2, pp. 138–139.

56 Gillet, 'Histoire', *RBHM*, Vol. 28, No. 2, p. 141.

57 Overmans, 'Die Kriegsgefangenenpolitik', p. 778.

58 Gillet, 'Histoire', *RBHM*, Vol. 28, No. 2, p. 143.

59 Gillet, 'Histoire', *RBHM*, Vol. 28, No. 3, p. 224.

60 Gillet, 'Histoire', *RBHM*, Vol. 28, No. 4, pp. 302–303.

61 Léa Buchkremer, L'engagement féminin dans la Croix-Rouge de Belgique pendant la Seconde Guerre mondiale (1939–1945) : une réelle contribution à l'émancipation? (Master's Thesis, University of Louvain, 2021), p. 59.
62 Pierre Kalmar and Alphonse Fouilhoux, *Lettres à ma mère*, (Le Mont-Doré: Crébu Nigo, 2012), p. 53.
63 Fabien Théofilakis, *Les prisonniers de guerre français en 40*, (Paris: Fayard, 2022).
64 Jean-Claude Catherine, *La captivité des prisonniers de guerre : histoire, art et mémoire 1939–1945*, (Rennes: Presses universitaires de Rennes, 2015), p. XLVII.
65 Gillet, 'Histoire', *RBHM*, Vol. 28, No. 3, p. 229.
66 Gillet, 'Histoire', *RBHM*, Vol. 28, No. 3, p. 246.
67 Gillet, 'Histoire', *RBHM*, Vol. 28, No. 3, p. 230.
68 Gillet, 'Histoire', *RBHM*, Vol. 28, No. 3, pp. 242–243.
69 Overmans, 'Die Kriegsgefangenenpolitik', p. 778; Gillet, 'Histoire', *RBHM*, Vol. 28, No. 3, p. 243.
70 Jean-Marc Vanderlinden, 'La réinsertion socio-professionnelle des anciens de la « Légion Wallonie ». Première approche', in: *Journal of Belgian History*, Vol. 1 (1991), pp. 203–222.
71 Gillet, 'Histoire', *RBHM*, Vol. 28, No. 1, p. 48.
72 De Wilde, 'De Belgische Krijgsgevangenen', p. 105.
73 De Wilde, 'De Belgische Krijgsgevangenen', p. 121.
74 De Wilde, 'De Belgische Krijgsgevangenen', p. 108.
75 De Wilde, 'De Belgische Krijgsgevangenen', p. 112.
76 Bruno de Wever, 'Militaire collaboratie in België tijdens de Tweede Wereldoorlog', in: *Bijdragen en mededelingen betreffende de geschiedenis der Nederlanden*, Vol. 118, No. 1 (2003), pp. 22–40.
77 De Wilde, 'De Belgische Krijgsgevangenen', p. 114.
78 De Wilde, 'De Belgische Krijgsgevangenen', p. 114.
79 Yves Durand, *Nouvel ordre européen nazi (1938–1945)*, (Paris: Complexe, 1990), p. 234; Jonas Campion, 'Être gendarme en Belgique occupée. Droits et devoirs d'une profession au regard de la répression pénale d'après-guerre (1944–1950)', in: *Journal of Belgian History*, No. 24 (2011), p. 188. Warmbrunn, *The German Occupation of Belgium*, p. 188. Conway, *Collaboration in Belgium*, p. 145. Benoît Majerus and Xavier Rousseaux, 'The World Wars and Their Impact on the Belgian Police System', in: Cyrille Fijnault (ed.), *The Impact of World War II on Policing in North West Europe*, (Leuven: Leuven University Press, 2004), pp. 59–60.
80 De Wilde, 'De Belgische Krijgsgevangenen', p. 116. Van Coppenolle was subsequently head of the gendarmerie from February 1943 onwards. Much to his disgust, Verreydt was forced to accompany Van Coppenolle, who had clearly been preferred despite the former's leadership of the LDWK.
81 De Wilde, 'De Belgische Krijgsgevangenen', pp. 118–119.
82 De Wilde, 'De Belgische Krijgsgevangenen', p. 116.

4 Escapes From the Reich

Escapees and Their Motivation

Through the detailed work of Georges Hautecler, we know that 768 Belgian servicemen were recorded as having (successfully) escaped from the Stalags and Oflags inside the Reich. This total represents approximately 1% of the Belgian prisoners still in German hands in 1944 although it is impossible to say how many additional unsuccessful attempts there were. Nevertheless, the overall impression is that only a small minority of prisoners ever seriously tried to escape captivity. That said, it is a much lower figure than the 4.37% of successful escapes by French servicemen – a percentage that itself was described as 'poor' (*faible*) by Yves Durand.[1] As we have seen, by 1941 most of the Flemish servicemen had been repatriated and the overwhelming majority of the men still in captivity were francophones whose homes were in the provinces of Liège, Hainault Namur, Luxembourg and Brabant. The detailed statistics provided by Hautecler show that escapes took place across all four years of the war, with the majority taking place in 1942 and 1943.

Table 4.1 Escapes by Belgian Prisoners of War 1940–1944[2]

Month	1940	1941	1942	1943	1944	Total
January	–	2	33	6	19	60
February	–	1	28	4	16	49
March	–	–	40	4	27	71
April	–	3	16	15	10	44
May	–	5	13	11	19	48
June	–	9	17	11	15	52
July	–	13	15	30	6	64
August	–	12	18	30	7	67
September	1	25	30	62	3	121
October	–	26	31	31	5	93
November	–	19	18	16	–	53
December	1	13	5	24	3	46
Total	2	128	264	244	130	768

DOI: 10.4324/9780429027697-5

The propensity of prisoners of war to attempt an escape from captivity was determined by a wide range of factors, those that encouraged flight and those that acted as deterrents. Given that the majority of Western Allied prisoners did not even try to escape, it can be assumed that it was the deterrent factors that loomed largest in their minds. Having survived the fighting and been taken prisoner, they were now in enemy hands but held in Stalags, Oflags and *Arbeitskommando*, where they could expect to be fed and to receive Red Cross parcels and personal parcels from home. In the early stages of the war, they were unlikely to be subjected to Allied bombing, not least because the majority were employed in the countryside. As long as the work they were required to do was tolerable, they were in a relatively safe position to see out the war. While their circumstances would sometimes make absconding a possibility, escaping was inherently dangerous and could lead to injury or death on the run, or the prospect of punishment if caught. It was no accident that prisoners were usually taken as far as possible from their homelands, so that the majority of Belgians initially found themselves in East Prussia or Pomerania where the sheer distances to be traversed were a major deterrent. While the railway network offered the prospect of travelling long distances in a relatively short time, the controls at stations and on the trains made this inherently problematic for fugitives lacking money and valid identity documents. Moreover, if the motivation for leaving the comparative safety of captivity was to return home, even success had potential long-term consequences, with the possibility of families being victimised, losing the rights to the prisoner's service allowances and for the individual to have to live 'underground' for however long the conflict lasted. Being out of the war therefore had its advantages, and most prisoners chose not to take the risks involved in going on the run.

In the following chapters, we are concerned primarily with the motivations of the minority of captives for whom other factors carried greater weight. These were many and various. For some, it was a positive desire not to stay idle and to rejoin the fight against the Nazis, either at home with the domestic resistance or by finding a way to join the Allied armed forces. For others, the claustrophobia of a prison camp was enough to create an obsession with getting out, often referred to as barbed-wire fever. In some cases, and this would be particularly true of officers who were not required to work, it was almost an intellectual pursuit in trying to devise ways of outwitting their guards and escaping. These were the psychological factors, but there were also more practical considerations. There might be a reticence about working for the Germans, or conditions in camps or *Arbeitskommando* might be so bad that escape was seen as a safer option. This became more prevalent in the later stages of the war when more prisoners were moved to urban areas where they were exposed to repeated bombing, or where they were deployed in far more dangerous work, such as mining and quarrying. Opportunities also played a role. The proximity of a neutral frontier, or that of Belgium itself, was often germane, and it is no surprise that the majority of successful escapes took place from the camps closest to Belgium and the Netherlands. Finally, there were the personal factors – long separation from wives, sweethearts and families could become intolerable over time or exacerbated by specific events such as illnesses, marriage breakups or deaths. All of these issues and more besides can be seen in the stories chronicled here.

The detailed information we have also tells us where the escapes took place – or at least which camps the men involved were attached to. Perhaps not surprisingly, the greatest number of successful 'home runs' came from Stalag VI-F (Bocholt), a camp that was only around 4km from the Dutch border and around 190km from the closest Belgian soil. Other camps in Wehrkreis VI (Münster), close to the western borders of the Reich, also had a disproportionate number of successful escapes. While still a considerable distance to travel, they were a good deal closer than the camps in East Prussia and Austria that housed most of Belgian prisoners throughout the war.

In addition, we also know their military ranks. The preponderance of ordinary soldiers should come as no surprise as they were by far the largest group of prisoners, but the numbers of *Sergents* is probably out of proportion to their overall numbers. As NCOs, they were not required to work under the terms of the Geneva Convention, but were placed under increasing pressure by the Germans as the war continued.

Of those who escaped, 270 were known to have continued the struggle against the Axis in one form or another, either joining Allied forces or underground organisations in Belgium, while the remainder just returned to their homes in Belgium.[3] However, in order to paint a picture of what escape meant to these men, it is important first to look at how they described their individual decisions and then to the practical issues they had to overcome. These include identifying possibilities for escape, the attempt itself and then the other issues that arose once they were outside the wire. These soldiers' contemporary accounts of their experiences provide a multiplicity of examples and show that no two escapes were completely alike.

Table 4.2 Escapes by Camps and Locations

Camp	Location	Number of escapees	Belgian POWs registered to camp	%
Stalag VI-F	Bocholt	102	726	14.00
Stalag II-C	Greifswald	94	5,670	1.65
Stalag I-A	Stablack	55	6,487	0.83
Stalag XI-B	Fallingbostel	50	3,688	1.35
Stalag VI-D	Dortmund	40	650	6.15
Stalag VI-C	Bathorn	38	1,344	2.82
Stalag X-B	Sandbostel	26	1,702	1.52
Stalag XIII-A	Nürnberg/Sulzbach	24	1,787	1.34
Stalag XVII-A	Kaisersteinbruch	24	802	3.00
Oflag II-A	Prenzlau	23	2,617	0.87
Stalag XIII-C	Hammelburg	23	4,648	0.47
Stalag IX-C	Bad Sulza	22	674	3.25
PG 82	Laterina (It)	27	166	16.00

Table 4.3 Escaping Belgian Prisoners of War – By Rank

Rank	Active	Reserve	Total
Soldats	46	471	517
Caporaux	11	63	74
Sergents	48	71	119
1st Sergents	9	5	14
Adjutants	1	9	10
Sous-Lieutenants	10	3	13
Lieutenants	13	2	15
Capitaines	1	–	1
Commandants	1	–	1
Majors	1	–	1
Civilians	–	1	1
Unknown	2	–	2
	141 + 2	625	768

One of the most forthright and comprehensive statements on why he escaped came from Georges Even, who clearly hated the Germans and had a burning desire for revenge:

Here is a summary of all I can say. I escaped from the German camp [in Wehrkreis I] (Königsberg) because:

1. I wanted to fight the Boches
2. I would have died of cold.
3. This nation revolts me, from 1914 to 1918, my uncle and my cousin fought. My cousin was killed on the battlefield and my uncle died soon after because he was badly treated by the Boches. Therefore, I had promised to avenge them during this conflict.[4]

Georges Even was true to his word as he joined the *Armée Secrète* resistance organisation soon after he reached Belgium in 1942. A similar motivation can be seen in the testimony of Frédéric Dalimier, a soldier from Liège, who was also vehemently opposed to the Germans. Previously punished by his captors for Anglophile speeches, he planned his escape to Switzerland in May 1941, declaring that he preferred 'a thousand times to be interned by the Swiss rather than being forced to work for the Germans'.[5] While escaping to avoid working for the enemy could be portrayed as a patriotic gesture, there were also more prosaic reasons. Some men, primarily conscripts, did not escape to continue the fight or to inconvenience their captors, but to flee the rigours of forced labour. As Félix Dumont candidly summarised: 'In 1942, we decided to escape because the work was too hard and there was too much discipline in Kommando III-B'.[6] Émile Dandois was equally unhappy with his circumstances: 'Not wanting to work and being constantly beaten by guards, I decided to escape'.[7] Captivity was a dull and uncertain experience, far from family and home. While not all Belgians were resolved to fight the enemy, most found that working for the Germans was difficult to bear. As Frédéric Dalimier explained:

> Having no information, we expected to be brought to an internment centre in Switzerland and it seemed much better to be kept by the Swiss rather than being forced to work for the Germans. [Moreover], having escaped from Germany, it looked easier to leave Switzerland for the unoccupied part of France.[8]

These accounts that encompass radical anti-German feeling, patriotism and self-preservation are only a snapshot of the reasons given for escaping from camps and *Arbeitskommando* in the Third Reich. Many successful escapees did not reflect on their reasons for acting as they did, perhaps seeing it as a natural response to captivity or regarding it as an obvious course of action that did not need to be justified. Others were more concerned with telling the story of their adventures 'on the run' and what happened to them subsequently – so that we only have a partial picture of what drove this small proportion of Belgian prisoners of war to act as they did.

Escaping the Enemy: The Soldiers

To understand the realities of what it meant to escape and be on the run inside the Third Reich, what follows are the detailed recollections of several servicemen who managed to flee their captors and find their way home to Belgium. Their experiences are many and various, but as will become apparent, they also shared some common features that assisted in their success.

Perhaps the most individual of the escapes was that of Joseph Delvigne, a 33-year-old serviceman in the Namur air territorial guard who escaped from *Arbeitskommando* E 34. Like many of his countrymen, he had been taken initially to Stalag I-A (Stablack), at the time the furthest prisoner-of-war camp from the Belgian frontier, and from there allocated to a work detachment in Tilsit, a city in the far north-eastern corner of East Prussia and close to the frontier with the USSR. In his own words, he had been brought up as an orphan from the age of four after effectively being given up by his mother. From the ages of 14 until 20, he had lived in every corner of Belgium and had tried many trades, sleeping more often under the stars than in a bed. He had thus endured a lot of hardships but had acquired a physical and moral resistance to any test. On 28 July 1941, just over a month after the beginning of Operation Barbarossa, he absconded from the *Arbeitskommando* having made meticulous preparations. Without saying anything to his fellow prisoners, he acquired civilian clothes, a compass and a map. He also had a 'solid cutlass' to serve as a tool as well as a weapon, some food and a supply of matches.

As he knew only a few words of German, he avoided inhabited areas. Crossing East Prussia was extremely difficult. At night he was devoured by mosquitoes and during the day by leeches as he crossed the marshes. His provisions were quickly exhausted and he then had to live on what nature offered him: fruits from the woods, raspberries, blueberries, wild chicory, small animals that he managed to kill, frogs' legs and eggs that he found. One day he was confronted by a large lake that he swam across after placing all his clothes on a small makeshift raft that he pushed in front of him. When his hunger became too great, he got closer to the villages, milked cows sleeping in the meadows and pulled vegetables or picked fruit in the gardens. Sometimes he was forced to traverse villages so he seized a farming tool, wheelbarrow, shovel or rake and walked confidently like any farm worker.

Crossing a huge forest took him three days and was particularly painful. Starving to death, he fed himself on slow-worm tails and snails. However, he was lucky to find a deer injured by a hunter that came to die in a thicket. Using the cutlass, he cut a leg that he took with him. His feet were injured by the constant walking with bad shoes. He wrapped them with plantain leaves and pieces of shirt. Inevitably and despite all his precautions, Delvigne could not complete this extraordinary crossing of Germany without meeting anyone. He was apprehended four times. He managed to escape twice without difficulty, but on another occasion he had to knock out two curious German rangers with a club. Once he was even hunted down in a wood by a whole troop of the Hitlerjugend, but he had become a real man of the woods and escaped them without difficulty. Crossing the major rivers Oder, Elbe, Weser and Rhine posed particular problems. Road bridges were heavily guarded and impossible to traverse without the appropriate papers. Delvigne solved this by following the bank of the river to a railway bridge, walking up the track to a station or a steep curve of the track, and then jumped onto a train. Three times he did this with freight trains, but on the fourth occasion he was more comfortably installed on a wagon filled with straw. After thirty-five days on the road, Delvigne crossed the Belgian frontier at Hertogenwald in Eupen. He had traversed a total of 1,200 kilometres at an average of 34 kilometres per day. From then on, he lived underground in Belgium, not telling his mother of his return as he had authorised her to receive his allowances as a military prisoner and knew very well that she would have denounced him in order to be able to continue to receive those allowances.[9]

Delvigne's early experiences seem to have prepared him well for life on the road, yet even then, traversing such a long distance on foot while living off the land and avoiding detection when any man of working age would be regarded as suspect is testament to his single-minded desire not to remain in German hands. Unusually, he used the railways not to travel long distances but merely to cross specific obstacles such as major rivers where bridges were heavily guarded. One last element of note here is the lack of family ties involved in his desire to escape, given that he thought his mother would probably betray him to the authorities if she knew of his escape.

A more common form of escape was to make use of the German railway system.

Nestor Gillot, Auguste Marcq, Louis Morelle and Paul Nussbaum had been incarcerated at Stalag II-C (Greifswald) and then sent to Arbeitskommando XII/101 Bredow, where they were members of a 22-strong party of prisoners of war working for the Brandt Construction Company. They were employed alongside five volunteer Belgian civilians in building a huge concrete shelter for the civilian population of Stettin. According to Gillot, 'tired of the insufficient food supplied for the heavy work to which they were obliged to do, eager for freedom and constantly harassed by nostalgia for their homeland', they decided to escape. By selling their tobacco and cigarettes to Polish workers, they easily obtained Reichmarks in large quantities. Two of the Belgian volunteers, Cyrille Tack and his son Germain, who worked at the same site, agreed to help them in their attempt. These two civilians had been helping the prisoners of war as much as they could. On each trip back to their homeland they took dozens of clandestine letters from prisoners of war to their families, and on their return brought back the answers and parcels. At the request of the four would-be escapees, the Tacks returned to Germany with civilian clothes provided by the men's families. They hid them in their camp and, at 8pm on the day before the escape, Germain Tack threw them over the barbed wire into the camp. The men were also provided with a good compass and a railway guide which indicated that permits for volunteer workers were suspended between 20 December and 10 January. This meant that they had to escape before this date.

On 12 December 1941, the four men, under the pretext of carrying out repairs, carefully dismantled the window of their barracks and made an opening in the plank partition of the German garden of the camp. The whole thing was carefully camouflaged and put back in place so as not to attract attention. Each escapee carried a suitcase containing clothes, food, and soap. Later that night, avoiding waking up the three German guards sleeping in the barracks, the four Belgians left through the dismantled window, passed through the plank fence via the prepared opening, crossed the garden and reached the neighbouring street. From there, they made their way to Stettin station and acquired coupons to Berlin. Through a Polish worker from the Brandt firm, they had obtained stationery and envelopes from the firm, as well as a stamp from the site manager. A French prisoner who was well versed in German had typed letters with the following text.

Head of Personnel of Brandt in Stettin to Head of Personnel of Brandt in Aachen.

Today we are sending you the two scrap metal workers (*aide-ferrailleurs*) you need for the new building in Aachen. The documents concerning these two men will be sent to you by post at the request of the Arbeitsamt.

Heil Hitler,

Signed Folmann.

Armed with this certificate, they had had no difficulty in obtaining tickets to Aachen. Marcq and Morelle placed themselves in one of the first carriages of the train and Nussbaum and Gillot in one of the last. Arriving in Berlin, they followed Tack's advice and used the U-Bahn to reach the Friedrichstrasse

Station. At 8.35am they boarded the train to Aachen, making the same arrangements as on their first train.

According to Gillot, their tickets were checked along the way, but not their identity papers. As for Marcq, he reported a random check by two *Feldgendarmes*, a control that he and Morelle managed to avoid. Around 7pm, the four arrived in Aachen and managed to leave the station, again without their papers having been checked. Morelle and Gillot knew the city well and brought their companions to the tram stop to Siegel. When the tram arrived they were, with a German NCO who regarded them with suspicion, the only occupants of the tram. Arriving at the terminus of the line, they moved quickly into a dense woodland. This was fortunate because they soon saw the glow of a dozen electric torches at the edge of the wood: the German NCO had probably given the alert. Fortunately, the Germans did not dare to penetrate deep into the woods and soon everything calmed down. They crossed the woods and reached some cultivated land. They walked in line at the limit of their vision with Marcq, the custodian of the compass, in the lead. Moving across different terrains with a compass is not easy. Thick hedges, ponds, and potholes forced detours. After several hours of walking, they clearly felt lost. They took a path heading southwest and came across concrete blockhouses and anti-tank lines. Near some concrete shelters, they saw the glow of electric lamps. Were these soldiers or smugglers? They thought it better not to check and moved away as quickly as possible. In their haste, they fail to notice the position of a Flak spotlight. A persistent fine rain began to fall. Marcq recounted 'We were tired in the extreme, our shoes made us suffer excruciatingly and we were discouraged because we saw no way out of our situation'. They decided to wait for dawn and, despite the cold of that December night, they laid against each other on the wet ground and thus managed to sleep for a few hours. At the first light of day, they resumed walking and found themselves only two hundred metres from a road, which they crossed quickly and disappeared into a dense wood on the other side.

Using their compass, they continued to travel westwards until daylight forced them to take refuge under a fir tree, where they were invisible under the low branches. They spent the whole day there (December 14) with enough to eat but nothing to drink. To assuage their thirst, they sucked the drops of water beading at the end of the fir needles. Once darkness came they resumed their journey. Walking through the wood was very painful. Their second-hand suitcases, soaked in water, could not withstand this ordeal and, one after the other, began to disintegrate. Fortunately, Marcq had brought string with him and made makeshift repairs. After a few hours of progress through the woods and coppices, they came upon a paved path heading westwards, which they followed for about 500 metres until they reached a large structure that appeared to be a customs post. They retreated and discovered a small stream where they could finally quench their thirst. Unfortunately, Marcq had used his torch and they were spotted. In terror, they heard guttural calls and saw the glow of torches whose owners were approaching at pace.

They immediately fled in all directions, which baffled the pursuers who soon abandoned their hunt.

Marcq, who had hidden under a bush without making a sound, found himself alone. Unable to shout for his companions, he continued through the woods. He reached a clearing and then a road parallel to a railway. As the road headed westwards, he decided to follow it and arrived in a village where he saw cafes and shops with inscriptions in French. He thought he was saved. Leaving the village, he met a young man and a young girl tenderly embracing. Having apologised for disturbing them, he asked them where he was. The answer was discouraging: he was in Moresnet, a village annexed to Germany in May 1940. The young man offered to help him but he must first accompany his fiancée home. He suggested Marcq hide behind a hedge and wait for his return. A little sceptical and ready to flee at the slightest danger, Marcq obeyed, but his worries proved unfounded as the young man soon returned and took him back to his parents' house. The son admitted that he had also been a Belgian prisoner of war at Stalag II-C, but had been repatriated in August 1940 as a '*Volksdeutscher*'. On the farm, Marcq was very well received and slept a few hours in the barn.

The young man then took Marcq to another farm, telling him that the farmer would surely help him as long as he did not betray him. Entering the courtyard, he found the farmer who was initially reluctant to assist because the Germans were using fake escapees to destroy networks. He was surprised at the good condition of Marcq's civilian clothes, but Marcq retorted that there was nothing strange as these were his own clothes sent secretly to Germany. Having seen Marcq's identity documents and some photos taken at the Stalag, the farmer's attitude changed, and he was received with open arms. At 3pm, a worker from Montzen station picked up Marcq and took him to the marshalling yard. Marcq left his suitcase with the farmer, taking only a few biscuits and packs of cigarettes. At the yard there was a train to Hasselt. All the crew were Belgian except the driver who was German. The guard had been warned and he smuggled Marcq into his compartment while the Belgian railway workers diverted the German's attention. At 4.20pm, the train got under way and soon arrived in Visé. A railway worker then led our escapee to the train to Liège. Marcq avoided returning to his home and lived in hiding in Brussels until the liberation.

The other three escapees managed to find each other after they split up in the woods. Without Marcq and his compass they decided to move through the woods in single file at the limit of their visibility. Nussbaum led, followed by Gillot and then Morelle. At the end of the wood, Nussbaum waited for his companions. He was joined by Gillot, but Morelle got lost a second time. Enervated and soaked by the rain, Nussbaum and Gillot re-entered the wood in search of him, but without success. They decided to find a railway track and follow it into Belgium. On their way they found an old abandoned shack and took refuge there until dawn. When day came, they set off again and arrived at a large village. Nussbaum went on alone as a scout while Gillot, hidden in a small wood, waited for the result of his reconnoitre. Nussbaum returned quickly but empty-handed as it was still too early and he had not met any inhabitants, but he was afraid of still being in Germany, because he had seen portraits of Hitler in the storefronts. The two escapees had no idea what to do next.

Soon a woman headed in their direction. Gillot stopped her, saying that they were two Belgian workers lost while trying to return to Belgium illegally. The lady, a little frightened at first, quickly recovered her composure and disappointed them by saying that they were in Moresnet. While she could not receive them in her house she assured them they could approach Vincken the pastry chef. Taking her advice, the two found they had nothing to complain about. They were very well received, could wash and dry their clothes, and then rest after a good meal. Around 3pm, they left this hospitable house to go to the Locht farmhouse in Homburg. They had barely left when the Mother Superior of the convent at Moresnet warned the pastry chef about German customs officers on the path to Homburg. Vincken immediately sent his son on a bicycle to warn the two escapees, who caught up with them and then acted as their guide via another path to their destination. Once there, they were immediately taken to the barn and provided with a change of clothes, while their own clothes were allowed to dry out. The farmer did not dare bring them into the house because the customs officers on duty at the nearby railway line came in at all hours to rest. Nussbaum and Gillot spent the night in the barn and were provisioned by the farmer's sons. In the afternoon the sons provided them with detailed instructions on how to cross the border. The two men asked to be able to stay in the barn one more night and leave the next morning. At 5am on 20 December, the farmer came to awaken them and wished them good luck. The night was pitch black and the rain was falling again. Following the farmer's advice, they carefully crossed the railway track, bypassed a few farms, crossed hedges and fields and arrived at a beautiful asphalt road that formed the border. They hurried across the road as it was heavily guarded and entered the fields on the other side. After half an hour of walking, they arrived at the village of Rémersdael. They encountered a housewife opening the shutters of her house who offered them breakfast and the chance to wash and dry their clothes.

At 10am they set off for Aubel, then on to Liège. Gillot stayed one night with an uncle in Liège, then one night with an aunt in Ohey, before going home. After an evening with his family, he took refuge in the Ardennes where he joined the resistance. As soon as the territory was liberated, he enlisted as a volunteer in the new Belgian army. Gillot was recognised as an armed resistance fighter in the secret army group from 1 June 1942 to 14 October 1944. Returning home on 20 December 1941, Nussbaum was able to have his status regularised through the good offices of Major Degaye of the OTAD. He was registered as having been legally repatriated on 15 February 1942 and was appointed to the Office of Comfort and Assistance to Families (O.R.A.F.) in Liège. He also became involved in the resistance, a branch of the liberation army, and played the role of liaison between Sector IV and Sector V. Denounced to the Germans by an anonymous letter, he was arrested at home at 8am on 30 August 1943 and taken to the Saint-Léonard prison. Nussbaum denied any resistance activity and admitted that he was an escaped prisoner of war. Given his name had Jewish origins, it was much better for him to be considered a prisoner of war than a political prisoner. His ruse succeeded, and on 12 October 1943 he was handed over to the Wehrmacht and returned to Stalag II-C on 18 October, from where he was repatriated on 23 May 1945. As for Morelle, he was recaptured trying to cross the border and initially sent to the Stalag VI-H at Arnoldsweiler/Düren. He made another escape attempt, again without success and was then sent back to his original Stalag where he was not punished for his attempted escapes but repatriated as medically unfit during the course of 1942.[10]

This extensive and detailed narrative of escape provides us with a great deal of information, but also raises a series of questions. The success in some of the men reaching Belgium is in no small part to careful preparation and a number of favourable factors. Obtaining German currency from other workers in exchange for cigarettes seems to have presented no problems. Their contact with Belgian civilian workers in Stettin seems to have been crucial in communicating illicitly with home and in obtaining civilian clothes. Perhaps even more important was the travel information they could provide, as is evidenced by their passing on details of dates when foreign workers would not be allowed to access trains. That said, the four men armed with a false set of orders seem to have had little difficulty in buying train tickets and travelling long distances across the Reich without being challenged – and this without having any viable identity papers. This seems to speak against the idea that rail travel was notoriously difficult because of the controls on stations and in trains, but it may be the result of checks being confined to valid tickets or down to sheer luck that these four avoided being challenged, both on the trains and in stations.

What they could not know with certainty was that crossing the frontier would be far more difficult and that checks at the border would soon expose them. The train to Aachen got them within a few kilometres of Belgian soil, and a local tram a stage further, but then they were forced to travel on foot, with only a vague idea of where the border might be. Here they seemed to have had good fortune in finding help, despite the fact they were in a German-speaking part of Belgium that had been annexed to the Reich. Although one of the four was arrested at the frontier and returned to captivity, this narrative shows how a combination of planning, favourable circumstances and luck could combine to produce a successful conclusion.

In a similar way, François Gobillon also travelled substantial distances across Germany with few if any problems. He had been in Stalag IX-C (Bad Sulza) but had been allocated to *Arbeitskommando* 552 in Gera.

Having obtained civilian clothes and a sum of 80 Reichsmarks, Gobillon went to Gera station and bought a ticket to Erfurt. From there, in short journeys by train, he arrived at Düren. He decided then to continue on foot and, two days later, was in Malmedy. He went to a café in an attempt to contact local smugglers, but they refused to help him as the dangers were too great. He then tried to cross the frontier alone and had the good sense to get rid of his suitcase and everything that might identify him as an escaped prisoner of war if he were searched. Near the border, he unexpectedly encountered a German customs officer who proceeded to question him. Gobillon responded in German that he had crossed the border the night before to buy bread and flour. He tried to gain the customs officer's sympathy by telling him about an 80-year-old mother who was starving to death in Belgium and that he did not know that he had entered Germany. His story was so touching that the customs officer was convinced and about to let him continue on his way when a superior officer arrived. Gobillon was taken to the customs office and searched carefully. The 43 marks he still had were confiscated and he was questioned. Gobillon claimed that he had left his ID card in Belgium so as not to worry his 80-year-old mother. When asked where the money found on him came from, he said he had found it. The sceptical customs officers claimed that it was the result of selling Belgian products in Germany. Gobillon vigorously denied this. He was then offered a bowl of soup and taken to the gendarmerie in Malmedy. He arrived there at 8pm and was locked in a dungeon. The next day at 7am, he was taken for further questioning. He did not change a word of his statements to the customs officials, despite the threats from his interrogators. Tired of the war of attrition, the gendarmes drove him back to his dungeon. Half an hour later, he was picked up and taken to the Sicherheitspolizei (Security Police) headquarters. He was placed in a room with several doors and left waiting for an hour. At all times, doors opened and then closed abruptly. Police officers rushed through the room wielding a large-calibre revolver. Gobillon understood that they were trying to frighten him, but he kept calm. He was then brought into an office where he was confronted by four civilians. One of them asked if he spoke German – which he denied. Gobillon then admitted that he understood a little German, but spoke it very badly and that, moreover, he did not know what was written in the two reports that he had not signed. The mollified interrogator then asked him for his wallet and dutifully returned it, but found only 120 francs. He then asked him, in French, how he dared to pretend to have come to buy in Germany with such a ridiculous sum. Gobillon retorts that he was also in possession of 43 marks, but that they had been confiscated by the customs. The policeman jumped up and Gobillon heard him tell his colleagues in German that the suspect's quarrel was with the customs officials who had confiscated the money. Gobillon was handed back to the gendarmerie who told him he would be incarcerated for about fifteen days – time to have his declarations checked in Liège.

However, he was almost immediately confronted again by the customs officer who proceeded to fine him 5 Reichsmarks for entering German territory illegally and gave him two hours to leave the country with the threat that a repeat offence would earn him a month in prison. Now freed from custody, he was able to walk to the frontier via the main road and was allowed to cross by the customs officials there. Whether his story was believed or not, he seems to have successfully played off the tensions between the *Zollgrenzschutz* (Customs Border Guards) and the Sicherheitspolizei in order to escape. Once back in Belgium he claimed to have been repatriated on the grounds of ill-health, but in a twist to the tale some four months later, the German police came to search his house at 4am in the morning, but he managed to escape and lived underground until the liberation.[11]

Here again, the fugitive prisoner does not seem to have had too much difficulty in crossing Germany by train unchallenged – or at least being able to avoid controls. His decision to use local trains – that were probably less well policed – was probably a considered one, but he also knew that crossing the frontier would be the most difficult part of the journey and that trains were inherently dangerous. The only alternatives were local public transport or on foot. Doubtless like many other fugitives, he was apprehended by the border police or customs officials, but unlike others he was able to talk his way out of trouble and return home. One last surprising element of this story is that Gobillon's house was later raided by the German police, but whether they were specifically looking for him or had some other reason for doing so remains a mystery.

The railway system therefore clearly played a crucial role in many escapes – allowing prisoners to travel substantial distances in a relatively short time. This was certainly the case with Joseph Laret, a soldier from the 34th Artillery Regiment who was deployed in *Arbeitskommando* 2392 (Auerbach) attached to Stalag XVIII-A (Wolfsberg). He had attempted to escape once previously in October 1942, but had been recaptured at Regensburg station. Undeterred, he and a French soldier, Albert Lucas, made a second attempt on 8 July 1943.

They cut the *Kommando* fence wires and found their way to a railway embankment, staying a whole day hidden in a wood near this railway line until at night they managed to climb onto a freight train which, heavily loaded, was moving very slowly. Unfortunately, when they arrived in Linz, their wagon was directed onto a siding for repair. Managing to leave it without being noticed, they hid all day under a tank wagon. In the evening, they took refuge in a brakeman's cabin but were discovered there by a German railwayman. However, the latter mistook them for foreign workers trying to escape wagon-loading duty and in great anger, he sent them to join their supposed workmates. Delighted with the mistake, the two escapees hastened to obey. Taking advantage of the general inattention, they then climbed on a train heading towards Vienna. The next day, their train stopped at a goods station. Laret and Lucas ventured into town, because they were hungry and thirsty and they tried to clean themselves up. They washed quickly in a fountain, then went in search of the Vienna-West station, from where, according to the information they had, a train left every day for Brussels. They searched all day, but to no avail and they were forced to sleep under the stars. The next day they were no more successful and they spent the second night in a damaged wagon on a siding. Finally, the following night, they managed to slip under the bogies of the Vienna–Paris express.

At 6 o'clock in the morning, their arduous journey began and for 25 hours they were exposed to burning cinders falling from the express locomotive and the outfall from the carriage lavatories. By way of compensation there were not many stops and these were perforce short. In Châlons-sur-Marne, completely exhausted, they left their uncomfortable hideout and were discovered by French railwaymen who took them in. Washed, fed and rested, life seemed worth living again. The railway workers agreed to take them home. Laret followed one of them to Reims, then another railway worker took him to Charleville, and a third took him to Givet where he was given into the care of a Belgian railway worker who brought him to Dinant across the border in Belgium. From October 1943, Laret was hidden in Anhee but, keen to reach the United Kingdom, he crossed France but was caught by the Germans near the Spanish frontier at Irun and sent by rail back to Germany. However, he was able to escape a second time by jumping from the train and taking refuge with the French resistance at Tonnerre (Yonne) where he stayed until March 1944 when he returned to Belgium and joined the *Armée Secrète* in Dinant.[12]

The prisoners deployed in railway yards did not just assist fugitives, but also used their position to escape themselves. Pierre Jauquet escaped from *Arbeitskommando* 2311 attached to Stalag VIII-A (Gorlitz), accompanied by a certain Georges, a butcher from Liège on 6 September 1943. Jauquet worked with about twenty prisoners of war at Gorlitz goods yard, and because they knew the destinations of the wagons they were loading, could take advantage of this information. Discovering wagons heading for Belgium, the two men decided to act and each returned from the *Kommando* barracks with a suitcase stuffed with food and Jauquet's carpentry tools. Arriving at the wagon, they found it was already sealed, but Jauquet went to the brakeman's cabin and made an opening there, allowing him to enter the interior of the wagon. During this time the other prisoners in the *Kommando* distracted the sentry with a lively game of football. After four hours' relentless work, Jauquet and Georges made an emergency door in the wall of the wagon. The wagon was completely full with crates, and the crates still had to be pierced to be able to sit inside. Jauquet was still in the brakeman's cabin trying to remove the traces of his work when he was surprised by a German railway worker.

Jauquet, who spoke German, admitted that he was about to escape. The railwayman was sceptical because the brakes would be checked at each major stop. Jauquet ventured to offer him five packs of American cigarettes as the price for his silence and the German accepted. He didn't discover the door made in the wall, so Jauquet's work had been successfully put to the test. The two fugitives climbed into the wagon and a few minutes later, it was shunted towards a train being formed. Around midnight, the train left and the two escapees disposed of some boxes in the middle of the countryside to make life a little more comfortable. Around noon the following day they drank their last drop of coffee, and from that moment began to suffer horribly from thirst. During a sudden stop, Jauquet was thrown against a wall of the wagon and stunned, remaining unconscious for a few minutes, much to the fear of his companion. The train spent the night at a busy station and they dared not leave their hiding place. The following evening, they arrived in Breslau.

Through an opening between the planks, they could see a nearby tap and decided to take advantage of this once night had fallen. Unfortunately, a train loaded with ammunition destined for the Eastern Front stopped between their wagon and the tap. Jauquet, carrying the two canteens, ventured onto the tracks and crawled under the ammunition train. Unfortunately this train was guarded, and a German sentry stood between Jauquet and the tap. He therefore made a cautious retreat and was lucky not to be spotted. On his return to the car, his companion was desperate and talked about surrendering, but Jauquet persuaded him to hold on. At dawn the train left and with unbelievable luck, rain began to fall, and they were able to collect water coming from the roof of the wagon – quenching their thirst and filling their water bottles. The following night, the train stopped in the countryside. And they were able to slip outside, cool their hands and faces with the wet grass and pull white cabbages from a nearby field before returning to their hiding place.

On the fifth day of the journey, they arrived in Düsseldorf. German railway workers came to work under their wagon but did not discover them. While the train stayed in the station, the two did not dare to move for fear of causing the boxes to tumble. On the following night they crossed the Belgian border and, at dawn, saw Belgian customs officers. As they were still in uniform, it seemed dangerous to stay on the train as far as Brussels and they decided to jump off at the first opportunity. Taking advantage of a slowdown in the train, they left their hiding place for good just beyond Hasselt. Flemish peasants working in a nearby field thought the two dirty, unshaven Belgian soldiers in uniform were ghosts. They explained their situation and went to a nearby farm where they received food and the loan of some civilian clothes. They then separated and returned to their respective homes. Jauquet did not stay long and took refuge in a hotel in Schaarbeek. Living illegally, he was dependent on ration cards from the resistance. He also asked the Red Cross to redirect his prisoner-of-war parcels, but this was refused as parcels were strictly reserved for prisoners who had remained in Germany. To survive, he worked illegally in a small workshop in Ixelles until the liberation.[13]

Travelling illicitly in goods trains had the advantage that one needed neither civilian clothes nor identity papers as the task was to remain undiscovered for the entire journey to friendly territory. The problem for Jauquet, as for others who made similar attempts, was that there was no way of knowing how long such journeys might take. Ordinary goods trains had a low priority for the *Reichsbahn* and would be placed in sidings for long periods, while military traffic and passenger trains were prioritised. Crossing the whole of Germany from East Prussia to the Belgian border was bound to take many days. As was apparent here, access to food and water was at a premium and nearly forced these two men to give up their attempt, and it was only the rain and a fortuitous stop in the countryside at night that saved them.

While the railway system played a major role in many escapes by providing a relatively speedy transit across German soil, it was by no means the only method of escape. As we have already seen, it was possible to traverse long distances on foot if one had the stamina and the wherewithal to stand the strictures of weeks on the road, but there were alternatives. For example, Maurice Massart had been allocated to *Arbeitskommando* 180 in Moritzburg from Stalag IV-D (Dresden) and worked as a forester on the estate of the Prince of Saxony. He also visited the Prince's castle – three quarters of which had been converted into a museum – to do odd jobs and made the acquaintance of the mostly elderly guards there. In exchange for chocolate, tobacco and cigarettes, as well as English and American parcels, he acquired a German military map, two civilian suits, a Tyrolean-type backpack, an inner tube and a bicycle tyre, and some tools. On 8 August 1943, before going back to the *Kommando* dormitory, he entered the basement of the castle cellar and stole the Prince's son's bicycle, which he knew was kept there. Leaving the castle by the rear entrance, he collected all his other belongings as well as some food and then hid everything in the forest.

The following day at 5.30am, Massart went with his companions from the *Kommando* to the *Gasthof* where the daily ration of bread was distributed and where the prisoners of war took their breakfast. The meal over, Massart told his companions that he had to go to the castle, which everyone found normal, but instead, headed into the forest. Finding his belongings and the bicycle untouched, he changed into civilian clothes and buried his military uniform. Travelling westwards, he successively passed through Moritzburg, Coswig, Chemnitz, Gera, Weimar, Erfurt, Gotha and Eisenach. He rode during the day and sought shelter at night. The rain was persistent and Massart suffered from the constant humidity. On the third evening, he could find no shelter and was forced to stay in the woods. Fortunately, he had the canvas from his military tent and this afforded him some precarious shelter.

At dawn, after a very bad night, he set off again. Coming out of the woods, he came across a German carrying a gun and a white armband on his arm. The German asked him what he was doing there. Massart pointed to the Tyrolean bag attached to the bicycle rack. Believing that he was dealing with a poacher, the German bent down to open the bag. Unfortunately for him, he put his rifle on the ground. Massart seized it and, with a few well-applied blows from the butt, knocked out his unwelcome acquaintance. Leaving quickly, he set off via Alsfeld towards Giessen.

Massart was aware that he still had to negotiate the most dangerous part of the journey – crossing the Rhine. The bridges across the river were heavily guarded by the military and the security police, so travelling without identity papers he had little or no chance of success at either Cologne or Koblenz. Instead, he headed for the much smaller town of Linz. Approaching the bridge, he noted that the sentry was carefully checking the identity papers of individual civilians making the crossing. Massart stayed hidden for two hours and then managed to mingle with a group of German factory workers crossing the bridge. Overwhelmed by numbers, the German sentry let everyone pass without checking anything. Massart then followed the Ahr valley passing Ahrweiler and Adenau. He took refuge in a forest. The rain had finally stopped and, exhausted and hungry, he decided to rest. Despite his discomfort, he immediately fell into a heavy sleep. When he woke up on 16 August, a week into his journey, the sun was already high on the horizon.

His legs were stiff and he had to massage them vigorously to be able to get back on his feet. Full of optimism, he hoped to cross the border the same day. Having eaten the last of his food – two potatoes and an apple – he drank water from a stream, then washed and shaved. Around 8.30am he set off towards Prüm.

Having cycled only a few hundred metres, he saw a German policeman arriving on a motorbike from the opposite direction. Impossible to avoid, he chose to continue riding as if nothing had happened. Unluckily the policeman stopped him and began to ask him specific questions: surname, first names, nationality, identity documents. Massart claimed to be a French volunteer worker coming from Adenau and travelling to Prüm to visit friends there, but the policeman was not convinced. He pulled out a revolver and ordered Massart to ride towards Prüm where his statements would be checked. Demoralised by failure so close to his goal, he set off, followed by the policeman.

Suddenly Massart could no longer hear the motorbike. He looked back and saw the German policeman leaning over his machine and trying to get it back on the road. Massart continued to ride away as if nothing had happened, but a mad hope was born in him. On his right there was a small, fairly narrow road, but in good condition and leading down into a thick forest. He turned in and ran down the slope at high speed. At the end of the forest, the road passed through a small village. Massart rushed through at full speed and almost landed right in the middle of a group of villagers in their Sunday best on their way to mass. He narrowly avoided a collision. He gathered all his strength to pass this village, heedless of threats made against him by the furious villagers. He then saw a small hill and another dense forest. He continued to use secondary roads and avoided settlements. Around 6.30pm, he arrived in St. Vith. He stopped at a café. Massart's arrival went unnoticed, but he realised that both Belgian and German money was in circulation and heard both German and Walloon French being spoken. Massart still had 400 Belgian francs and 35 Reichmarks sewn into the lining of his trousers and decided to put them to use.

In the café, he took a seat at the counter and ordered a glass of beer. Beside him a young man searched his pockets to see if he was still rich enough to afford a drink. Massart offered him a glass of beer and a packet of cigarettes. The conversation thus became very cordial and Massart asked his new friend to be able to speak to him confidentially. Leaving the café, Massart admitted to being an escaped prisoner of war and offered the young man the 35 Reichsmarks for help in crossing into Belgium. The young man accepted and revealed that there was a good chance that the customs officers, having had their meal, would no longer be watching the road. He went in front of Massart and signalled to him to hurry because the road was clear, and at 8.30pm, the fugitive finally arrived in the Belgian village of Cominster.

After more than a week on the road, Massart was completely exhausted and found refuge in a hayloft before moving on again, but his problems were not yet over. Asking for help in Belgium was still dangerous and he had neither identity papers nor a permit for the bicycle. One man he approached was sympathetic but could not shelter him as his son had evaded the labour draft and his house had already been raided by the police. He did, however, provide two addresses of farms where Massart might be taken in and a postcard to send to his family. Soon afterwards he collapsed completely and was taken to a nearby café. A teacher named André who had been an officer with the *Chasseurs ardennais* was there, and he took Massart to a doctor who questioned him at length before agreeing to treat him. Massart lost consciousness again and did not reawaken until the following afternoon.

Subsequently, he lodged at the teacher's brother's farm for about five weeks. He was given a Belgian identity card and he then moved to his brother-in-law's residence in Jemeppe-sur-Sambre. He lived there in hiding until the liberation in September 1944 when he presented himself at the military hospital in Namur where he was declared unfit for military service.[14]

We also have an account of a 'classic' escape from agricultural employment in the early years of the war, showing how planning and ingenuity could pay dividends. On 12 October 1941, Hubert Rassart, a 33-year-old sergeant of the 25th Artillery Regiment, escaped from *Arbeitskommando* 1250 of Stalag XII-A, at Gladbach, Kreis Neuwied, near Koblenz. He claimed to have made two previous unsuccessful attempts, but there was no evidence for these in the German records. As a result of his experiences, he decided to escape alone and on a Sunday when surveillance was more relaxed, and hoped to be across the Rhine before the alarm was raised. Since 3 May 1941, Rassart had been working on the Winnen family farm and he prepared his escape carefully. He noted that the work clothes of the two Winnen sons were stored in an unoccupied room and that one of the sons more or less matched his height and build. A girl in the village, Edwige Litzenbach, was in love with a Belgian prisoner and was prepared to aid other prisoners. Through an intermediary, Rassart was able to acquire an excellent map of the Rhineland and eastern Belgium. Her father, the butcher in the village, allowed Rassart into his home to listen to the English radio and use his bathroom on a Sunday morning with the hot water created by the bread ovens. Another Belgian prisoner named Delys worked on a farm a long way from the village and had acquired a bicycle which Rassart knew he hid overnight. He obtained Delys' permission to use the bicycle in his escape and stole a small triangular flag from a passing car. He also acquired a supply of food and bought a few jars of brilliantine and a pair of glasses with tortoiseshell frames and neutral lenses.

On Sunday 10 October Rassart shaved carefully, bade farewell to his companions in the *Kommando* and at 7am went as usual to the Winnen farm to look after the horses. At 9am, the farmer and his wife left the farm to go to the church at the other end of the village. Rassart entered the farm through the kitchen window that had been deliberately left open, grabbed the civilian clothes which fitted him like a glove and left the farm hiding his unusual outfit under his Belgian artilleryman's greatcoat. He hid his food supply, his toiletries and a civilian raincoat in a parcel of dirty laundry. He then went to the place where Delys' bike was hidden and grabbed it. He quickly discarded his military coat and his non-commissioned officer's cap, flattened his stubborn hair with brilliantine, put on the raincoat and glasses, placed the Hitler flag on the frame of the bicycle and set off. He followed a truck driven by a Belgian prisoner of war from the *Kommando*, Permanne, who, knowing the region well, guided him to the bridge over the Rhine at Neuwied. At 10.10am he crossed the Rhine. He rode for the rest of the day and by nightfall he was between

Jünkerath and Stadtkyll. He spent the night in a fir forest but could barely sleep as he was freezing cold. At dawn, he got back on his bike and warmed up while pedalling. Around 4pm he arrived in Malmedy and reached the Café Maertens. After speaking to the owner in Walloon, the latter agreed to help him. He led him to the edge of the woods west of Malmedy and described in detail a route marked out by abandoned Belgian forts and ending in Cheveaufosse at the home of a pro-Belgian farmer. Rassart wandered all night in the woods, managing to avoid three patrols, and arrived at Cheveaufosse at 8am the following morning. He was welcomed by the farmer and took a few hours of much-needed rest. At 12 noon, taking advantage of the relief of the customs patrols, he crossed the border a mere 200 metres from the Cheveaufosse farm. Half an hour later, he was in Stavelot and went to the house of a career non-commissioned officer, Roger Parmentier, employed at the time by the Belgian national railway company, and the latter accompanied him to Liège, where the two men arrived on 14 October at 6.30pm. Rassart, who was a left-wing socialist militant, considered it more prudent to avoid returning home and he accepted Parmentier's offer to provide him with a rented room in the rue Warin. Via Jean Allard, municipal secretary of Jupille, and Charles Rahier, director of the clandestine socialist newspaper *Le Monde au Travail*, Rassart obtained false papers in the name of Jean Hubert. Using this alias, Rassart worked as chief checker at the Martinrive shipyard (Aywaille) of the Pieux Franki company, in charge of rebuilding a bridge over the Amblève. Later, Rassart changed his identity once again and became Jean Davernay, a student at the University of Liège, thanks to the intervention of Baugnet, municipal secretary of Aywaille and Fernand Dehaisse, professor at the university. On 7 September 1944, Rassart took part in the liberation of the city of Liège.[15]

As we have seen, most escapers attempted to cross directly from Germany into Belgium, albeit that the annexations in 1940 had created a buffer zone populated by people, many of whom still regarded themselves as Belgians and where they were more likely to find sympathetic help. Aachen as a major railway hub was especially appealing as it was only a few miles from the frontier. In much the same way, some thirty-eight escapees found their way home via the Grand Duchy of Luxembourg, a small number when compared with the 374 that crossed directly from Germany into Belgium and even more surprising as the two frontiers were of much the same length. However, because the Grand Duchy had been annexed to the Third Reich, its eastern frontier was unguarded and the local population was almost universally hostile to the Germans.[16]

On 13 March 1942, Léon Dandoy, a soldier from the IIIrd Army Transport Corps, François Mirgain, a sergeant in the 1st Regiment of Chasseurs Ardennaises, and Albert Wilmet, escaped from Stalag IX-C (Bad Sulza). They had prepared very carefully and were aided by a tailor in the camp who provided them with suitable civilian clothing. They used the chore of taking coal before 6am every day to the German barracks to light the fires there. Their civilian clothes were concealed in the bags of coal which they carried on their shoulders. They hid in the barracks until 9pm. Taking advantage of the darkness, they then crossed the barbed wire in an unguarded place. It was very cold and the roads were covered with a thick layer of snow.

Hoping to catch the 12.42am train from nearby Apolda, they got lost and had to wait for the next train at 4.36am. Travelling via Bebra, they arrived in Kassel where they had to wait for two hours for the train to Giessen. They went to the canteen but sat apart and in order to eat their food, they went to the station lavatories. At 9am they boarded the train to Giessen and on arrival bought tickets valid for Luxembourg. Dandoy and Mirgain travelled in the same compartment, which also contained a German soldier. Wilmet had gone missing in Giessen. In Trier, a German policeman in civilian clothes examined the identity papers of travellers. When he arrived in Dandoy and Mirgain's compartment, he spoke first to Dandoy. The latter held out his Belgian identity card. The policeman asked for his leave entitlement document but, at that moment, the train started moving. The policeman shouted to the German soldier to keep an eye on the suspect until Luxembourg, while he himself went to warn (telephone) the police there. As the train arrived in the capital of the Grand Duchy, Mirgain got up quickly. The soldier ordered him to stop but Mirgain, who spoke German, protested violently, declaring that the Trier policeman said nothing about him and, taking advantage of the confusion as the train arrived at its destination, disappeared into the crowd. By this time it was around 11pm. Mirgain set off on foot towards Steinfort, to the home of Madame Oswald, a distant cousin. After walking for two hours, he arrived and was very well received. On the night of March 16 to 17, he crossed the Belgian border with the help of Madame Oswald's son, who served as his guide. He reached Brussels [...] He later tried to reach England but was stopped trying to cross the Line of Demarcation in France at Chaumont-sur-Loire. Considered by the authorities as an ordinary criminal, he was released a few days later. On his return, he joined the armed resistance until the liberation.

Dandoy was entrusted to the custody of three Luxembourg policemen by the German soldier. He was carefully searched and thoroughly questioned, inventing a story that the Luxembourgers pretended to believe. He was then taken by one of the policemen towards the police station. Along the way Dandoy tried to evince help from his captor and the latter, named Trivière, seemed well disposed. At the police station, he intervened on behalf of Dandoy and the commissioner decided to release him, simply requesting that he not admit to having already been arrested in Luxembourg if he was apprehended again while trying to cross into Belgium. Dandoy bought a train ticket for Esch (close to the French frontier) and arrived there at 4am. He immediately set off towards Belgium. At the border, he encountered a German guard whom he despatched with a vigorous punch in the stomach. Once on Belgian soil, Dandoy attempted to change the 40 Reichsmarks he had left into Belgian francs at Athus. He spoke to a passer-by and the latter, a local hairdresser, immediately understanding the situation, took Dandoy to his home, fed him, gave him clothes and a shave and changed his money.

On the evening of 18 March, only five days after his initial escape, Dandoy returned to his home in Gilly (Charleroi) and lived there in hiding until the liberation.[17]

Escaping the Enemy: The Officers

Escapes were not confined to ordinary soldiers; officers, whose status precluded them from work, had more time to plan and execute their plans. That said, they were kept in closed compounds and generally more closely guarded than in the Stalags and *Arbeitskommando*, and escaping often required a greater degree of ingenuity to breach German security measures, as the following accounts make clear.

On 6 February 1942, Maurice Minne, a Reserve Lieutenant in the 40th Engineer Battalion, escaped from Oflag II-A at Prenzlau, in the company of second lieutenant Paul Charlier of the artillery reserve. Their plan was developed over several months by carefully observing the entrances and exits of the camp. This is how they noticed that the Belgian prisoners from nearby *Kommandos* no longer came for consultations in the camp infirmary accompanied by a German sentry, but were brought by their employer. Charlier was able to search the doctor's confidential papers one day and discovered the official form which German farmers had to present to the guardhouse when they brought their prisoners for a medical examination. This information and document allowed Minne and Charlier to formulate an escape plan.

The entrance to the camp was through the guardhouse and there was a German sentry at both doors. Charlier, who was fluent in German, was to play the role of the employer and Minne that of a Belgian soldier with his arm in a sling, going for a consultation. The escape committee in the camp, known as the Bolle Organisation, approved these two men's ingenious plan and provided the dyes to create acceptable civilian clothing. The two officers chose a day when it was very cold and, shortly before the changing of the guard, presented themselves at the first exit door. Charlier was in civilian clothes and Minne dressed as a Belgian soldier. The sentry, thinking he was dealing with a soldier who had come for a medical consultation, opened the door and the men reported to the gatehouse. The officer in charge, absorbed by the changing of the guard, did not see if the two men had come from outside or inside the camp, and Charlier declared that he had come from outside with a sick soldier. He filled in the entry and exit notebook for the camp accordingly and received written permission (pass) to enter the camp. They left the guardroom and proceeded into the camp. They headed towards block D, which housed the infirmary, but, as soon as they were in the block, they took refuge in a general's room where they had concealed everything necessary for their escape: German money, map, compass, etc. Minne put his civilian clothes under his uniform and Charlier supplemented the German pass with a prescription for medicine authenticated by the seal of the German doctor. They waited all the time necessary for a real medical examination, then re-presented themselves at the first exit gate of the camp. The sentry who saw them come in made no fuss about opening the door for them, and the two Belgian officers, with pounding hearts, entered the guardhouse. There everything went well and Charlier received written authorisation to go out with his prisoner, passing through the second door without difficulty.

The road to freedom, all white with frozen snow that crunched under their feet, opened up before them. They had to control themselves so as not to run for joy but to get away quietly. At the first appropriate place, Minne disposed of his military clothes, which he hid under the snow, and the two of them headed to Prenzlau station with the snow falling ever more heavily. They boarded a train bound for Pasewalk which brought them to Stettin, then on to Berlin where they arrived at 11pm on 7 February. At 1am, they boarded the express for Cologne. On the way there was a check on identity documents. Minne was lucky to escape, but Charlier was apprehended and his comrade saw him walking away – flanked by two policemen. At 9.15am, that is to say at the time of the roll call at Oflag II-A, Minne arrived in Cologne. Around 3pm, he boarded a train to Aachen – arriving there around dusk. Their original plan had been to walk from there to Gemmenich (close to the Belgian border) where Charlier knew a Belgian patriot, Mr Martin Altenhof. Unfortunately, it was Charlier who had been carrying the map and the compass. Minne tried to follow the railway line, but in the dark night he soon completely lost his way. Snow was still falling heavily and Minne, sinking up to his knees in this snow, realised the impossibility of crossing the border alone, not least because he did not know exactly where it was. He therefore retraced his steps and met a German civilian and asked him the road to Gemmenich. With good directions from this German, Minne found the route and headed west but did not persist for long because he realised the dangers of encountering customs officers late at night with no possibility of escaping, as the snow would allow them to easily follow his trail. He returned to Aachen station and noticed that no one asked for identity documents and so bought a ticket to Gemmenich. A train was just leaving and Minne just had time to jump on board and 10 minutes later, he reached his destination. He was shown to Altenhof's residence and was welcomed there with open arms. There he remained until 11 February, awaiting a favourable moment. Before then, the moonlight had been too bright but finally the sky darkened and crossing the frontier became possible. At 8.30pm in the company of two smugglers, Minne set off and arrived the next morning at the Belgian village of Clermond at around 7am. One of the smugglers, Peereboom, from the nearby municipality of Henri-Chapelle, accompanied him to Thimister where Minne could catch a train. Minne wanted to compensate his rescuers, but they refused any reward. Minne then went home where he lived underground without ever receiving the visit from the German police.[18]

This story includes reference to the Bolle Organisation within the camp, which functioned as a coordinating escape committee. Created in August 1941 by Lieutenant-Colonel Paul Bolle,[19] it was intended to provide leadership, information and material aid to would-be escapers – advising on the best methods of leaving the camp, traversing Germany and crossing into Belgium or neutral Switzerland. It was essentially the initiative of one man but grew to substantial proportions. According to Bolle, information as well as certain material means, such as clothing, tools, money and false papers, were sourced from Belgium after finding correspondents prepared to take charge of such things. Other elements came from German sources and were obtained by trickery, theft, even by purchasing after carefully considered approaches. There was also the formation of work teams for the substitution of clandestine parcels, the establishment of a watch, the creation of various workshops with the appropriate equipment and the identification of men with the skills who were suited to carry out specialist work for everything required for escapes: from detailed maps, identity papers and travel orders to tools, keys, compasses and even ventilation equipment for tunnels. This took more than four months to create, and it was only at the beginning of 1942 that the organisation began to be effective in helping escapees from the Prenzlau camp.[20]

The process of obtaining information and materials was aided by the soldiers on fatigue duties, who were permitted to leave the camp each day and were charged with bringing back information about the locality and, when possible, stealing maps, documents and parts of uniforms. The organisation also made contact with an *Arbeitskommando* of six ordinary Belgian soldiers working in Prenzlau who became indispensable to the success of escapes. It was noted that after an escape, the Germans mounted a major operation employing local police and their dogs, Gestapo, railway staff, Hitler Youth and locally stationed troops to erect roadblocks and carry out meticulous checks of all identity papers. However, after six days, this would be abandoned and the situation returned to normal. As a result, it was decided that once outside the wire, all escapees would be sheltered locally until the hue and cry had died down – thus giving them a better chance of getting away. Where possible, the men were placed in sealed railway wagons heading for Belgium, but the organisation also created a second relay, another Belgian *Arbeitskommando*, in Berlin and the beginnings of a third in Kassel before Allied bombing dispersed them both. The network even extended to safe houses close to the border, for example the farmhouse at Ober-Emmels near St. Vith where escapees were hidden before being taken across the frontier by the daughter of the house, Lucie Moutschen.

One example of the organisation's significance can be seen in the following account of six escapees from the camp in July 1943.

On a hot day in the summer, it was noticed that between block C and the watchtower, there was a place which was very difficult for the sentry to watch, and as an added diversion a boxing match was taking place on the terrace of one of the camp buildings. Escapees could take advantage of a slight slope in the ground, barely noticeable to a standing man. Colonel Bolle and his deputy, Commander Renier, sanctioned the attempt and Lieutenant Jean Mentior and Lieutenant Emile Sibenaler volunteered to create a breach in the barbed wire. Lots were drawn and Mentior won. Operations started at 11.30am when the shadow cast by the barrack block covered the chosen location and where the watchtower sentry was blinded by the rays of the sun. The latter seems to have suffered particularly from the heat and fidgeted like a caged bear. When he turned his back on the chosen location, a newspaper read by a lookout was closed and folded. Another lookout placed at the corner of block C then gave the signal for action. At 11.30, prompted by the lookout, Mentior rushed towards the barbed wire. He had the only wire-cutting pliers in the camp, manufactured from metal bed posts and, 40 metres from the watchtower, he courageously began the creation of a 50-centimetre breach in the wire. To be able to recover the pliers in case of misfortune, they were attached to a long rope leading to block C. After 16 minutes of hard work, Mentior finally created a breach in the fence. The pliers were hauled back into the camp and at a favourable moment, Mentior rushed towards freedom, crossing a garden and the wooden fence along the adjacent road before hiding in a nearby wood. After this, the other escapers followed one by one. When the sentry turned in the wrong direction, the first lookout opened his newspaper and operations were suspended. Similarly, a halt was called when the watchtower sentinels were relieved, but fortunately neither the incoming nor the outgoing sentries saw the breach in the wire. After a time waiting to establish the pattern of the new guards, the escapes resumed. Each escaper had to lay close to the breach for fifteen minutes to wait for an opportune time. However, at 2pm, Colonel Bolle suspended the action because the sun's position no longer provided sufficient cover. By that stage, twelve men had successfully traversed the wire unseen: Mentior, Sibenaler, Lieutenant Florent Ledent, Major Victor Legrand and second-lieutenants Albert Janssen and Joseph Vranken, and six others.[21]

It was impossible to determine when the Germans realised the network of barbed wire had been breached and started to search. Ledent and Legrand found their way to the Belgian *Arbeitskommando* at Prenzlau station, where the soldiers hid them and looked after them. The men were to stay in Prenzlau for a few days and wait for the search for the escapees to be scaled back. They were joined on the third day of their escape by Mentior, who had spent two nights in the woods. The Bolle Organisation had provided the three escapees with civilian clothes and papers identifying them as Belgian volunteer workers. After an eight-day stay in Prenzlau, Mentior boarded a train towards Switzerland. His papers were examined by the railway police, but they were deemed to be in order and he was not interrogated. He got off the train about a hundred kilometres from Switzerland and continued his journey on foot, sheltering in woods or haystacks. Arriving near Schaffhausen, he redoubled his precautions and crossed the border at night on 3 August 1943 using a compass. He arrived in Zürich where he presented himself to the Belgian consulate. The consul, in view of his identity card, recognised him as a Belgian officer and granted him an advance on his salary, but refused to facilitate his passage to England. On the contrary, he reported Mentior to the Swiss police. He declared that the English had enough Belgian officers and no more reinforcements were needed. Mentior was placed under house arrest in a hotel in Bern, then sent to Lausanne, where he was joined by lieutenants Sibenaler and Albert Henry.

As for Legrand and Ledent, their plan was to head for Sweden. After a seven-day stay in Prenzlau, they left for Danzig by train where they hoped to find a ship. They arrived there without incident and hid in a French workers' camp. Unable to get to the ships in the harbour, Ledent twice managed to swim out to a Swedish ship. On the first occasion, the ship set sail but then returned to the quay, and after twenty-six hours on board, Ledent was forced to abandon it. On a second attempt, he was discovered by the crew and ordered to leave or face being handed over to the German police. He swam back to shore. On 4 September with their supplies all but exhausted, they returned by train to Prenzlau and the station *Kommando*. They stayed with four Belgian volunteer workers and managed to make contact with Colonel Bolle through Belgian soldiers from the camp and received food, money and new identity papers as Belgian workers. Travelling by train via Berlin, Kassel and Cologne, they finally arrived in St. Vith. There, they went to an address given to them by the Bolle Organisation and were very well received by a mother and her three daughters. Contact was then made with the transit service. The next night Lucie Moutschen and her grandfather came to take charge of the two escapees. Using overgrown paths, the *passeurs* brought them to their own house close to the frontier and took them across the following night, 16–17 September 1943.[22]

Their stay in their homeland was only to be a short one as their intention was to continue their journey to join the Allied war effort. Nevertheless, their experiences in fleeing the Reich had demonstrated the many unknowns in any plan of escape. Getting to a port did not mean there was shipping to a neutral port, and no guarantee that even if such ships were in port the captain and crew would entertain stowaways. The story also highlights the importance of outside help, and specifically the scope and adaptability of the Bolle organisation, not just in organising and co-ordinating escapes, but also in providing contacts and help when plans went wrong.

Emile Sibenaler followed the same trajectory as the others when he escaped the barbed wire – making his way to Prenzlau railway station. Six days later, he had made it to Schaffhausen via Eberswalde, Berlin, Dessau, Memmingen, Tuttlingen and Engen. Sibenaler had a major advantage in being from the German-speaking part of Belgium and therefore spoke the language fluently. The night of 27–28 July, he crossed the Swiss border using his compass. Arrested by Swiss border guards, he was taken to Bern where he was held for 21 days, then transferred to Lausanne under house arrest where he encountered Mentior and Albert Henry, who had escaped from Oflag II-A on 9 December the previous year. Here they were helped by M. and Me Biart, delegates of the Belgian Red Cross and directors of the organisation 'Aide aux prisonniers et internes belges'.[23]

Mentior, Sibenaler and Henry were all determined to continue their escape to England. On 11 October 1943, Reserve-Lieutenant Duchamps, working for the Belgian Information Service, furnished the men with false French identity papers and provided details of a French escape network. They were joined by a Belgian reserve officer and all four, with the complicity of a Swiss border guard, crossed the barbed wire between Switzerland and France on the night of 13 October 1943. They stayed in the village of Saint-Julien-en-Genevois then took a bus to Annecy and from there travelled by train to Narbonne where they had to find a smuggler. They lost a whole day finding one. The man, a wine merchant, agreed to lodge them but insisted that the next departure for Spain would not take place for another eight days.

Henry and the reservist agree to go to a castle where escapees awaiting passage into Spain were housed, while Mentior and Sibenaler decide to take their chances immediately. They were hidden by French railway workers in a freight car due to pass through Spain. Unfortunately the wagon, which already held a Dutchman and Frenchmen, remained in a siding at Cerbère. After five days, starving and thirsty, Mentior and Sibenaler abandoned the train and returned to Narbonne. There they found Henry and his companion, who had had no better luck. The same evening they had arrived at the castle, it had been raided by German police and it was only by pure chance that they were able to escape. As for the escape network, it was obvious that it had been completely compromised. Disgusted with the French network, the reserve officer decided to return to Switzerland, and he was replaced by a Sergeant Tchene, who had recently arrived from Belgium. The escapees once again contacted the French railway workers whom they trusted and were installed in another railway wagon on 29 October 1943. That evening, one of the railway workers came to warn them that a German patrol was approaching. The men hurriedly left the wagon and jumped on a moving freight train. Arriving in a tunnel guarded at one end by the Germans and at the other by the Spaniards, they left their train and walked towards Spain. While still in the tunnel, they encountered a Spanish train that took them to Portbou in Spain.

Janssen and Vrancken also had their fair share of adventures. Janssen provided a fulsome account of their escape and peregrinations across Germany.

Five past midday, the signal for my departure was given. I took some leaps to cross the forbidden space and they brought me against the fence; a second signal and I made my way through the wires; finally a third signal and I ran across an open space of twenty metres, then a jump, one of the finest of my life over a second barricade and I hid in the neighbouring thickets where I waited for my teammate who didn't take long to appear. The first step, but by no means the easiest, had been taken.

Our first concern, after checking our equipment, was to put a distance between us and the camp as soon as possible, just in case our escape was discovered prematurely. As quickly as possible we set off in a northerly direction, traversing covered and deserted places as far as possible and using the sun as a guide. For food, we had been provided with 2 pockets filled with sugar and 2 chocolate bars each. We each had about 200 German Marks, products of miscellaneous sales of foodstuffs to German sentries and officers in the camp. Around 5pm we arrived at the outskirts of Pasewalk and in the fields, we met the first group of civilians who looked at us with astonishment, but their mistrust was conquered thanks to our greetings of "Heil Hitler". Resolutely we entered the small town and asked where the station was (we both spoke good German). After a few minutes' wait we were lucky to catch a train to Neubrandenburg and from there we continued by train to Hamburg where we arrived around midnight. Because our fake papers were for workers employed in Hamburg, we were already much more comfortable. We spent the night in Altona station, stretched out on the benches, side by side with German missionaries who were surprised to see young people like us in plain clothes. We reassured them by saying that we had been discharged from hospital and were now on our way to a new naval unit training in Bremen.

On 23 July at 5.30am we left for Bremen via Harburg and Rothenburg. Around 8am there was the first close call – identity checks by an Oberfeldwebel of the Kriegsmarine. I showed my leave certificate, but he asked for my passport as well as that of my friend. I declared that I indeed had a passport, but that my employer had told me that I did not need it and that the leave document was sufficient, so I had left it at my business in Hamburg. My friend fortunately had an old Belgian identity card that matched his German leave certificate. All our papers were removed and taken to another carriage, I guess for verification. We weren't going anywhere. To our surprise and something that remains inexplicable to me, after a few minutes, the Oberfeldwebel brought us back our papers with a new stamp, a real one, and then moved on. We arrived in Bremen around 8.45am and left at 9.15am towards Osnabrück and from there to Rheine and then to Burgsteinfurt. In this last city, we bought tickets for Vreden that we had agreed ourselves to be the last train stop. Between Burgsteinfurt and Ahaus, a second close call with a check carried out by a Gestapo agent. Our papers were found to be in order, but we were asked what we were doing on this route because our leave documents gave our destination as Liège. This time we explained that a brother of my comrade worked in Vreden [and] we were going to say hello before returning to Belgium. [The explanation] was accepted (I said to myself that if I'd had this chance before, I would have succeeded in my escape [attempt] more than 2 years earlier).

Judging that we were close enough to the Dutch border and as it was impossible to try to cross the frontier by train without having passports perfectly in order, we decided to continue on foot from Ahaus. Around 4pm we set off on our way westwards, guided by the sun and avoiding inhabited areas as much as possible. After walking for about 3 hours through fields and woods, we had a third close encounter. In crossing a firebreak we saw a cyclist in uniform, probably a customs officer, accompanied by a police dog, about 100 metres away but heading in our direction. We retreated hastily but immediately afterwards we heard barking and the dog soon reached us. As he was about to throw himself on me, I welcomed him with a masterful kick under the jaw, which knocked him dead. Miraculously, chance had once again favoured us and, without waiting for any further reaction from the customs officer, we ran as far as we could through the woods. About half an hour later we met a German girl and because we no longer had any means of orienting ourselves, we explained to her that we were Dutch and lost in the forest and that we wanted to know the way back. She answered us mischievously: "But it's very simple. Just carry on straight for a quarter of an hour and you'll be in

Holland, but be warned that there is a customs post in this direction" (pointing in the direction of the danger).

Not wanting to make the same mistake twice, we took the route she suggested, taking good care to avoid those who might still stand in our way. Around 8.15pm I suddenly noticed a board nailed to a tree which was marked in Dutch '*Verboden toegang. Strafwetboek nr 241*'. So we had arrived in a friendly country, without daring to believe it. Further on, at the edge of a wood, we reached a farmhouse. We noted with satisfaction that a broken pane has been replaced by a piece of cardboard with 'Rotterdam' printed in large characters on it. Going around the building, we found ourselves in front of a little old woman babysitting her child. We approached boldly and asked her where we were. Her answer makes us jump for joy. "You are in Rekken, near Eibergen in Holland. You've probably come from the other side". On our affirmative answer, the little old woman offered us a bowl of milk and some old toast, which tasted better to us than a princely meal. She showed us the road that would take us to the village safely. Only a few moments later we reached Eibergen. A man followed and we asked him where we could find a drink, he put us at ease with a few words and led us to a place where soon we were joined by other young people who asked us to tell our story. They were mostly young people who were hiding as *refractaires* [labour draft evaders]. Suddenly a lookout came to warn us that we would have to keep our eyes open that night as the Feldpolizei were preparing for a patrol. We were shown a quiet place near the football pitch and we spent the night under the stars, tired and happy.

The next day, July 24, we left early and, thanks to the information that we were able to collect at Eibergen, our journey continued without further incident: a bus from Eibergen to Neede, then another from Neede to Doetinchem before getting a train to Weert, via Zevenaar, Arnhem, Nijmegen, 's-Hertogenbosch and Eindhoven. From Weert, a region that I knew perfectly for having spent part of my youth there, we continued on foot to cross the Dutch–Belgian border, avoiding roads and paths. Fortune smiled on us again as the 'black guards' [*Marechaussee*], the border guards at this place, had been removed a few days earlier without being replaced. We thus reached without hindrance the farm of J. Vrolix, my father's employee at a place called 'T'Broeck' to the north of Bocholt in Belgian territory.[24]

These two escaped officers were also determined to continue their escape to England. In August 1943, armed with false identity cards, they reached the south of France and arrived in Pau. Unfortunately, they couldn't find a guide to go to Spain. All the escape lines that they had been told about had been rolled up by the Germans. Others were only accepting liaison officers from London and (political) prisoners escaping the death penalty. Vrancken returned to Namèche in Belgium where, on 15 September 1943, he joined the resistance in the 025 Corps of the Belgian partisan army, under the command of Guiot. One of his relatives met him in Liège and Vrancken told him: "Everything is in order. The day after tomorrow, I'm leaving by plane with six other Belgian officers for London". Unfortunately,

Vrancken's group was denounced to the Germans and he was arrested at the Villa des Roses in Namèche on 1 January 1944 and imprisoned in Saint-Léonard prison in Liège. OTAD, made aware of Vrancken's arrest, attempted to intervene with von Falkenhausen, asking that he be returned to the Oflag, but was told that he was being held "for reasons other than his escape". In May 1944, while still in Saint-Léonard, he married, by proxy, Régine Voue, at whose home he had been arrested. On 1 June 1944, he was transferred to Germany. He was known to have been interrogated at Düren on 2 June and his parents received a letter dated 4 June from Arnoldsweiler. He was taken before the military tribunal of Wehrkreis VI in Münster and then sent to Siegburg prison. He is presumed to have died at Schande-lah in March 1945, and he was posthumously recognised by the Belgian authorities as a political prisoner.

As for Janssen, he tried to cross into Switzerland in February 1944, but he was apprehended by the federal police and taken back to the border. He then returned to Belgium and joined the secret army zone IV, western sector but, surprisingly, was never recognised as an armed resister by the post-war Belgian state.

The relatively few stories of escapes provided here are no more than examples from the 768 men known to have successfully escaped from Germany during the war. They nevertheless provide an insight into the experiences of men who were not content to sit out the war in captivity. Their stories of narrow escapes from being unmasked or arrested bear testimony to the difficulties involved in travelling by train and in crossing frontiers and also provide clues as to why other escape attempts were unsuccessful. Likewise, the Rhine and other major rivers in Germany were a major obstacle with bridges heavily controlled by the military and security police. On the positive side, the German annexations in 1940 had brought alienated populations within the Reich borders, and thus escaping prisoners could find more sympathetic help and assistance on the German side of the frontier when crossing into Belgium, France or the Netherlands than might otherwise have been the case. As we have also seen, fugitive Belgian prisoners, and indeed their French counterparts, benefited from the existence of countrymen working as volunteer or forced labourers in the German war economy who could act as helpers and intermediaries for those on the run. The fact that there were so many francophones inside the Reich made it possible for prisoners to be cloaked and assume false but credible identities while travelling and not raise any immediate alarms. While the German authorities spent a great deal of time and effort looking for escapees, they were hampered by the increasingly cosmopolitan nature of the country's labour force as the war progressed.

The stories of escapes here have also focused on those who not only escaped from German captivity and made their way home, but then decided on the equally perilous path of trying to join the Allied cause by making their way across France and into neutral Spain. Their knowledge about the peril they faced and the people who helped them was often perforce limited and therefore not reflected in their subsequent accounts, but the following chapter provides some further insights into how these fugitives were treated by the Spanish authorities, how they were helped by escape networks and Allied organisations based in the Iberian Peninsula and how they finally joined Belgian formations in the United Kingdom.

Notes

1 Yves Durand, *La Captivité. Histoire des prisonniers de guerre français* 1939–1945, (Paris: FNCPG, 1980), p. 156.

2 Georges Hautecler, 'Statistiques au sujet des évasions réussies de prisonniers de guerre belges en 1940–1945', in: *Revue belge d'histoire militaire*, Vol. 19, No. 8 (1972) cited in: 'Les Prisonniers de Guerre Belges en 1940–1945', *Mensuel de l'Amicale des Anciens Prisonniers de Guerre de Stalag XIIIB (Weiden)*, n° 251, 1975, p. 10.

3 Hautecler, 'Statistiques', p. 13.

4 AGR, Ministre de la justice: dossiers relatifs à l'octroi de la Croix des Évadés, 1940–1945, file 1071: Georges Even.

5 AGR, Ministre de la justice: dossiers relatifs à l'octroi de la Croix des Évadés, 1940–1945, file 276: Frédéric Dalimier.

6 AGR, Ministre de la justice: dossiers relatifs à l'octroi de la Croix des Évadés, 1940–1945, file 985: Félix Dumont.

7 AGR, Ministre de la justice: dossiers relatifs à l'octroi de la Croix des Évadés, 1940–1945, file 282: Émile Dandois.

8 AGR, Ministre de la justice: dossiers relatifs à l'octroi de la Croix des Évadés, 1940–1945, file 276: Frédéric Dalimier.

9 MRAB, Fonds Georges Hautecler, 59/43, Rapports sur les évadés.

10 AGR, Ministre de la justice: dossiers relatifs à l'octroi de la Croix des Évadés, 1940–1945, file 1330: Nestor Gillot and file 2306: Auguste Marcq.

11 MRAB, Fonds Georges Hautecler, 59/43, Rapports sur les évadés.

12 AGR, Ministre de la justice: dossiers relatifs à l'octroi de la Croix des Évadés, 1940–1945, file 1933: Joseph Laret.

13 MRAB, Fonds Georges Hautecler, 59/43, Rapports sur les évadés and AGR, Ministre de la justice : dossiers relatifs à l'octroi de la Croix des Évadés, 1940–1945, file 1735: Pierre Jauquet.

14 MRAB, Fonds Georges Hautecler, 59/43, Rapports sur les évadés and AGR, Ministre de la justice : dossiers relatifs à l'octroi de la Croix des Évadés, 1940–1945, file 2358: Albert Massart.

15 MRAB, Fonds Georges Hautecler, 59/43, Rapports sur les évadés. It should be noted that Rassart is not among the men who received the Escapees' Cross, although his file might have been destroyed.

16 MRAB, Fonds Georges Hautecler, 59/43, Rapports sur les évadés.

17 MRAB, Fonds Georges Hautecler, 59/39, Rapports sur les évadés and AGR, Ministre de la justice : dossiers relatifs à l'octroi de la Croix des Évadés, 1940–1945, file 283: Léon Dandoy.

18 MRAB, Fonds Georges Hautecler, 59/43, Rapports sur les évadés and AGR, Ministre de la justice : dossiers relatifs à l'octroi de la Croix des Évadés, 1940–1945, file 2465: Maurice Minne.

19 Bolle had been with the 1st *Regiment de Defence Terrestres Contre Aéronefs* and was captured at the abbey of Sint-Andries-bij-Brugge on 27–28 May 1940.

20 MRAB, Fonds Georges Hautecler, 59/43, Rapports sur les évadés.

21 AGR, Ministre de la justice : dossiers relatifs à l'octroi de la Croix des Évadés, 1940–1945, file 2041: Victor Legrand.

22 AGR, Ministre de la justice : dossiers relatifs à l'octroi de la Croix des Évadés, 1940–1945, file 2003: Florent Ledent.

23 AGR, Ministre de la justice : dossiers relatifs à l'octroi de la Croix des Évadés, 1940–1945, file 3070: Emile Sibenaler.

24 AGR, Ministre de la justice : dossiers relatifs à l'octroi de la Croix des Évadés, 1940–1945, file 1723: Albert Janssen. There is no file for Vrancken in the archives of the Escapees' Cross.

5 Escape and Evasion to Neutral States
Spain, Switzerland, Sweden

The three major European states that declared themselves neutral at the outbreak of war all represented possible havens for those fleeing Axis-held territory. That said, it was widely recognised and understood that Spain under Franco and Sweden because of its strong economic ties to Germany were both initially inclined towards the Axis and unlikely to be sympathetic to its enemies beyond the requirements of international law. Switzerland was in the unenviable position of being completely surrounded by Axis or Axis-dominated territories after June 1940 but has subsequently been even more widely castigated than either Spain or Sweden for bankrolling the Nazi war economy, for its indifference if not outright hostility to victims of Nazi persecution and for callously profiting from their deaths.[1] At the time, however, the British saw Switzerland as a haven (as it had been in the Great War) and prized its humanitarian role as a protecting power and as the home of the ICRC.

While this pro-Axis bias in neutral states was evident when German armies were sweeping across Europe and continued while the outcome of the war was still in doubt, all three states had to take cognisance of their obligations under international law with regard to citizens of belligerent countries, and this included the governments-in-exile of the various German-occupied states of western Europe. Under the terms of the Hague Convention on the Rules of War (1907), escapees from German or Italian captivity were permitted to travel onwards, if that could be arranged, and return home. Anyone who identified himself as an escapee would normally be allowed access to the relevant military attaché to facilitate this, a process that reputedly took minutes in Switzerland, hours in Sweden and weeks or even months in Spain.[2] Conversely, belligerent servicemen entering a neutral state having evaded capture by the enemy were supposed to be disarmed and then interned for the duration of hostilities.[3] This provision was especially pertinent for Switzerland as the war in France came to an end on 20 June 1940 when 42,000 men of the French 45th Corps, including 12,000 Poles, crossed into Swiss territory to avoid capture by the Germans. They were interned according to law but eventually the French were allowed to return home. While other neutral states did not see the same masses of military internees in 1940, they were nevertheless the recipients of both military and civilian evaders and escapers throughout the war. In this context, it is perhaps also worth noting that they represented only one issue in the highly complex and multi-faceted diplomacy between belligerent and neutral states.

DOI: 10.4324/9780429027697-6

The Iberian Peninsula: Way-Station to Freedom

Spain played a crucial role in the trajectories of many escapers and evaders during the war. As France was overrun in the summer of 1940, Spain became an obvious destination for those fleeing the Germans or unsure about the new French regime under Marshal Pétain. The Civil War had only just ended, and the country was still in the grip of the retribution being handed out by Franco's victorious Nationalists against the defeated Republicans. The country's neutral status and long border with France, as well as the various available options to leave the country for an Allied-controlled territory, were crucial criteria. Travelling to south-west France was not a major problem for most Belgians. Speaking the language, familiar with the culture, they blended in easily, avoided checkpoints and benefited from local help so that their first main hurdle was a natural barrier: the Pyrenees. This frontier had been a route out of the country for masses of Republicans who found temporary sanctuary in France, but in 1940 the flow was reversed with political and racial refugees fleeing to safety inside the Iberian Peninsula. They were joined by French and British servicemen who presented themselves independently at their country's Vice-Consulates in the northern cities or were detained by the authorities. This latter group often spent a few days in local prisons or police cells before being sent to internment camps, the most important of which was Miranda de Ebro.[4] This had been an internment/concentration camp for Republicans since 1937, but by 1940 contained only a small number of International Brigade veterans. It was subsequently used to house civilian refugees as well as soldiers and NCOs. These included primarily French, Polish, Dutch and Belgian nationals as well as 'Canadians' (whose presence is explained below) and an appreciable number of stateless individuals, primarily Jews from Eastern and Central Europe.[5] While the stories of escapes across the Pyrenees and of Spanish internment form part of the narrative for many groups sought by the Nazis, we are concerned here with the Belgian servicemen and civilians and how their experiences dovetailed with those of other Allied nationalities, and how they were helped once they had arrived in Spain.

Networks

As the previous chapters explained, escaping from Belgium was at first a lonely adventure made with limited planning and support by brave individuals. The men who fled during the battle of Dunkirk or in the first months of the German occupation often relied on luck alone. Once it became clear that only a fierce struggle could drive the Nazi forces out of Europe, escape routes and underground networks were created both by British and Belgian agencies. While they played an important part during the conflict, it should be remembered that not all escapees were helped by these organisations. Until the end of the German occupation, various Belgians managed to flee the country without outside help. Likewise, others only relied partly on clandestine networks.

After the fall of France, the British Secret Service, in the form of MI6, had begun the process of creating a clandestine network between Marseilles and Barcelona to carry intelligence from north-west Europe and to assist evaders and escapees in returning to the United Kingdom. Such was the initial Foreign Office antipathy towards any action that might antagonise Anglo-Spanish relations that Donald Darling, the man charged with creating the network, was not based in Spain but was despatched to faraway Lisbon as a Vice-Consul.[6] His activities inside Spain continued to incur the wrath of Ambassador Sir Samuel Hoare, and much of his work relied on the good offices of lower-ranking diplomats and various other individuals. The former included Michael Cresswell, an attaché at the Madrid Embassy who spent a great deal of time and energy ferrying evaders through Spain and across the frontier into Gibraltar. The Consul-General in Barcelona, Francis Patron, while having apparently little time for Darling, nonetheless also contributed his own time and money to helping, even when this was not sanctioned or indeed tolerated by the Ambassador.[7] Rather than creating his own networks, Darling managed to inherit initiatives begun elsewhere. For example, Captain Ian Garrow of the Seaforth Highlanders, who had escaped to Marseilles after his regiment's rear-guard action at Saint-Valery-en-Caux, had teamed up with the Scots Presbyterian pastor from Paris, Donald Caskie, to provide aid and assistance to British servicemen who found their way to the French port.[8] They were put in touch with Darling and the first tenuous network was established. Ultimately, this became the so-called 'Pat' Line, named after Patrick O'Leary, the alias of Albert Guérisse, who took over the organisation when Garrow was arrested by the Vichy police and interned in

Figure 5.1 Miss Frieda Moore (@Archives de l'État en Belgique)

October 1941.[9] Despite Ambassador Hoare's hostility toward MI6's actions, other lower-ranking members of the Madrid Embassy were involved in helping Belgian and British escapees. One figure in particular, an attaché, was to become a post-war celebrity within veterans' circles. Miss Frieda Moore systematically tracked Belgian citizens captured and interned at the Miranda camp. She managed to bring food and moral support to the inmates and intervened with the Spanish authorities on several occasions to negotiate their early release.[10]

The Belgian contribution to the British desire for escape and evasion networks was markedly enhanced when the Consulate in Bilbao received a visit from three men and a woman. Arthur Dean, the Vice-Consul who interviewed them, discovered that one man was Colin Cupar, a British private, while the other two were Belgian officers. Their leader was the woman, Andrée de Jongh, nicknamed Dédée, a commercial artist from Brussels and a volunteer nurse at the beginning of the war who had travelled to Spain with the other three to offer the services of her network of safe houses from Belgium through France to the Spanish frontier. With the offer of British money and some other help, but retaining its independence, this network, initially known as Postman but then re-christened *Comète*, became one of the major conduits for aircrew escaping or evading from occupied Europe.[11] Operating from the summer of 1941, it benefited from the connections of one of its benefactors, Arnold Deppé, who had worked as a cinema technician in the south of France. His local network proved extremely useful. Despite de Jongh's arrest in January 1943, *Comète* continued to operate, first under the leadership of co-workers Baron Jean-François Nothomb and, later still, by Mme Elvire de Greef, who had established the network's jumping-off point for journeys into Spain at Anglet, near Bayonne. Overall, *Comète* is credited with having conducted 356 people into Spain, of whom 288 were Allied aircrew. A further seventy-five were handed to other networks when operations were disrupted by the Gestapo, while a further 356 were hidden after the D-Day landings until they were liberated by the Allied invasion of France and Belgium.[12]

There were other clandestine organisations that, while more famous for other activities, also played some part in helping military escapees. These included *Dutch-Paris*, created by Jean Weidner, that reputedly helped many hundreds of Jews escape to Switzerland or Spain, but also accommodated spies and servicemen on the run.[13] Others were smaller scale and more specialised. The *Marie-Claire* operation was the work of a single woman, Mary Lindell, who, as the Comtesse de Milleville, had many connections in Parisian society. She was responsible for the transit of several officer-evaders across the line of demarcation to Caskie's operation in Marseilles before being arrested by the Gestapo and serving a nine-month gaol sentence. Released in November 1941, she continued her work but was soon forced to flee into Vichy France and, fearing a second arrest, made her way to Britain via Spain in July 1942.[14] After training by MI9, she returned to France in October of the same year and recommenced operations but was finally arrested by the Germans at Pau railway station and was deported to KZ Ravensbrück, where she survived the war.[15] Likewise, *Burgundy* was Georges Broussine, a French officer who ran an important network in north-western France in 1943–1944 and was linked with the Shelburne network, which created a sea escape line from Brittany to Cornwall.[16]

For its part, the Belgian government-in-exile also maintained diplomatic representation in the Iberian Peninsula with embassies in Lisbon and Madrid and consular offices in these capitals as well as in Barcelona. Loosely attached to all three (in the sense that they were controlled directly from London and not by the diplomats) were branches of the *Sûreté de l'État* that were responsible for, amongst other things, liaising with what became known as the Belgian *Service de Renseignements et d'Action* (SRA).[17] This had begun with the *Benoît* network, which was based around Belgian servicemen remaining in the unoccupied zone of France. In theory it could still operate legally, but under pressure from Vichy and the Germans, its activities became increasingly clandestine and were helped by men such as Jacques Lagrange, the Belgian representative attached to the US Consulate in Lyon, who was able to supply identity papers and allowed the network access to the diplomatic bag for communications with the outside world. Offices to help evaders were created in Marseilles, Macon, Lyon and Vichy, and in Montpellier where the focus was on moving servicemen, reservists and especially aviators across the Pyrenees into Spain.[18] This was assisted by Max Polchet, who was living in Spain and sought out contact with *Benoît* to expedite clandestine travel across the frontier. Beginning in December 1940, this was a fully fledged operation moving men and information across the line of demarcation and across the Pyrenees by the summer of 1941.[19] On arrival in Spain, the fugitives were held at safe houses near the border for two or three days before being sent on to Barcelona and thence to Madrid. En route to Portugal, they were taken to Badajoz and then across the frontier to Estremoz, where they were sheltered on the Quinto do Carmo estate of a wealthy Englishman, Victor Reynolds. Reynolds was already working for the British secret services, having been well known to the British diplomats in Lisbon as a trusted member of the British expatriate community.[20] Accounts of his exploits give a flavour of how the work was organised. In the first years, the Portuguese authorities refused transit visas for many nationalities and those of military age, and it was essential for them to be smuggled across the frontier. This took many forms and involved several different routes. Thus, while the British expected most of the fugitives to cross at Marvão because it was the most direct way between Madrid and Lisbon, Reynolds suggested a second reception centre at Elvas, where accommodation was easier to find and the trains were more reliable. Moreover, he seems to have had access to unlimited resources, with one commentator describing him as spending 'rivers of money' on whisky, game and other gifts for the local frontier police. Sometimes the only way to cross the frontier was by boat across the river Caia, where Reynolds had a flat-bottomed boat for the purpose.[21] Once safely in Portugal, the fugitives were parcelled out to farms on the estate and looked after by the locals.

Later in the war, Reynolds received as much co-operation from the local Spanish authorities as he did from the Portuguese. It was not unusual for the Spanish border guards to inform him that they had captured an Englishman, and he would then arrive and 'liberate' the prisoner, for example in exchange for a kilo of coffee.

Reynolds' operation allowed the British network to control the numbers of men travelling to Lisbon for onward transit to the United Kingdom. Those with valid papers could travel by train, but others were smuggled in the diplomatic cars that made frequent visits to the estate. While the primary focus was on British Commonwealth escapees, it has been estimated that more than sixty Belgian soldiers passed through Quinto do Carmo between February and June 1941. Among them was cadet (later General) Roger Dewandre, who with five comrades was penniless, starving, frozen stiff, and in danger of arrest from the Portuguese frontier police before being rescued by Reynolds. Without his help with food, accommodation and transport to Lisbon, Dewandre was convinced that their chances of getting to Britain would have been remote.[22]

Other networks were also created at much the same time, and often overlapped with *Benoît* and those of the British. Pierre Schul was originally sent to Barcelona by *Benoît* but was later charged by the Lisbon branch of the SRA with providing assistance to all Belgian nationals of military age, and specifically to airmen and soldiers who had escaped from Axis captivity. His routes often paralleled those of Polchet, but he also instigated another line that went north via Aragon, Valladolid and Orense, and in addition there was a southern route via Madrid and Seville. Schul worked alongside the *curé* Simon Leclef, who had been appointed in December 1941 by the SRA to minister to Belgians interned in Spain. The *curé* seems to have been heavily implicated in clandestine work and had his own contacts with the British through Michael Cresswell and also for a time with a Polish organisation that had safe houses in Madrid. Ultimately in April 1942 he was instructed to cease this element of his work lest it jeopardised his primary task of ministering to the Belgians interned at Miranda de Ebro and elsewhere. In addition to these various routes, another network was established from occupied France into the Basque country by Charles Schepens, an ophthalmologist who had been in the Belgian Air Force but had become involved in resistance and had fled to France in 1942. Using the alias Jacques Perot, he reopened a sawmill in the July of that year in the Basque French village of Mendive/Mendibe near the Spanish frontier to act as a conduit point for Belgians on the run. From there, fugitives were taken across the border by Jean Sarotxar, a local shepherd, and then to San Sebastian where they were handed over to the Belgian Consul Luis Lizarriturri. This continued until the Gestapo net closed around Schepens and he also fled to Britain.[23]

There was also the *Sabot* organisation, established and run by Pierre Bouriez. This had begun when Pierre Vandermies, a Belgian aviator who had already escaped to Britain via Spain once, was parachuted back into France to organise a more effective way of evacuating Allied aircrew and other servicemen still hiding in France and Belgium. Sabot was charged with three tasks: transmitting messages for the SRA, facilitating the passage of 'parcels' (escapees and evaders) to Spain and gathering information inside France. From his base in Montpellier, Bouriez created a substantial network in unoccupied France to facilitate all three tasks until he was betrayed to the Gestapo in Toulouse in January 1943. While many elements of his network were rolled up, some of its intelligence-gathering cells remained.[24]

Escapes and Evasions

Most Belgians who chose the road to Spain remembered primarily their transit across the mountains. This formidable obstacle had one main entry point: the French department of the Pyrénées Orientales. Finding someone to guide them through the mountains was a challenge in itself. Albert Pauly, who had been captured in May 1940 but had managed to escape, reached the south-west of France in 1941. Unable to cross the Pyrenees immediately, he found a job in the region to wait for the end of the winter season. In April 1942, he finally identified an escape network based in Montauban. With its help, he left with a group of ten other escapees escorted by two Catalans. Soaked to the skin during the trip across the mountains, he was immediately arrested by the Guardia Civil after crossing the border.[25]

Reaching Spain on foot was fraught with difficulties in its own right, but so was finding help. Henri Ferval, a Belgian stuck on the French side, was trying to find a *passeur* in a café when he was approached by the owner:

> "The weather! Brr! It is said that it is snowing in the mountains. There will not be many hikers there," he said, looking mysterious.
> "Hikers?" I said deliberately.
> "Yes," said the big man, looking me in the eyes. "Hikers… who like sport! It happens sometimes, by accident, that they go down on the other side of the Pyrenees: this can happen to everybody, right?"
> "Of course," I replied. "But I assume they do not go alone into the mountains?"
> "No," answered my interlocutor. "No, they can be helped."
> I had understood; luck was on my side. No need to waste time.
> "Listen, boss, let us talk straight," said I. "I want to go to the other side as quickly as possible. Can you help?"
> "Who are you?" he said. "You are not French?"
> "I am Belgian, and I must go today. And money is no object."[26]

Ferval slept above the café and was woken up the next day. He agreed to pay 10,000 francs, a substantial sum of money, to be guided across the Pyrenees. Walking for hours, facing several dangers, he managed to reach the border. Like many others, he was arrested inside Spanish territory by the Guardia Civil. Most escapees were abandoned before reaching their final destination by their *passeurs*, who could be either professional smugglers, Spanish Republicans, members of the French resistance, cynical adventurers on a mission for easy money or even convinced fascists. More than one escapee was denounced by his *passeur* or led into a trap.[27] It was not unusual for a guide to walk for the first few kilometres before abandoning his group and leaving it on its own. When Carl Bachelart got lost in the mountains near the border with Andorra in July 1943, he was rescued by a French shepherd who brought him to Spanish territory. Once on the other side, he was once again helped by Spanish shepherds who offered him food and a blanket to rest for a few hours. In the morning, they advised him to surrender to the police, claiming that escapees were released very quickly.[28] Étienne Plissart, who travelled with the help of the *Benoît* network, had a smoother experience:

> In Toulouse, a group was formed. Ten Belgians, including Michel Taymans, Gaston de Gerlache and me. The three of us were going to experience all the dangers of the Pyrenees and Spain. We left the train at the Bourg-Madame border station, 1,100 metres above sea level and 30km east of Andorra. This rail line leads to Barcelona but basic prudence demanded that we avoided the border controls and tried to cross the Pyrenees illegally and by night with the help of an experienced guide. The guide was a Spaniard, a 'Rojo', a red anti-Francoist and resistance fighter, as were all his colleagues. Nightfall came at 8pm. The guide took the lead and the ten followed in single file. Very quickly, we climbed a rocky and narrow path. Our sticks proved very useful because there were obstacles... and the emptiness. The wind was stronger but was still manageable. After 3 hours of walking, we saw the mountain pass; it was relatively easy. It was about 1,600m high, taking into account the 1,100m at Bourg-Madame. But at the summit, on the south side, [there was] an unexpected and moving sight: thousands of lights shining peacefully in villages and along the roads. What a contrast with the blackout imposed by the Nazi regime in the occupied territories, including 'Free' France! Spain looked like a country at peace. [Although] a relative peace as we were to discover...[29]

Even well-organised clandestine networks found it difficult to cross the Pyrenees. The sources clearly demonstrate the organisational chaos experienced by *Sabot* and its Barcelona branches. Expecting to help at most twelve men per week, they were sometimes sent twenty or thirty souls. This surplus alarmed the network on both sides of the border. Unable to cross from France to Spain safely in such numbers, the escapees were likewise too numerous to be hosted in the capital of Catalonia.[30]

Occasionally, luck was on the escapee's side. Commandant Louis Legrand had been captured near Wielsbeke by a German unit in May 1940. The same day, he managed to escape and returned to his native city of Namur. On 3 August 1940, he left wife and children en route to Spain in order to reach Britain. He stopped first at the Spanish embassy in Brussels where the diplomatic authorities provided him with a certificate proving that three of his relatives had been killed during the Spanish Civil War while fighting against the Republicans. He tried to cross the border between France and Spain legally but was turned down as he did not have a French exit visa. On 14 August, he noticed that the priest in Cerbère was a French veteran of the First World War. Counting on his patriotism, he asked for help and was told how to reach Catalonia illegally. Once there, he was arrested by the police, but the certificate provided by the Spanish embassy proved invaluable as Legrand was granted an *Intrada* (entry permit). Unlike many of his fellow countrymen forced to travel illegally, the Belgian officer was able to board a train to Madrid where he applied for a Portuguese visa. By 30 August 1940, he was on an aeroplane to Britain.[31]

As we have seen, most Belgian escapees crossing the border were arrested immediately when stepping into Spanish territory. What followed was a period of incarceration in local prisons before transfer to the facilities adapted by the Franco regime to deal with foreign nationals escaping German-held Europe. The overwhelming majority ended up at the Miranda de Ebro camp, situated in the province of Burgos and between the cities of Burgos and Bilbao. Built in 1937 by the Nationalists to house Republican prisoners during and immediately after the Civil War, it was subsequently pressed into service as an internment centre for both military personnel and civilians who had found their way illegally onto Spanish soil.[32] In theory, the officers were meant to be held at Jaraba, but questions about status and identification meant that they often remained at Miranda de Ebro camp for the duration of their incarceration. Even without this severe overcrowding, conditions were notoriously bad and food inadequate for the inmates. There were many reports of scabies, diarrheic diseases and even a typhoid fever epidemic in 1943.[33]

Sir Samuel Hoare, the British Ambassador in Madrid, estimated that around 30,000 people managed to cross the Spanish frontier illicitly during the conflict, although how he arrived at such a figure is unclear. Of these 30,000, he thought that around 16,000 had been subsequently arrested by the Spanish authorities and had spent some time interned at Miranda de Ebro.[34] As soon as the first British evaders were interned there, the British diplomats in Spain mobilised to expedite their release and evacuation. International law dictated that evaders who entered neutral territory were supposed to be interned for the duration of hostilities, but escapers were free to find their way home and continue to serve in the war.[35] As most of those arriving in Spain were intent on participating in the war effort, it was in

Figure 5.2 The camp of Miranda de Ebro (@CEGESOMA/Archives de l'État en Belgique)

their interests to claim some form of capture and escape. This allowed them access to the relevant military attaché or local diplomat and the chance of help for their onward journey. However, the initial attitude of the pro-Axis Spanish authorities was to make this as difficult as possible, and access could often take weeks or even months. Albert Pauly, for example, was held at Miranda de Ebro from April 1942 to June 1943.[36]

Most Belgians were captured once on the other side of the Pyrenees. However, a few escapees left France unnoticed and more often than not headed first towards Barcelona, where they were helped by various networks of Belgians or Spanish Republicans. Étienne Plissart managed to avoid the border guards. Once in Spain, he was helped by a local family. He explained:

> We were hosted by a pleasant family. We could see that they looked favour-
> ably on us. And it was for the same reason as the peasants of the day before:
> they were reds too, anti-Franco and loving the English who were fighting
> against Hitler and Mussolini, the allies of Franco. But to these common feel-
> ings, our Barcelona family could add its strong attachment to the culture and
> independence of Catalonia. The father proudly exhibited in his library a ten-
> volume dictionary of the Catalan language.[37]

Travelling through Spain was no easy task as controls were numerous and the authorities were actively looking for suspicious individuals with foreign accents. Étienne Plissart's journey through Spain ended when a train guard heard his group speaking French.[38] Belgian escapees helped by underground organisations were sometimes provided with fake papers. These counterfeit documents were not always expertly made – for example, a residence card that still bore the coat of arms of the Spanish Republic! Money and strict instructions on how to behave once in Spain were also given. Escapees were forbidden from drinking alcohol, smoking in trains, speaking or carrying bags. They were also supposed to obey their guide and dress inconspicuously. In reality, these rules were frequently broken. The Belgian escapees were sometimes described as unpleasant, demanding, and unable to resist alcoholic beverages.[39] Yet such unruly behaviour was easily explained; the clandestine travellers had faced weeks or months of stress in Belgium, France and Spain and had sometimes spent long periods of hiding in confined spaces. In these circumstances, spending their allowance on wine proved all too tempting. Trains were considered as the fastest and safest way to travel around the peninsula, but regular controls made such journeys hazardous. Fugitives were given advice on how to avoid them, but luck remained a determining factor. Members of the *Sûreté de l'État* even advocated the acquisition of a car to drive escapees from Barcelona to Madrid, but acquiring a vehicle with a Spanish licence plate proved extremely difficult. Alternatively, it was suggested to travel by night and walk next to the railway lines.[40]

For the Belgian escapers and evaders who managed to reach Spanish soil, it was clear that some subterfuge was required if they were apprehended by the authorities, as many of them were. Their entry into Spain had been, by definition, illegal. There was a real chance that, as citizens of an occupied country and of military age, they could be handed back to the German authorities on the French side of the frontier. In January 1941, for example, fourteen Belgians were returned to the Germans by Spain.[41] This had been Spanish policy in the early part of the war, and knowledge of this undoubtedly influenced the behaviour of those who came later. When arrested, they needed an appropriate cover story that would at least cause the Spaniards to make further enquiries. Masquerading as an escaping Allied soldier was the obvious choice, but claiming to be British would swiftly be exposed by a lack of linguistic competence. The solution was to insist on being Canadian, which would simultaneously bring them within the protection of the British diplomats in Spain and at the same time explain their fluency in French as a native tongue. It seems that all the escapees crossing through Spain knew this trick. Albert Adam recounted how this worked when he and others were arrested in Figueras:

> Here we are in front of the officials of the police of Figueras. Scowling looking, suspicious eyes, they examine the shabby, shaggy, wrinkled group, which stands facing them.
> The chief prods his pen holder into the solar plexus of the first.
> "*Como se llama*? (what's your name?)" said the penpusher.
> "Roger Dupont."
> "Profession?"
> "Tail gunner."
> "Home?"
> "Issy-les-Moulineaux, Canada."
> "Next!"
> "Pyotr Rebibovich. Front gunner. Born Bratislava, Canada."
> "Hector van Oldenbarneveldt, born Volendam, Canada, Middle gunner."
> And so on.
> But my turn comes, and I create a surprise. This monotonous brigade of the transatlantic annoys me. Let's put a note of originality, while remaining, well, "Anglo-Saxon". What the hell, Flemish will come to me at the right time.
> "You!..." The official gives me an unfriendly look.
> "Bertie Adams, doctor."
> The police look relieved. There were really too many machine gunners so far.
> "Where is your home, Canada?"
> "Not at all, Commissioner. I live in Bloemfontein, South Africa."
> "How?" cries the boss of these cops. "Is this true? But then," he said triumphantly to his acolytes, "*señores*, we finally have a real Englishman!"[42]

By the time Adam fell into their hands, the Spanish police seem to have been playing along with the subterfuge, perhaps at the behest of their masters in Madrid who were treading a fine diplomatic line between sympathy for the Axis and pressure from the Western Allies. Whatever the reason, there was no question now of *refoulement* back into France. Nonetheless Adam's attempt to pass himself off as Afrikaans with his supposed knowledge of Flemish gave the local Guardia Civil a welcome change from the mass of 'Canadians'.

Once moved on to Miranda de Ebro, the façade continued as evidenced again by Adam:

The weekly food truck, sent by the English embassy in Madrid, to which the escapees owe a huge debt, stops in the middle of the camp. The man in charge climbs on the hood, list in hand, to ensure a fair distribution. And here's what we hear:

"Belgian Canadians, parcels!" followed soon by: "French Canadians, parcels!" then "Polish Canadians, parcels! Yugoslav Canadians, parcels!" Czech, Dutch and Luxembourg Canadians are not forgotten. But the closing of the call sounds a particularly delightful note: "Canadian Canadians, by the way!" There were two! Real ones...[43]

By the latter months of 1943, conditions in Spain for evaders from occupied Europe had improved still further. Two officers, Lieutenant Florent Ledent and Major Victor Legrand, who had escaped from Oflag II-A (Prenzlau) with the aid of the Bolle Network, had already found their way back to Belgium but were keen to join the Allies. Arriving in Liège on 17 September, they were able to contact another escape line. After only four days in the city they crossed into France, but here things went wrong. The network turned out to be almost non-existent and the two escapees were left to their own devices.[44] After two months of fruitless searching, they finally found a reliable *passeur* and they successfully crossed into Spain on the night of 16–17 November. Arrested by the Spanish authorities, they were held under house arrest in Irun for fifteen days and then in Madrid for a further fifteen days. Perhaps because they were officers, there had been no question of their being sent to a prison camp. After their incarceration they were able to travel on to Portugal where, after ten days of waiting, a seaplane brought them to England on Christmas Eve 1943. Both were enlisted in the Belgian Brigade on 5 January 1944.

Two other escapees from Oflag II-A had different experiences. Lieutenants Jean Mentior of the 2nd Regiment of *Chasseurs ardennais* and Emile Sibenaler of the 14th Artillery Regiment had found their way back to Belgium from captivity in Germany but were keen to continue the fight. As outlined in Chapter 4, they had already made unsuccessful attempts to cross from France into Spain but remained undeterred. Having boarded a goods train with the aid of French railway workers, they found themselves at the Col de Belitres tunnel that marked the border between the two countries. Disembarking there and walking into the tunnel they were able to board a train bound for Spain.

In Portbou, Mentior and Sibenaler, with the complicity of a Spanish railway worker who had discovered them, hid on a freight train bound for Barcelona. [...] In Girona, the train stopped, and the two escapees decided to continue the journey by passenger train. They were apprehended in the train by the Spanish Civil Guards and on 31 October were incarcerated at the police prefecture of Barcelona, then at the Carcel Modelo (penitentiary) of that city. At the end of November, they were transferred to Miranda de Ebro camp and liberated on Christmas Eve, without knowing who had accomplished this. They then made their way to Madrid to await visas for Portugal, but it took a month of incessant pressure to obtain these due to the apathy of the staff of the Belgian Consulate. On 26 January 1944, they finally arrived in Lisbon where they were greeted with open arms by Major Gilliaert, head of the 'military evacuation' service of the Belgian legation. On 2 February 1944, Mentior left by seaplane for England, but Sibenaler was retained in Lisbon by Gilliaert, who was short of a deputy. This did not amuse Sibenaler, who finally managed to obtain authorisation to reach England from the ambassador. Alas! As the day of his departure neared, the English authorities stopped granting visas. Sibenaler was then appointed as Deputy Military Attaché to Algiers. He arrived there on 20 May 1944 but never gave up on the idea of getting to England and managed to be designated a place on the first available convoy. On 2 August 1944, he left Algiers for Plymouth where he arrived on 10 August. After a stay at the Victoria Patriotic School until the end of that month, he was then posted to the First Belgian Brigade that had already landed in France. Sibenaler [… finally] arrived in Normandy on 6 September and joined the Brigade only after it had reached Belgium.[45]

This account is interesting for several reasons. These two lieutenants were clearly committed to continuing the fight and joining the Free Belgian forces in Britain. Their choices of actions may not always have been the right ones, and they were eventually swept up by the Spanish authorities despite the efforts of both French and Spanish railway workers to help them. Ultimately incarcerated in Miranda de Ebro camp, they had no idea why they were released. The unseen hand (*intervention inconnue*) may have come from the Belgian or British diplomatic missions but may equally have been the result of the Spaniards thinking they had served enough prison time for illegally entering the country. Certainly, the international situation at the end of 1943 made greater Spanish accommodation with the Allies more likely. Their continuing frustration with their own diplomats over the time it took to get a Portuguese visa may well have been misplaced as it relied as much on the Portuguese authorities to co-operate. In the end, it took Sibenaler more than ten months to get from occupied Belgium to rejoining active service, and fifteen months from his initial escape from Oflag II-A.

Miranda de Ebro

Irrespective of their nationality, Allied escapees who entered Spain who were caught by the Spanish authorities in the Pyrenees followed a similar itinerary. First, they were jailed in a local prison or in the cells of the Guardia Civil before being transferred to a provincial detention centre or to the Carcel Modelo of Barcelona.

There, they were held in appalling conditions. Prisoners were shaved and expected to sleep in overcrowded cells, from where they witnessed the executions of Republican Spaniards on a regular basis. Foreign citizens were expected to salute the flag in the fascist fashion during each roll call. Violence and the creation of petty frustrations were core principles applied by the guards. From Carcel Modelo, the evaders were transferred to Miranda de Ebro. Usually referred to as a concentration camp, it had been built to accommodate 2,200 prisoners but often held many more as the numbers of fugitives increased. For example, Spanish sources indicated that there were 3,406 inmates in late 1942, including 534 officers and 425 NCOs.[46] At least one Belgian managed to escape during the transfer. Jules Rutten explained his unusual story after the war:

> We spent the night at the fortress of Figueras and, the next day, chained, we were brought to Barcelona. After a few hours, we were sent to Miranda de Ebro. We were six in the compartment with two *Guardias*. My obsession was to escape! I fell asleep but awoke suddenly. The train was climbing a hill slowly. Night had fallen. I asked to go to the toilets. One *Guardia* blocked the door open with his foot, but he had to remove it to let a traveller pass by. I closed the door, slipped through the small window and climbed onto the wagon's roof. I went down onto the [carriage] platform and then threw myself off. I followed the railroad tracks and, after a few kilometres, reached the station at Manresa.[47]

Those who arrived at Miranda were usually shocked by the conditions. Edouard Cuvelier explained in a post-war manuscript what the first hours were like:

> '*Campo de Cencentracion*'. These tall letters were written above the gate serving as the camp's entrance. This camp was about 300 metres by 200 metres surrounded by a small one metre fifty concrete wall, on top of which there was barbed wire. Outside, a path and fences of barbed wire at about three metres on each side. Each thirty metres, concrete guard towers. A third of the entrance was occupied by administrative buildings and by the guards. The camp was about five hundred metres from the station and is next to the Bilbao rail line.[48]

Arriving prisoners were brought to the police post to complete identity forms before being handed over to the military authorities of the camp. Each arrival was the opportunity to share information. The Belgians newly arrived in Miranda were soon informed by veteran prisoners that they were facing many months behind bars. Each man was given a dirty blanket and an aluminium canteen before discovering the camp's infrastructures. Almoner Simon Leclef of the Belgian Navy described the sleeping accommodation:

> Beds were rare, and were reserved for the old and infirm, or for officers. Practically everyone slept and spent the day on the ground on the trodden

earth, lying on wretched straw sleeping-bags, and only issued with a dirty and torn threadbare blanket, or failing that, a big piece of old rag. In summer the heat would be sweltering and parasites were a positive torture. In winter there was no heating of any kind and hardly any glass in the windows, at first anyway. As for lighting, there just wasn't any.[49]

There was a single source of water for the whole prison. Each morning, a line was formed even before the inmates were supposed to get up. The toilets were equally appalling, being cleaned once a day despite being used by thousands of persons. In 1941, medical help was provided by a doctor belonging to the Spanish army and an Argentinian national who claimed to be a doctor but was obviously not qualified. The lack of hygiene and food, and the dirt and harsh winters caused several epidemics of rash, ulcerations, breathing troubles, dysentery, etc. An illegal infirmary manned by Belgian military doctors and supplied by Miss Moore and Major Griffith from the British embassy provided a little relief.[50]

Prisoners from twenty different countries lived together. The camp was subdivided into two basic groups, the German group that included all those whom the Third Reich regarded as its citizens – Germans, Austrians, Czechs, Hungarians – and the Allied group that comprised the British Commonwealth, French, Belgian, Dutch and later Americans, although the French were by far the largest contingent.[51] The oldest inmates were foreign Republican fighters. There were also vast numbers of self-proclaimed Canadians, in fact French, Polish and Belgian citizens. Before June 1941, there were no more than thirty Belgian internees. This number swelled by July 1942 when there were over 300, in December 450 and in February 1943, 555. In total, thousands of Belgians passed through Miranda. American, British, Dutch, French and Czech inmates also formed unified groups. According to Edouard Cuvelier, there was even one Filipino. The presence of Jews from Poland was also noted in his manuscript. Each nationality had a central bureau and a leader who worked closely with his consulate. He was also in charge of money distribution, food, clothes, and communication with the Allies and the Spanish authorities.[52]

The day was punctuated by several rituals. The first roll call was at eight in the morning. The fascists' flag was raised while the band played and the prisoners were supposed to salute. Breakfast followed. Lunch was announced by a bugler. To keep themselves busy, the Belgian prisoners organised conferences and classes. All topics were addressed, even how to buy tickets in a train station. Others tried to learn how to play the guitar or the mandolin. At six in the evening, a new roll call preceded the last meal of the day. Food was far from plentiful and had to be complemented by outside deliveries. The Belgians relied on help from the British consular staff and more rarely from delegates of the Belgian Red Cross.[53]

Living conditions were so poor that the Belgian and Polish inmates decided to go on a hunger strike on 6 January 1943. They were convinced that other prisoners would follow them and that public opinion would be alerted. For seven days, the strikers stayed in bed during the day, agreeing to stand up only twice a day during the roll calls. During the five first days, the local military authorities seemed unmoved but when it became clear that Spanish civilians had heard of the strike, things changed. On 10 January 1943, Edgard Évrard, a medical officer in the Belgian army, was summoned by the commander of Miranda and was allowed to meet the director of the Spanish Red Cross to explain why the inmates were refusing to eat. Évrard indicated that the Spanish authorities were not respecting the Geneva Convention of 1929. Together, they toured the camp to inspect the most salient issues. A few days later, on 12 January, the prisoners learned that those aged less than 18 or older than 45 years old would be freed. Living conditions were also supposed to be improved. This convinced the inmates to suspend the hunger strike.[54] This impact of this action has been interpreted differently by various witnesses and historians. While the hunger strike may well have prompted changes, it is also possible that the Spanish authorities decided on improving living conditions for Allied soldiers because the war was becoming more favourable to their side.

Escaping from Miranda was not an easy task, even for seasoned evaders who had often already managed to leave their Stalags in Germany and crossed the Pyrenees. What made the deed particularly dangerous was the knowledge that a failed attempt was systematically punished by death. Edouard Cuvelier witnessed the tragic death of a Polish prisoner who was shot in the leg outside the camp and ended up with a bullet in the head. He also mentioned other more successful examples, such as the tunnel dug from the chapel by three men who managed to escape and disappeared. Similarly, a Belgian *gendarme* claimed to have a medical problem and was diagnosed with peritonitis by the Belgian doctor Évrard, who was in fact an accomplice. Once in a hospital, he managed to slip through a window and ultimately reached London.[55]

There were, nevertheless, good reasons not to escape from Miranda as incarceration was known to be limited in time. The Belgians knew that eventually, sometimes after a few weeks, more often after several months, they would get out and have a chance to join the Allied forces. This method of release from internment came about through an agreement between the British and the Belgians that the former would 'recognise' around thirty of the Belgians each month as escaped Allied soldiers – which explains their cover stories as 'Canadians'. Once released, they could legitimately be provided with documentation such as the *Salida de Espana* (Spanish exit visa), as well as entry and exit visas for Portugal which would permit transit to their final destination (mostly the United Kingdom or the Belgian Congo). Other conduits seem to have been arranged by the Benedictine priest Simon Leclef, as head of the 'Service des internés et prisonniers Belges en Espagne'. Leclef had been nominated as an almoner for the Belgian Navy and had arrived in Bilbao on board a fishing boat in June 1941. Initially interned at Miranda de Ebro, he was rapidly released and then ministered to the Belgian internees in the camp and managed negotiations with the Spanish authorities, his status as a priest being invaluable in a very Catholic country. Prior to this, the Belgian diplomatic service had been in a state of disarray with only the Belgian chancellery in Madrid (kept open after the Embassy was shut) and the two consulates in San Sebastian and Barcelona to represent the country's interests.[56] Even after Leclef had created this new organisation, there were ongoing tensions between him and his nominal superior

Max Creners as head of the Chancellery – with Leclef resented for by-passing Crener and maintaining direct contacts with other Belgian and foreign agencies.[57] While Leclef received some praise for his work from Sir Samuel Hoare, both he and Crener were heavily criticised by some internees themselves. One such critique will have to suffice.

> Little by little he completely lost the confidence of the Mirandians, he was the invisible and distant Belgian delegate who we did not see and who very rarely responded to letters and requests from internees. There are very many who, in particular cases, have the right to complain about the lack of services of the Chaplain. [...] No visit, no gesture during the hunger strike unlike all the other groups. [...] There is an incomprehensible negligence in his services, he knows nothing, he no longer knows anything and it is Mr. Lizarriturri, with admirable dedication who must push him, advise him, even lecture him. [...] Only at that moment I realised that the Chaplain could no longer do anything for Miranda and that unless he intervened independently, the Belgians would no longer be released.[58]

While the frustration of those held in internment and in appalling conditions was likely to manifest itself in this way, it is clear that there were problems with the Belgian organisation. It is also worth noting that the real lynchpin of the whole enterprise was André Motte, the Ambassador in Lisbon, who helped coordinate the removal of Belgians from Spain and helped them with documents for their onward journeys. However, the internees were also faced with interventions of a different type. Georges Marquand, a Belgian national with luxury hotels in various European countries, became a presence as a 'representative' of the Belgian Red Cross. Ostensibly neutral but in practice fervently pro-German, he proceeded to persuade/ cajole internees into returning to Belgium. Working in concert with Hubert Chabot, a Belgian consul in Madrid, he was responsible for the handing over of at least ten individuals – some of them pilots – back into the hands of the Germans.[59] In addition, there were some interventions credited to the Spanish Ambassador in London, who ostensibly arranged the freedom of certain individuals in exchange for raw materials such as cotton, metals and cereals.[60]

In general terms, it was the Belgian service personnel that found it easiest to leave internment. As desirable assets for the British, their recognition was often fast-tracked, and their release thereby expedited for onward travel. This was especially true for trained aircrew, but other soldiers were also beneficiaries. Many were evacuated from Spain via Lisbon, there to be sent by ship to Britain, unless they were considered high priority when they were sent by aeroplane. Others could be sent legitimately via Gibraltar where they could again be shipped or flown out to the United Kingdom. This also applied to those who were not discovered by the Spaniards, but who then had to be smuggled illegally out of Spain.

As far as the British were concerned, they were more than happy to work with Belgian-based networks such as *Comète* and *Sabot* if it aided the return of valued Allied aircrew from occupied Europe into Spain, but they also had to deal with a much broader range of fugitives who were keen to continue the fight. This became explicit in November 1941 when Joseph Bech, Foreign Minister of the Grand-Duchy of Luxembourg, asked for help with their citizens in Spain. This prompted a comment from an unnamed member of the Foreign Office Central Department that noted the existing difficulties of 'escapees' in Spain and that 'neither the Madrid Embassy, nor our own secret organisation will, I am sure, welcome the idea of adding the Luxembourgers to the mixed bag of Allied volunteers which they already have to deal with'.[61] This was echoed by Arthur Aveling, the former Counsellor to the British Embassy in Brussels, who pointed out that there would be no skilled airmen among the Luxembourgers and 'presumably no officers or men with military experience'.[62]

Subsequent British experience seems to have borne out the reservations voiced towards the end of 1941. Many Belgians who were processed through Spain and Portugal had no military backgrounds whatsoever and included students, clerks, secretaries, engineer cadets and munitions workers. Some had been resident in North Africa or France rather than coming from Belgium, but they also encompassed young men who had reached military age and/or who were now liable for labour conscription. They included Paul Nopere, a student who had been put to work at the Acierie Aubert et Duval at Ancizes, a specialist steelworks between Clermont-Ferrand and Montluçon, having been arrested in France in August 1941 on his way from Belgium. According to his testimony, there were at least sixty Belgians with similar stories employed there. He had managed to escape from the factory on 15 November and subsequently found his way into Spain.[63] Others who had lost their jobs in Belgium as a result of the occupation had been incorporated into the German labour force, such as Louis Genart, a 38-year-old singer who had been employed by the *Arbeitsamt* (labour office) in several German factories in and around Aachen from August 1940, but absconded on 13 September 1941.[64] Likewise, Leopold Remaut, a fisherman, and Charles De Jonghe, a hotel worker, had been sent to Wimereux in France to work on the Atlantic Wall for the Organisation Todt. They had been given a *contrat de travail* that was open ended and were allowed periods of leave, but returning to Belgium without permission would mean no further support from the Belgian labour exchange and, more importantly, the loss of their ration cards. Despite this, these two left their employment and travelled together across the line of demarcation and across the Spanish frontier.[65] While all these men were able to provide some limited intelligence about conditions inside occupied Europe and the specifics of particular enterprises, none of them appeared to have any specialist military skills. Despite this, they had all been 'recognised' by the British and had been transported to Britain.

Reaching Gibraltar was often described as a memorable moment by those who had experienced captivity for months or years. As Étienne Plissart explained:

The contrast between Miranda and Gibraltar was marvellous. There, captivity was lived in a sinister place, here it was freedom in a decorum of beauty: the sea, the African coast so close, the blue sky, the sun, a hymn to joy, creation in all its beauty. It was the most beautiful place, the best days since Tongeren.[66]

The relative abundance and the sense of freedom contrasted heavily with the prisoners' camps or the occupied territories. The mood was perfectly captured by Jean-Baptiste Piron, who later became the commander of the 1st Belgian Infantry Brigade of the Free Belgian forces:

> In Main Street, a house, the Spanish Pavilion, is the welcoming centre where we are warmly greeted. We are served big bowls of tea and very good sandwiches with thick slices of excellent Cheddar. I was hosted at the mess of the Joint Intelligence Centre presided by Major Haslam. I made two friends. One, Roger Keyes, was the nephew of the famous admiral. I was lodged in an empty house. Early in the morning, an orderly woke me up to offer me tea. I would have liked to sleep longer but the thought of breakfast meant I did not hesitate. I was literally starving and welcomed the mess table, even though it did not manage to reduce my appetite completely. Tea time found me at a bakery, where I swallowed a respectable quantity of brioches. Gastronomy had become a major part of life for the citizens of the occupied territories.[67]

Gibraltar was usually the last stop before Britain, but leaving the southern tip of the Iberian Peninsula was dangerous owing to the presence of German submarines. Eager Belgians were required to wait for their transport to join a convoy under the protection of the Royal Navy.

Enemy Agents

As the route to the United Kingdom through Spain and Portugal became more established, there is no doubt that the Spanish authorities tolerated at least some of the illicit actions carried out by Allied diplomats on their soil, not least the 'cloaking' of European evaders as escaping 'Canadians'. Indeed, the Spaniards, while their official sympathies were weighted towards the Axis, had to walk a narrow path between the two warring sides and were prepared to turn a blind eye to the evaders being smuggled through their country with the collusion of diplomats and secret services. While their German counterparts may have been publicly displeased by the latitude afforded to their enemies, it did allow them to use the same routes to smuggle its own spies into the United Kingdom. To be convincing, these individuals needed to be nationals of Allied countries such as the Belgians and be furnished with believable cover stories to account for their escape from occupied Europe.

According to his initial testimony, Alphonse Timmerman had been born in 1904 and had gone to sea in 1919, serving on Norwegian and Belgian steamers until 1925 when he undertook military service in the Army Medical Corps for a year. Returning to his former employment, he was out of work between 1933 and 1935 before resuming work on the Belgian Channel boats until the outbreak of war in 1939. Transferring to the SS Ville de Namur, his ship was torpedoed en route to

Liverpool in June 1940, and he was picked up by Spanish fishermen and taken to Bilbao. He was to spend two months there before being sent home by train to Belgium via Hendaye and Bordeaux. Ostensibly unemployed between August 1940 and April 1941, he then made his way back to Spain via Dunkirk, Lille, Paris and Hendaye. He supposedly crossed the border on foot and was arrested at Irun the day after his arrival. Subsequently he spent three months in internment at Nanclares camp[68] before being released and told to leave the country. He made his way to Huelva where he saw the British Vice-Consul and Belgian Consul. Sent on to Seville, he signed on as crew with the British ship SS Ulea and arrived in Glasgow on 1 September 1941. Ostensibly, his story was very similar to other evaders, but it did not ring true with his interrogators at the Royal Patriotic School when he arrived in London. They pointed out that by his own admission, he had left Belgium with £100, $500 and Rm200 – substantial sums under any circumstances and certainly for someone who had been unemployed for nine months – but had arrived in the United Kingdom after four months with most of the money intact. They found his escape and travel across France and Spain 'strange and unbelievable'. Moreover, they had discovered an envelope containing a suspicious white powder among his possessions.

Two days later, a further interrogation elicited a very different story, with Timmerman confessing to be a German agent, apparently unaware of the consequences of such an admission. In fact, he had been approached by the Germans in February 1941 but was only formally recruited by German naval intelligence at Antwerp in April of that year when he was asked to go to England as a spy. His task would be to collect information on coastal defences, convoy preparations, minefield, airfields, munitions factories and the like. He was subsequently collected from his home in La Panne around seven or eight times for briefings in Antwerp, including ones on the use of invisible ink and appropriate stationery. At the end of July, he was given a false German passport in the name of Alphonse Hoffman and taken with two other Belgians to Paris and then to Hendaye, Bayonne and across the Spanish frontier. Here he was in the hands of another agent, Jose Aiguabella, who relieved him of the German identity documents but intervened when Timmerman was apprehended by the Spanish Secret Police at Vitoria. Interviewed by the civil governor, he was initially interned at the Nanclares camp, but after three days Aiguabella appeared with Spanish certification that Timmerman had been interned for three months. Released, he was returned to Vitoria and then proceeded to contact the British and Belgian consulates in Huelva and Seville. His explanation for being selected by the Germans as an agent was that he was a seaman, knew England well and could speak good English.[69]

Timmerman was subsequently incarcerated in Wandsworth Prison, but given his full confession and capture with appropriate stationery and invisible ink, the British MI5 decided to use him for their own purposes by sending messages to his *Abwehr* contacts in Lisbon.[70] This project was soon judged a failure, and to make sure that the *Abwehr* knew that Timmerman had never been at liberty, he was tried *in camera* before Mr Justice Humphreys on 20 May 1942 in a 'rapid, secret hearing' and executed by hanging in the prison on 7 July.[71]

Other Belgians recruited as German agents were also routed through the Iberian Peninsula. Pierre Neukermans had arrived at Poole Airport in the United Kingdom on 16 July 1943, having been flown from Lisbon. His initial story was that he had been a soldier in the Belgian armed forces until being invalided out in 1938. After the German occupation he had tried and failed to leave Belgium on at least two occasions before managing to journey through France and cross the Pyrenees on foot with the help of a *passeur* and contacting the British Consul in Barcelona, who had arranged his illegal entry into Portugal and onward evacuation from Lisbon.[72]

On 23 July, he was transferred to the London Reception Centre where his story was equally well received by the officials there, and he was released into the hands of the Belgian government-in-exile soon afterwards. Deemed unfit for military service, he was given employment with the Belgian Ministry of Agriculture in London, and this would have ended matters had it not been for some crucial additional information that came into the hands of the security services. Towards the end of the year, the British authorities became aware that in groups of three escapees arriving in Spain, one was likely to be a German agent. In his initial interrogation, Neukermans had mentioned the two men he had travelled with between Brussels and Paris – and who had also subsequently been screened and cleared by the authorities. On the strength of this intelligence, all three were re-arrested on 2 February 1944 and interrogated at the Oratory Schools and later at Camp 020. Within days, Neukermans had confessed to being a German agent and gave details of his mission and his methods of communication to his handlers.[73]

His real story was a very different one, having apparently been recruited by German intelligence even before May 1940. Having had a number of assignments in the early years of the occupation, he was then persuaded to go to England as an agent. Rather than travelling clandestinely into Spain, he was in fact taken by car across the frontier by his handlers and with the collusion of Spanish officials before appearing at the British Consulate in Barcelona. Thus filtered into the Allied escape line system with a believable story, he was able to cloak his true purpose and very nearly succeeded. During his time at liberty, he claimed to have sent only eight coded messages to recipients in neutral countries, but this could not be independently verified.[74] Tried and convicted *in camera* before Mr Justice Macnaghten on 28 April and 1 May, his appeal was also rejected and he was executed at Wormwood Scrubs Prison on 23 June.

The report in *The Times* included not only details of his crimes, but also the names of the German agents in Belgium who had supposedly helped him, namely Louis de Bray and Georges Hollevoet.[75] There was some disquiet voiced by the Belgian security services about naming his accomplices, but the British reply made clear the calculations.[76]

The decision to expose de Bray was taken because it was felt that, by allowing these two men to continue their evil work, loyal Belgian patriots were being exposed to the greatest possible risk; as you know, extensive losses have been suffered by these good people as a result of the activities of de Bray and Hollevoet.

It is recognised that, by revealing these names, we have deprived our-selves of a number of advantages. Not least of these benefits was our knowl-edge that anyone arriving here with the assistance of de Bray or Hollevoet must be treated as gravely suspect. The conclusion reached was that the probable advantages to be gained by revealing the names outweighed the disadvantages.[77]

According to British historian and intelligence officer Harry Hinsley, Neukermans was the only incoming German agent who managed to slip through the British security net for any length of time, and subsequent commentators have not con-tradicted him. Of the sixteen German agents executed by the British under the Treason Act, three were Belgian nationals. They could be prosecuted under Brit-ish law because Belgium (or rather the recognised government-in-exile) was for-mally allied to the United Kingdom. Of the three, Timmerman and Neukermans had come via the Iberian Peninsula, but the third, Joseph Jan Vanhove, had arrived via a different route.

Vanhove was 23 years old in 1940 and had been working as a waiter in Antwerp but was suspected by the Belgian police of black-market activities. He had spent some time in France but returned to Antwerp and in 1942 offered his services to German intelligence. Employed initially to spy on Belgian and French workers in northern France, he was then given training in secret writing and the intention was to send him to the United Kingdom as an evader via Switzerland. This plan mis-fired and he returned to Antwerp but was then furnished with seaman's papers and signed on to a German steamer *en route* for Stockholm. Once there he jumped ship and contacted the British Embassy, saying that he wanted to fight for the Allies. Although suspicious, the British sent him to the United Kingdom where he was arrested on arrival on 11 February 1944. Under interrogation, he admitted he was working for the Germans. Tried before Mr Justice Hallett on 23–24 May 1944, he was convicted and executed a month later on 27 June.[78]

Sweden

There were only nineteen Belgian prisoners recorded as having made it to Sweden during the conflict. The Baltic Sea was a major obstacle and heavily patrolled by the Germans. Moreover, prisoners were unsure of the welcome they might receive as the Swedes, while neutral, were reputed to be sympathetic to the Axis. Never-theless, this neutral haven in Scandinavia did have some attractions for prisoners held in the far north of Germany as the fortunes of war changed. A few days af-ter the Allies had landed in north-west Europe, five Belgians and four Frenchmen from *Kommando* VI/1203 of Stalag II-C (Greifswald), working for the Buchholz boatyard, made such an attempt. Working on boats all day made the men eager to attempt an escape. As none of them were sailors, they tried to educate themselves and managed to obtain maps of the German coast. The yard built speedboats for the navy and lightweight boats for towing seaplanes to their shed. As our prisoners were never certain if the boat they were working on would be the one they would use, they worked conscientiously and never considered sabotage. The opportunity arose when the yard completed a towing boat, 8.25 metres long and 2.25 metres wide, equipped with a 50-horsepower, three-cylinder semi-diesel engine that could reach speeds of around 15 miles per hour.

On two occasions the mechanics, Belgian Guy De Ridder (Sergeant in the *1er Regiment d'Artillerie*) and Jacques, one of the Frenchmen, accompanied Buchholz to the island of Rügen to break in the engine. They carefully took the opportunity to familiarise themselves with the engine and steering the boat, as well as noting the locations of navigation buoys. On 15 June, they overheard a conversation between Buchholz and the captain of a coastguard cutter being repaired at the yard. The two men were planning a hike around Peenemunde, about 70 kilometres away, where the boat was to be delivered. In anticipation of this trip, Buchholz asked the mechanics the average consumption of the engine, and they, profiting from his ignorance, told him it required triple what he would actually need. Buchholz therefore had two 150-litre drums of fuel oil placed near the launch as well as having the two 70-litre tanks of the boat filled. The prisoners calculated that all this fuel represented about double what they needed to reach Sweden, a journey of around 170 kilometres.

In the evening there was a major discussion at the *Kommando* as this seemed such a favourable opportunity. Once the decision was made, at midnight the men forced the bars barricading their barracks' windows and headed towards the boatyard. They had barely arrived when the air-raid sirens sounded, forcing them back to the barracks because after the alarm there would be a check. Fortunately, all the men made it to their bunks and pretended to sleep when the German officer arrived. The latter left completely reassured but cursed such a useless chore as the aeroplanes in question were a long way off and the alarm only lasted twenty minutes. The men hastened back to the shipyard, loaded the reserve fuel and hoisted stolen German naval flags fore and aft. Around 1am they cast off, intending to row the 1,500-metre channel leading to the sea to avoid attracting attention, but it was high tide and the current was too strong – so the boat made no progress. While starting the engine was dangerous because of the noise it would create, there was little choice. The engine started first time and the boat headed towards the open sea at around 18 km per hour. There was a further setback when the engine stopped right in the middle of Greifswalder Bodden. De Ridder and Jacques worked feverishly by the glow of a flashlight and found it was just the pump from the cooling system that had stalled. The repair was quickly effected, and with the pump primed, they set off again. As they did not know if the entrance to the Greifswalder Bodden was guarded, the crew approached apprehensively and with caution, but either there was no defence or the garrison was asleep because there was nothing out of the ordinary.

Arriving in the open sea, De Ridder opened the throttle and the brave little engine happily forced the pace. De Ridder and Firmin Maghe (soldier of the *1e Régiment de Ligne*) were at the helm. They had themselves acquired a good little compass from a chocolate-loving Hitlerjugend kid. They used this to navigate for about an hour, heading N.N.E. 28°, because they had to stay in the channel separating Rügen from the German coast. All their good work in identifying the marking buoys turned out to be useless because the night was dark and they saw none of them. Finally, they were parallel to the Peenemunde lighthouse, which signalled the exit of the channel. The men had a momentary fear that someone would notice them, but the Baltic Sea was a German sea and thus very poorly guarded. As the boat reached the open sea, De Ridder changed course and headed north, skirting the disturbing dark mass of the island of Rügen. Around 6am, the west wind picked up and an hour later, it blew in a real storm. The small boat was badly shaken and the crew that, until then had behaved well, was routed: all four Frenchmen and two of the Belgians fell ill. Only valiant Ridder, Maghe and Gervais Gousseau (corporal in the *27e Régiment de Ligne*) remained. De Ridder and Maghe took turns at the helm and the compass, while Gousseau took care of the tanks and tried to bail out the seawater that weighed the boat down. The engine was working well, but the headwind was stronger and the boat seemed to have remained almost static. The boat pitched terribly and the improvised sailors, for whom this was their first voyage at sea, barely managed to stay the course. Some rivets in the bow failed and this served to increase their anxiety. Around 9am, Rügen was left behind and gradually disappeared from the horizon. De Ridder passed the helm to Maghe and laid down. He was so tired that he fell asleep immediately. Suddenly a convoy of three German freighters following the same route as our heroes approached, then passed them and disappeared over the horizon. About 1pm, the wind fell and the little boat made good progress. Suddenly five German seaplanes appeared, approaching rapidly. Alert on board: everyone hid under the tarpaulin save Gousseau, who, in blue overalls and a German sailor's cap next to the naval flag, valiantly represented a sailor of the Kriegsmarine. One of the seaplanes dived towards the boat, passed very close then, visibly reassured, joined the other aircraft and all quickly moved away. The men, who believed their last hour had come, breathed a huge sigh of relief. Around 2.30pm, a coast came in sight. Maghe reduced speed and approached cautiously. Victory! It was the Swedish flag flying at the entrance of a small harbour. Full throttle and triumphant entry to the Swedish port around 3pm. Even the sick who, until then, were wallowing in a pile on top of each other, bathed in a mixture of seawater, oil and vomit, were suddenly cured. The Swedes looked with amazement at the arrival of a German naval vessel but when they understood the circumstances, they gave the heroes a triumphant welcome. They had arrived at Rachenfud, a small fishing port located at the extreme south-eastern tip of Skåne, west of Ystadt. By 17 June 1944, they were in Stockholm and arrived in England four months later where they attached to the Belgian armed forces – at least three of them to the Section Belge of the Royal Navy.[79]

Switzerland

Numbers of Belgian soldiers also found their way into Switzerland as the French war effort collapsed and were, in accordance with the Hague Conventions, disarmed and interned by the Swiss authorities. Such was the case of 18-year-old Carolus Dendoover, an ordinary soldier from Ghent, who in peacetime had been a labourer.

Surrounded by enemy troops, his unit was in danger of being overrun and he was able to cross the frontier by train on 17 June 1940 with around 200 other soldiers and with the permission of his commanding officer. He was then interned in a series of camps at Lac Noir, St. Stephan, Reichenbach, Bettwiesen and finally Aberhofen. He attempted to escape from Reichenbach with one of his comrades and managed to travel around 30 kilometres before being apprehended by Swiss soldiers. For this, he and his comrades received twenty days in the cells (*cachot*). Undeterred, he and two other soldiers managed to escape from Bettwiesen. Having marched through the night, they were caught in a village by the Swiss police and once again returned to the camp, and, because this was his second offence, Dendoover was given fifty-eight days in a punishment block inside the camp. Transferred on two further occasions, he was ultimately repatriated by the Swiss to Belgium via Germany on 11 June 1941. Dendoover and his comrades were among the 104,000 foreign soldiers interned by the Swiss at some point during the conflict. They seem to have benefited from the agreement reached between the belligerent powers that the 30,000 men of the 45th French Corps interned in June 1940 could be returned home. This process had been completed by February 1941, but it can be assumed that the Swiss desire to be relieved of responsibility for as many internees as possible also facilitated the return home of the small numbers of Belgians in their hands.[80]

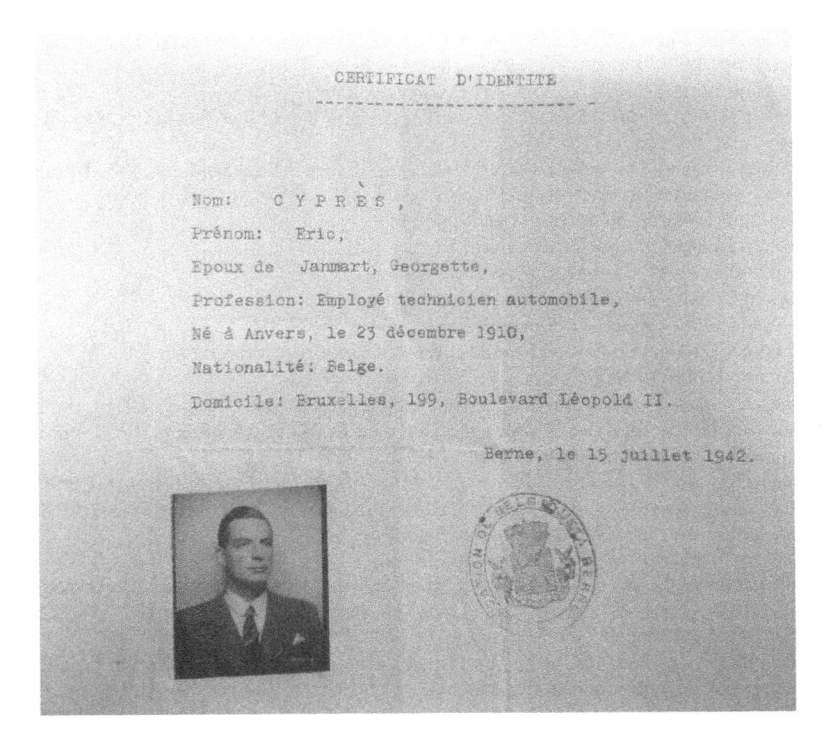

Figure 5.3 The identity certificate issued by the Belgian legation of Bern (@Archives de l'État en Belgique)

Later during the war, Switzerland did not seem to have attracted many escaped Belgian soldiers. The case of André Bounameaux is an uncommon one. Together with Paul Gaussin, he escaped from Stalag VIII-A (Görlitz) on 15 October 1943 and managed to board a train headed for Switzerland, where he arrived some four days later. This is, in itself, quite remarkable in that he managed to find a train travelling into Switzerland from Lower Silesia and was then able to hide himself there undiscovered for the duration of the journey. Unfortunately there are no other details of his escape. He stayed there for almost a year before leaving for France, Spain and Portugal.[81] Albert Henry, another escaped soldier, stayed months in Switzerland before going back to France and across the Pyrenees. The Swiss were not particularly strict with Belgian soldiers.[82] Most were under house arrest in Lausanne and enjoyed a level of freedom that those interned in Spain could only dream of. Leaving the country and crossing into France usually involved negotiating and barbed wire at the frontier, although it can be assumed that the Swiss were less concerned about individuals leaving their territory, and the French and their German masters likewise not looking for arrivals.

Notes

1 Neville Wylie, 'Switzerland', in: Neville Wyle (ed.), *European Neutrals and Non-Belligerents during the Second World War*, (Cambridge: Cambridge University Press, 2002), pp. 333–334.
2 Foot and Langley, *MI9 Escape and Evasion*, p. 19.
3 Neville Wylie, *Britain, Switzerland and the Second World War* (Oxford: Oxford University Press, 2003), pp. 316–317.
4 Matilde Eiroa and Concha Pallarés, 'Uncertain Fates: Allied Soldiers at the Miranda De Ebro Concentration Camp', in: *The Historian*, Vol. 76, No. 1 (2014), p. 36.
5 Eiroa and Pallarés, 'Uncertain Fates', p. 31.
6 Foot and Langley, *MI9 Escape and Evasion*, p. 44.
7 Foot and Langley, *MI9 Escape and Evasion*, pp. 76–77.
8 Donald Caskie, *The Tartan Pimpernel*, (London: Oldbourne, 1957).
9 Foot and Langley, *MI9 Escape and Evasion*, pp. 66, 73, 75.
10 CEGES/SOMA, Fonds sur Miranda : AA1491, reports on Frieda Moore.
11 Foot and Langley, *MI9 Escape and Evasion*, pp. 79–81.
12 Margaret L. Rossiter, *Women in the Resistance*, (New York: Prager, 1986), pp. 24–31. Sir Brian Horrocks, 'The Comet Line', in: *The Listener*, 14 January 1960, pp. 61–64. Pitchfork, *Escape from Germany*, pp. 14–15.
13 Megan Koreman, *The Escape Line: How the Ordinary Heroes of Dutch-Paris Resisted the Nazi Occupation of Western Europe*, (Oxford: Oxford University Press, 2018).
14 Foot and Langley, *MI9 Escape and Evasion*, pp. 86–88.
15 Rossiter, *Women in the Resistance*, pp. 35–42.
16 Guillaume Avalosse, Les activités de la Sûreté de l'État belge dans la péninsule ibérique, 1940–1944, (Master's Thesis, Louvain-la-Neuve University, 2022), p. 72. Foot and Langley, *MI9 Escape and Evasion*, pp. 209–213.
17 Jean Fosty, 'Les Réseaux belges de France. Essai sur l'histoire de Services de Renseignements et d'Action belges de France durant la Seconde Guerre mondiale', in: *Cahiers d'histoire de la Seconde Guerre Mondiale*, Vol. 2, (1972), p. 82 fn. 8.
18 Fosty, 'Les Réseaux belges', pp. 82–83.
19 Prosper Vandenbroucke, 'La route de Londres', in: *HISTOMAG 39–45*, No. 65, May–June (2010), pp. 42–49.

20 Alberto Franco (trans. Janet Reynolds), 'Victor Reynolds: Our Man in Estremoz', in: *British Historical Society of Portugal: Annual Report and Review*, Vol. 31 (2004), p. 15.
21 Franco, 'Victor Reynolds', pp. 16–17.
22 Franco, 'Victor Reynolds', p. 19. Reynolds was honoured by the Belgian Government as a Chevalier of the Order of Leopold II in 1954 and with the Order of Free Poland by the Polish Government-in-Exile.
23 Joseph P. Kahn, 'The Escape Artist: For This War Hero, Discretion Was the Better Part of Valor', in: *Boston Globe*, 15 April 2004. Meg Ostrum, *The Surgeon and the Shepherd: Two Resistance Heroes in Vichy France*, (Lincoln NE: University of Nebraska Press, 2004).
24 Jean Fosty, 'Les Réseaux belges', pp. 86–89.
25 Rens et al. (eds), *Évasions*, p. 180.
26 *L'Évadé*, March 1950.
27 Luis Bernardo y Garcia, *Miranda de Ebro ou l'internement des Belges en Espagne au cours de la Seconde Guerre mondiale*, (Brussels: CEGES/SOMA, 1995), p. 7.
28 Rens et al. (eds), *Évasions*, p. 214.
29 Étienne Plissart, *Souvenirs de guerre*, (2001), p. 43.
30 Avalosse, Les activités de la Sûreté de l'État belge, p. 79.
31 Louis Legrand, *Destin d'un homme*, (Brussels: L'Avenir), pp. X–9.
32 Eiroa and Pallarés, 'Uncertain Fates', p. 31.
33 Louis-Armand Héraut, 'Miranda de Ebro. État sanitaire du camp de concentration à l'automne 1943', in: *Histoire des Sciences Médicales*, Vol. 42, No. 2 (2008), pp. 210–213.
34 Eiroa and Pallarés, 'Uncertain Fates', p. 31.
35 Foot and Langley, *MI9 Escape and Evasion*, p. 19.
36 Rens et al. (eds), *Évasions*, p. 181.
37 Plissart, *Souvenirs de guerre*, p. 45.
38 Plissart, *Souvenirs de guerre*, p. 49.
39 Avalosse, Les activités de la Sûreté de l'État belge, p. 80.
40 Avalosse, Les activités de la Sûreté de l'État belge, pp. 81–82.
41 Avalosse, Les activités de la Sûreté de l'État belge, p. 86.
42 Adam, *S'évader*, pp. 78–79.
43 Adam, *S'évader*, p. 78.
44 MRAB, Fonds Georges Hautecler, 59/43, Rapports sur les évadés.
45 MRAB, Fonds Georges Hautecler, 59/43, Rapports sur les évadés.
46 Eiroa and Pallarés, 'Uncertain Fates', p. 33.
47 Rens et al. (eds), *Évasions*, p. 234.
48 CEGES/SOMA, Manuscript of Edouard Cuvelier, Villégiature en Espagne.
49 Belgian Ministry of Foreign Affairs (BMFA), *Belgium: The Official Account of What Happened, 1939–1940*, (London: Evans Brothers, 1941), Vol. IV, n° 11, December (1943).
50 *Le Journal des combattants*, 5 June 1966.
51 Eiroa and Pallarés, 'Uncertain Fates', p. 31.
52 CEGES/SOMA, Manuscript of Edouard Cuvelier, Villégiature en Espagne.
53 CEGES/SOMA, Manuscript of Edouard Cuvelier, Villégiature en Espagne.
54 Rens et al. (eds), *Évasions*, pp. 80–82.
55 CEGES/SOMA, Manuscript of Edouard Cuvelier, Villégiature en Espagne.
56 Joline Maenhout, Een Concentratiekamp op het Politiek Schaakbord van Franco, (Master's Thesis, Universiteit Gent, 2019), p. 100.
57 Maenhout, Een Concentratiekamp, p. 102.
58 Maenhout, Een Concentratiekamp, p. 104 cites CEGES/SOMA, Rapport R. Van Cutsem, 8 August 1943, AA 1333: Bestand Inlichtings- en Actiediensten (IAD) van de Veiligheid van de Staat, Simon Leclef.
59 Maenhout, Een Concentratiekamp, pp. 107–109.

60 Avalosse, Les activités de la Sûreté de l'État belge, pp. 90–91.
61 Richard L. Speaight, comment on The National Archives (TNA), FO371/26355. C12322 Belgium: Escaped Belgian Prisoners of War, 21 November 1941.
62 Arthur Aveling, comment on TNA, FO371/26355. C12322 Belgium: Escaped Belgian Prisoners of War, 2 December 1941.
63 TNA, WO208/3676. M.I.19 (RPS) 748, 29 May 1942.
64 TNA, WO208/3676. M.I.19 (RPS) 747, 29 May 1942.
65 TNA, WO203/3676. M.I.19 (RPS) 740, 28 May 1942.
66 Plissart, *Souvenirs de guerre*, p. 63.
67 Piron, *Souvenirs*, p. 80.
68 Nanclares de la Oca was built in the winter of 1940 as an overspill facility to relieve overcrowding at the Miranda de Ebro camp.
69 TNA, KV2/3854. Statement by Alphonse Timmerman witnessed by Lieutenant-Colonel W.E. Hinchley Cooke GS, 5 Se9tember 1941.
70 Timmerman was given the codename 'Scruffy' by his MI5 handlers.
71 Nigel West, *MI5: British Security Service Operations, 1909–1945*, (New York: Stein and Day, 1982), pp. 262–263. For details of the trial see, TNA, PCOM9/940.
72 TNA, KV2/53. MI5 Report, Pierre Richard Charles Neukermans, 27 February 1944, p. 1.
73 TNA, KV2/53. MI5 Report, Pierre Richard Charles Neukermans, 27 February 1944, p. 2.
74 TNA, KV2/53. Statement by Pierre Neukermans at Camp 020, 20 February 1944.
75 *The Times*, 'Spy Executed', 24 June 1944.
76 TNA, KV2/1720. Extract of memorandum from Lieutenant-Colonel Marcel Roost (Belgian Security Service), 29 June 1944.
77 TNA, KV2/1720. B. Lough to Lieutenant-Colonel Roost, 10 July 1944.
78 See, TNA, PCOM9/1044.
79 MRAB, Fonds Georges Hautecler, 59/43, Rapports sur les évadés.
80 AGR, Ministre de la justice : dossiers relatifs à l'octroi de la Croix des Évadés, 1940–1945, file 648: Carolus Dendoover.
81 AGR, Ministre de la justice : dossiers relatifs à l'octroi de la Croix des Évadés, 1940–1945, file 1236: Paul Gaussin.
82 AGR, Ministre de la justice : dossiers relatifs à l'octroi de la Croix des Évadés, 1940–1945, file 1568: Albert Henry.

6 Escape to the South

The Foreign Legion

Besides the Belgians who fought in their country's own forces or those of the Western Allied powers, there were also an appreciable number in the ranks of the French Foreign Legion. While some had joined before the outbreak of war, their presence had been increased because of Vichy policies towards young Belgians caught in the unoccupied zone trying to reach Britain. They were generally given a stark choice, either join the Foreign Legion or be consigned to one of France's many internment camps. To understand the complex trajectories of the Belgians who served in the Foreign Legion, we need to go back to the beginning of the conflict.

The history of the Foreign Legion during the Second World War is a complex one. At the beginning of the conflict, there were nearly 49,000 soldiers in its ranks, including many Spanish, German and Austrian exiles.[1] The presence of nationals of an enemy nation was a major difficulty for the Legion's leadership, especially as there was a desire on the part of the German secret services to infiltrate its ranks in order to weaken it. Left-wing refugees were also represented, as Belgian Legionnaire Joseph Debry witnessed: 'Most of the volunteers were at the time political refugees who had fled their country of origin before 1940: Spanish Republicans, Russians, Portuguese, Germans, Italians'.[2] There were also several dozen Belgians, often attracted by the distinctive history of this formation as well as by a certain taste for adventure. This was notably the case of Albert Desmoutier, who had enlisted on 5 May 1934, and René Scieur, who had joined on 14 October 1938. Both men were to experience the unique trajectory of the Legion during the Second World War. Between October 1939 and May 1940, some 6,000 volunteers were recruited and regrouped in the newly created 21st and 22nd *Régiments de marche de volontaires étrangers* (RMVE or Marching Regiments of Foreign Volunteers). Ill-equipped and ill-disciplined, these units were considered unreliable. Two other units, made up from veterans from Africa, formed the 11th and 12th *Régiments étrangers d'infanterie* (REI or Foreign infantry Regiment). There was also the GERD 97 (Foreign Legion Divisional Reconnaissance Group), attached to the 7th North African Division, and the 13th Demi-Brigade (Half-Brigade) of the Foreign Legion, better known as the 13th DBLE.

The military campaign in France in 1939–1940 was not the most glorious episode in the history of the Foreign Legion. Some units were severely mauled in the

DOI: 10.4324/9780429027697-7

fighting, such as the 11th REI, responsible for the defence of Inor Wood between the Meuse and the Chiers, close to the Belgian border, which lost half its strength between 27 May and 11 June 1940. GERD 97 held out for more than three weeks on the Somme through delaying manoeuvres against superior forces before being annihilated in a counter-attack on 9 June 1940. On 6 June 1940, the 12th REI had a third of its men killed, wounded or taken prisoner in fighting near Soissons. The newly created 21st RMVE was unable to resist the onslaught in the Ardennes on 10 June. The 22nd RMVE was more successful but lost half its strength in the vicinity of Péronne. The 13th DBLE took part in the ill-fated Norwegian expedition and was landed at Narvik but lost many of its officers. On its return to France, as the country surrendered, the 13th DBLE was embarked at Brest for transit to Great Britain.[3] On arrival, the men were harangued by General de Gaulle himself. He gave them the choice of fighting alongside the British or being repatriated to Morocco. Half of the 13th DBLE, including the Belgian Albert Desmoutier, chose to stay.[4]

The French armistice with Germany placed the Foreign Legion in an uncomfortable position. The regiments stationed in Algeria, Morocco, Tunisia and Syria fell under the authority of the Vichy regime and found themselves locked into a garrison life carrying out colonial police duties. These Vichy units were subject to regular inspections by the German authorities, who were anxious to monitor their numbers and arrest undesirable elements. Legionnaires of interest to the German authorities, such as German nationals who had opposed the Nazi regime, were generally transferred by the Legion to units based in Senegal, far from prying eyes. The fall of France also created a recruitment crisis for the Foreign Legion as it could no longer rely on a supply of foreign recruits, and this led to the idea of using escapees arrested in the non-occupied zone of France. Belgians who had managed to slip onto vessels bound for North Africa were no more fortunate. For these would-be escapees, often former soldiers, joining the Foreign Legion was the lesser evil. The appalling reputation of the French internment camp system, together with the desire to continue to fight, made the choice a simple one.[5] Victor Depireux, a volunteer who had fought in the Belgian Army at Fort Barchon in May 1940, was one of the Belgians who faced the uncomfortable situation of having to join Vichy troops. After capture, he was taken to Germany but escaped on 2 April 1941. Recaptured in France, he was forced to enlist in the Legion. Posted to Algeria, he deserted and managed to escape via Gibraltar to England in 1942 and subsequently fought in the ranks of the Allies.[6]

André Brusselmans had left Belgium on 10 May 1941 to join the Belgians in England. He had managed to reach Marseilles by 24 May but was arrested while waiting for a tram. Brusselmans explained the following:

> Without papers except for my identity card, I was taken to the police station. I spent the night in a cell. The next day, I was interrogated by a civilian officer of the state. He gave me a choice:
>
> If you do not join the foreign Legion or a working camp, you will be given to your country's authorities. I chose the Legion without knowing much about it but with something in my mind. In Africa, I could probably reach the Belgian Congo. On 25 May, the police brought me to the camp of

Saint-Joseph in Marseilles where the human race was represented by people allergic to national-socialism. There were mostly Spaniards, Belgians and Dutch people. The camp's commander took away my identity card, read the rules of enlistment and made me sign a contract. I was given a uniform and a meal. [...] The Belgians recognise themselves, talk, regroup. We only think of escaping, deserting... Luckily, among us is a Belgian gendarme, a man named Coulon. He calms us and warns us against foolish acts.[7]

Joseph Debry provides another example of this unusual form of 'escape'. In 1940, he had taken a train to the unoccupied part of France and had managed to spend the winter in Luchon. On 15 February 1941, he was arrested after having tried to cross the border into Spain. He was imprisoned at Saint-Michel near Toulouse and was then transferred to Récébédou Camp in Haute-Garonne. Later, he managed to escape from the camp at Argelès-sur-Mer. Apprehended again by the Vichy police, he was given the option of enlisting in the Foreign Legion. In January 1942, he was dispatched to Africa to join the 1st REI. Serving the enemy was frustrating, a feeling that he expressed after the conflict:

Yes, I served in the Foreign Legion under the orders of the Vichy government until the Allied landing on 8 November 1942. During this period the senior officers gave the appearance of being totally loyal to the Marshal, but this was only a facade: it disappeared in the first hours after the Allied landing. Before this, it was unwise to show anti-Vichy sentiments, and these opinions were sometimes paid for dearly, and some Belgians were the victims. When I was in the 4/4 Group in Saida, all the Belgians in the Group were arrested and put in cells. For two days we were interrogated relentlessly by plainclothes agents belonging to the political police of the Oran office. Four or five of us who had tried to escape to Spanish Morocco were sent to the 11th disciplinary company of Colomb Béchar. They were Cartiens, Trébor, Mory and Salut who also later moved to the Belgian Forces in Great Britain.[8]

The case of Hubert Leroy was also unusual. A native of Visé, he had been raised on the stories of the German massacres in the region in 1914. In 1941, at the age of 19, he decided to join the Allies and took the train for France with a friend. At the border, he was helped by a train manager and was able to reach the unoccupied part of the country. Hiding during the day, the two Belgians travelled to Marseilles. Once there, having no identity papers or money, they noticed a Foreign Legion enlistment poster and decided to join, thinking that they could get away from Europe. After three months of training in North Africa, Leroy was transferred to Fes and subsequently fought for Vichy.[9]

While Legionnaires were fighting on the Vichy side, the 13th DBLE, still based in England, was reinforced and sent to Sudan in February 1941, where it fought alongside British troops. It then moved via Jordan to Vichy Syria, where an astonishing episode took place on 8 June 1941. The unit was confronted by troops of the 6th REI, loyal to Marshal Pétain. Legionnaires were pitted against each other in battle. The men of the 13th DBLE had the upper hand but both sides suffered heavy losses. Several captured soldiers of the 6th REI were given the opportunity to change sides. From there, the 13th DBLE was sent to Libya where it participated in the defence of Bir Hakeim. On 2 June 1942, the unit distinguished itself by its resistance to the assaults by the Afrika Korps. After nine days of fighting, the legionnaires escaped at night through minefields. This famous incident, however, had caused the 13th DBLE to sustain some substantial losses. The Legionnaires nonetheless continued to be used in the campaign during 1942 and found themselves on the left of the Alamein Line.[10]

While there is no means of knowing how many Belgians fought with the Foreign Legion, there were at least seventy-seven known deaths, including eleven in Syria in 1941 and three at Bir Hakeim in 1942.[11] After the Allies invaded North Africa on 8 November 1942, which the 1st REI was supposed to resist, Vichy's legionnaires were deployed in the Allied cause. Joseph Debry was among those who were able to switch sides:

In the night, we were woken up and... locked for 48 hours. Two days later, when the Allied success was confirmed, all the pictures of Marshal Pétain which were in the official buildings were quickly removed and replaced by those of Weygand and Huntziger. The battalion chiefs, the company commanders and the section commanders who had seemed very loyal to Vichy became instantly pro-Ally. They were not for de Gaulle but agreed to be led by General Giraud.[12]

The Foreign Legion was reorganised and most of the Belgians, including Leroy, were placed in its 3rd *Régiment de marche de la Légion étrangère*, which was then deployed against the German forces in Tunisia commanded by Generaloberst Hans-Jürgen von Arnim and Generalfeldmarschall Erwin Rommel. Their regiment was encircled and then almost destroyed at Pont-du-Fah on 18–19 January 1943, losing thirty-five officers and 1,634 men. Those that remained ran out of supplies and attempted to break out to the south, but the ensuing debacle was described in detail by one of those who survived.

On 21 January 12.30pm, we attacked. All the fires of hell were unleashed on us. Lieutenant Mayot fell at the head of the company and the young officer Suchié took command. Of our section, there were only 4 fighters left: Sergeant Ludoski, as calm as in an exercise; Tabar, the machine gunner; Morgan, who still carried enough ammunition for the whole battalion and myself, who carried bags of grenades and generously bombed every hole that came up. A Wadi stood in our way. We ran to the other side and stupidly we got stuck in the open. The Germans had installed a machine gun that took us in a row: Tabar collapsed, Morgan had his head shattered, the sergeant was wounded, a bullet hit me in the head and I lost consciousness. When I recovered, a German armed with a machine gun was looking at me laughing. Of the 950 men of the battalion, only about fifty were able to break through. All the rest were dead, wounded or prisoners. This is captivity: a 300 kilometre walk with almost no supplies; Tunis where we embark into the bottom of a ship's hold with 3 Italian biscuits and two quarts of water per day: Palermo... with as food two cups of soup and a *pagnotte* [loaf] made from corn flour.[13]

Although captured by the Afrika Korps, the survivors were then handed over to the Italians, which was perceived at the time as something of an insult and 'outside the rules of the game'.[14] Like other Allied soldiers captured in North Africa, this group was transferred to Italy from Tunis in the hold of a merchant ship, arriving in Italy on 28 January. They were held initially at PG Camp 66 in Capua (Caserta), then PG Camp 62 in Grumello del Piano (Bergamo) and finally PG Camp 82 in Laterina (Arezzo). Again, precise numbers are impossible to ascertain. In a letter of 30 June 1948, the Belgian Embassy in Rome made reference to 147 Belgian prisoners of war, while the International Red Cross tabulated 163 and the prisoner of war service, 166. Of these, eighty-eight were known to have been deported to Germany after 8 September 1943, leaving seventy-eight unaccounted for. In the chaos that surrounded the Italian surrender, many prisoners chose not to stay put but disappeared into the countryside, either attempting to reach Allied lines, joining the nascent Italian resistance or just opting out of the war altogether.[15] Hautecler notes that there are records of only twenty-eight escapes but explains that: 'It is true that a legionnaire fights very well, but [he] writes very little'.[16]

One of those who did leave a record of his escape was Jean Sail, who was 34 when war broke out but who had been in the Foreign Legion since 1937. He was a sergeant in the 3rd *Régiment de marche de la Légion étrangère* who was captured on 18 January 1943 at Oued Kébir and was in PG 82 (Laterina) when the Italians surrendered and who escaped some eleven days later.

At 8pm, he managed to cross the barbed wire and forded the stream that ran a few metres away from the fence. To orient himself he had a small school map of Italy and set off in the direction of Arezzo by following the railway tracks. After 5 or 6 hours walking through the night, near a level crossing he heard a command, "Wer da" (Who goes there). As he fled immediately, two bullets whistled past his ears, and he decided to redouble his precautions. When day came, he rested in a vineyard, having only grapes and a few tins from Red Cross parcels for food. After a few days, he arrived at the heights above Arezzo which he avoided. Pretending to be a Sicilian, he addressed an old man working in a field. The old man was not fooled and took him for an Englishman. He exchanged his military shirt for a civilian one, and the old man offered him some bread and gave him directions for Perugia. After a few days of careful walking, Sail skirted Lake Castiglione and arrived in the vicinity of Perugia. He did not dare ask for help, because he feared the lure of the 26 gold lire offered to any Italian capturing an escapee. One afternoon, while resting on a small bridge in the countryside, he was awakened by an elderly woman accompanied by a child. They invited him to rest at their home and, as this was an isolated farm, Sail agreed.

After a day of rest, full of bread and cheese, he took the road to Poligno. His hosts had warned him to be suspicious, because there were many Germans and 'Camisa Nere' (Blackshirts) in the locality. However, he crossed Poligno without a hitch, skirted the Campello sul Clitunno, which he already knew having stayed there as a prisoner, and headed towards Spoleto. Crossing a very extensive wood, he discovered a shepherd's hut where he was surprised to find potatoes, sheep fat and bread. He seized it and continued on his way. Arriving near a stream, he stopped to cook his potatoes. While doing this, he was surprised by two Italian carabinieri. They asked Sail what he was doing in this deserted place. Sail told his story of being a Sicilian on his way south, but the two Italians laughed in his face, and pointed out that he had English military trousers and excellent Canadian shoes. Sail believed his adventure was over, until the two Italians confessed that they were also illegals and that they were hiding in the woods waiting for the Allies. Sail stayed with them for three days, spending the days in the woods and the nights in the barns of a nearby village. Every evening, in the village, they were offered a frugal meal that was most welcome: potatoes, beets and pure water. Sail wanted to continue south. His two friends advised him to avoid the roads, provided him with old civilian trousers and exchanged his good shoes for vulgar sandals made of poorly tanned cowhide fixed by straps. In this accoutrement he was no longer likely to attract attention. The two carabinieri accompanied him to Terni and showed him the way to Rieti.

Sail had to hide repeatedly to avoid German military convoys. He had the impression that as he approached the front, the Italian population became more and more hostile to the Germans. He was no longer afraid to ask for help and beg for food as there was a good welcome everywhere. He even had the opportunity to hear Radio Bari and thus knew the military situation. His plan was to go to Avezzano, but an Italian priest from Aquila strongly advised him to avoid this locality and gave him a detailed route to Castellafiume. In the mountains, he was surprised by a tornado and soaked to the bone when he met two young Italian women. The young girls questioned him and he told his little story, but although they did not believe a word they nonetheless led him to their home. There, Sail could finally explain himself in French, their father and brothers having worked for a long time in France. He stayed there for two days, well fed, and sleeping in a hayloft. Comforted, he then set off again, passing Capistrello and entering the forest of Abruzzo. In the late afternoon, he entered a charcoal hut and was stunned by the sight of five shaggy individuals. Fortunately, he heard them speak English and had time to tell them: "French Legion". These men were five South Africans who had also escaped from prisoner-of-war camps. Sail spent the night with them and at dawn headed towards Sora.

He remained in the woods overlooking the road, as it was cluttered with German columns and convoys. He even had the pleasure of witnessing a convoy being attacked by Allied aircraft. Two days later Sail was arrested by two civilians, a German and an Italian who asked for his papers. As he had none, he was brought before a German and an Italian officer, who interrogated him. Getting nothing from Sail, they sent him back to Tagliacozzo where he was locked up in a school with other prisoners who had escaped and been recaptured. Taking advantage of an air-raid, Sail and a Scotsman named Lucas managed to escape. Sail returned to Capistrello and decided to stay there and wait for the Allies as crossing the lines was too difficult. He was taken in by the Pizzi family and hidden in their barn. He was not discovered there despite two German raids on the farm. Sail remained there for three months, listening to Radio Bari every day and hoping for the rapid arrival of the Allies. Finally, the front line got closer. The Germans blew up electrical installations, water tanks and engineering structures. Believing the moment [of liberation] had arrived, Sail, the Pizzi family and the whole village and its cattle took refuge in the surrounding woods. They stayed there for 8 days in the middle of the front line, close to a German battery. One morning, it was strangely calm: the battery had gone. The villagers returned home, and Sail continued his journey south. On 6 June 1944, he was overjoyed to encounter British soldiers. He was carefully interrogated by an English intelligence officer and then invited to the non-commissioned officers' mess. He was transferred to Naples and the French Base No. 620 and embarked for Algiers on the steamship 'Gloire'. Rejoining the Legion, he subsequently participated in the operations of the 1st French Army. Finally demobilised on 4 October 1945 in Besançon, he settled permanently in France.[17]

Marc Cahay was an even more unusual example. Forcibly incorporated in the Foreign Legion by the French in March 1941, he was sent to Algeria in June of the same year. He also served in Morocco in December 1942 and in Tunisia in February 1943. Soon afterwards, his unit was destroyed by the Germans. Captured, he was transferred to the Italian custody:

In September 1943, I escaped from PG82 (Laterina) with other Belgian comrades including a man from Tournai, Jean [?] and one from Brussels named Roger Biard from my company. I stayed hidden in the countryside for a few months in the region of A[?]zo and, having tried to cross the frontline in the winter, I came back to my starting point, where I was recaptured by the Germans on 30 April 1944 and sent to Germany. First Stalag-VII, then Munich and Stalag II-B in Hammerstein Pomerania. On 30 January 1945, the camp was evacuated because of the Russian advance and I started an exodus of three months, a walk on foot of more than 1,000 kilometres in the snow.

On 15 April, I escaped from the column and after five days of walking in [?] the forest of Hanover, I rejoined the British forward posts in Celle. On 25 April, I was transferred by plane to Belgium.[18]

In March 1943, a group of legionnaires then serving in North Africa was given the choice to join their countrymen in Britain. René Scieur explained:

On 8 March 1943, I was removed from the Foreign Legion and, together with eleven other Belgians, we wore English Battledress for the first time – something I did not remove until the end of the war. We were taken by truck to Mers-El-Kébir where an English officer told us that we were free to embark on a Liberty Ship. Once in Gibraltar, fifty Belgians embarked for Glasgow where they arrived on 13 March 1943.[19]

In September 1943, other Belgian legionnaires still in Africa, including several escapees incorporated in these units, were also offered the opportunity to join the Belgian forces in Britain by the Belgian commander Claes. Those who made this choice were embarked on 10 September 1943 on the Belgian-registered ship René-Paul, which sailed from Lisbon to Gibraltar. On arrival on the rock, they were accommodated at the Moorish Castle before boarding the liner Eastern Prince and taken to the port of Greenock.[20]

The Road to Africa

Most Belgian escapees and evaders travelled to France in order to regain their freedom. From there a vast majority went through Spain but others, for various reasons, chose a different route.

In May 1940, Jean-Philippe Janssens, who was barely 18 at the time, went to Normandy before going to the south of France. Once in Marseilles, he learned of the Belgian capitulation and decided to try to reach Britain to carry on the fight in the Royal Navy. To do so, he joined a civilian ship, the French steamer Mariette Pacha, as a crew member and sailed to Oran. He was allowed to disembark with the help of a French official and joined a Norwegian ship as an ordinary seaman. He remained there until 22 June 1941, when he left with other foreign nationals on a small boat. For eight days, the group sailed in the direction of Malaga but were eventually intercepted by the Spaniards. The latter considered the Belgians as British and dispatched them to Gibraltar.[21]

Albert Rosenberg was another Belgian whose desire to join the British to fight led him to Africa. On 29 August 1940, he left Brussels by car for the Gironde. Stuck in Haute-Garonne until February 1941, he finally reached Marseilles by train. On 7 April 1941, having no papers and no French exit visa, he embarked illegally on the SS Gouverneur Laférière, which took him to Algiers. Once there, he was refused help by the Belgian General Consul, who instead offered to repatriate him to Brussels. Rosenberg took the train to Oran to meet a Belgian family. The next day, another train brought him to the border with Morocco. Crawling under the barbed wire, he reached the station at Oujda and travelled to Casablanca before going to the border city of Arbaoua, close to the Spanish enclave. On 19 April 1941, his luck ran out when he was intercepted by Vichy policemen. Arrested, he was sent to prison before being transferred to an industrial enterprise where most of the workers were Spanish Republicans. During the next seventeen months, Rosenberg experienced several camps, including Oued Akreuch, Oujda, Djerada, Bouarfa, Talzala, Menaba and Colomb-Béchar. Finally the Belgian authorities in Algiers were alerted to his presence by the French *Deuxième Bureau* in September 1942. Following their intervention, Rosenberg was evacuated on board HMT Ormonde on 9 November 1942.[22] Rosenberg's bravery cost him a lung and 20 kilos. Physically broken, he was unable to fight with the British army.[23]

Later during the conflict, Belgium's imperial territories were seen by several escapers and evaders as a suitable refuge. It should be remembered that the Congo, as a Belgian colony, had been at war with Germany since 10 May 1940. Despite the occupation of the metropolitan homeland, the Belgian Minister for the Colonies, Albert de Vleeschauwer, had gone to England with plenipotentiary powers over the country's African lands. From London, the government-in-exile continued to rule the colony in favour of the Allied cause. Its vast resources became extremely valuable and amounted to 85% of the Belgian contribution to the Allied war effort.

Most of those who ended up in the colony initially took the same route as those who arrived in England, namely travelling via Spain. Antoine Dupont, a soldier captured on 24 May 1940, escaped from Stalag XII-B and reached France on 16 October 1941. He was incarcerated at Miranda de Ebro from 5 June 1942 to 19 April 1943, and after his release was taken to Portugal and embarked on board one of the vessels regularly sailing between the Congo and the British Isles. He finally arrived in the port of Matadi in August 1943. After the conflict, he explained the last stretch of his odyssey:

> On 19 April 1943, [I was] liberated from Miranda, 3 weeks to rest at Cestona, near St Sebastian, then departure for Portugal at Curia near Camba where they selected those who could go to England. Only aviators and soldiers aged less than 30. The oldest and all the [other] ranks had to go to Congo to instruct and supervise the black troops, including some already in Egypt. [I] left Lisbon on 10 July 1943, reached Matadi on 1 August [and] enlisted for the duration of war with the FP [*Force Publique*] with the hope of being sent to the Expeditionary Corps. However, I was claimed by civilian mobilisation because of my job, despite all my protests and was forced to work for war production and sent to a cement factory. I stayed in the same line of work until December 1945. I was allowed to embark from Matadi on 18 December on the SS Mafuta and reached Antwerp on 2 January 1946.[24]

It seems obvious that the Belgian authorities in the Congo were not as desperate for military volunteers and were almost more interested in finding skilled civilians. When Maurice Tibeau escaped from Stalag XVII-B on 26 July 1943, he was first sent to England. After serving for nine months as a soldier, he was demobilised and dispatched by the Inter-Allied mission to Africa. In February 1944, he was recruited by the Belgian Ministry of Colonies.[25] Going to the Belgian colony was clearly not a choice but a matter of fate. NCO Van der Voodt had a similar experience as Antoine Dupont, leaving Portugal in July 1943 for Congo, but was more fortunate on arrival. He was allowed to enlist in the *Force Publique* and he thereby resumed his military career.[26] The *Force Publique* had been created in 1885 by the Congo Free State before being absorbed into the structures of Belgian colonial rule after 1908. This gendarmerie and military force was organised along racial lines, with the officers and NCOs exclusively Belgian and white, while soldiers were recruited from the native Congolese.[27]

Once in Africa, Belgian soldiers either stayed there or were dispatched to other fronts. Charles Vyt, also a career NCO, left Portugal in February 1943. Soon after reaching the Congo, he requested a transfer to the expeditionary corps stationed in the Middle East. When this unit was later disbanded, he was dispatched to Britain where he joined the SAS.[28]

The overall military contribution of the *Force Publique* was by no means negligible. Some 40,000 men were incorporated into three different brigades and were dispatched to serve outside the colony alongside their British Allies; in Italian East Africa in 1941 and after victory there, being redeployed, first to Nigeria and then to Egypt and Mandatory Palestine in 1943 and 1944.[29] Among the officers who served in these colonially raised units were several Belgians who had either escaped from German camps or had evaded capture altogether and found their way to West Africa to re-enlist.

Notes

1 Alexis Neviaski, '1919–1939 : le recrutement des légionnaires allemands', in: *Guerres mondiales et conflits contemporains*, n° 1 (2010), pp. 39–61.
2 Guy Weber, *Les Belges et la Légion étrangère*, (Brussels: Louis Musin, 1984), p. 78.
3 Weber, *Les Belges et la Légion étrangère*, p. 53.
4 Georges Blond, *Histoire de la Légion étrangère 1831–1931*, (Paris: France Loisirs, 1981), p. 244.
5 Weber, *Les Belges et la Légion étrangère*, p. 73.
6 AGR, Ministre de la justice : dossiers relatifs à l'octroi de la Croix des Évadés, 1940–1945, file 677: Victor Depireux.
7 Weber, *Les Belges et la Légion étrangère*, p. 80.
8 Weber, *Les Belges et la Légion étrangère*, p. 77.
9 Weber, *Les Belges et la Légion étrangère*, p. 73.
10 Blond, *Histoire de la Légion étrangère 1831–1931*, pp. 255–258.
11 MRAB, Fonds Georges Hautecler, 59/43, Rapports sur les évadés.
12 Weber, *Les Belges et la Légion étrangère*, p. 78.
13 MRAB, Fonds Georges Hautecler, 59/43, Rapports sur les évadés.
14 MRAB, Fonds Georges Hautecler, 59/43, Rapports sur les évadés.
15 Moore, *Prisoners of War: Europe 1939–1956*, pp. 145–151; Roger Absalom, 'Hiding History: The Allies, the Resistance and Others in Occupied Italy 1943–1945', in: *Historical Journal*, Vol. 38, No. 1 (1995), pp. 111–131; Roger Absalom, 'Allied Escapers and the Contadini in Occupied Italy, (1943–5)', in: *Journal of Modern Italian Studies*, Vol. 10, No. 4 (2005), pp. 413–425.
16 MRAB, Fonds Georges Hautecler, 59/43, Rapports sur les évadés.
17 MRAB, Fonds Georges Hautecler, 59/43, Rapports sur les évadés.
18 AGR, Ministre de la justice : dossiers relatifs à l'octroi de la Croix des Évadés, 1940–1945, file 15: François Calafice.
19 Weber, *Les Belges et la Légion étrangère*, p. 85.
20 Weber, *Les Belges et la Légion étrangère*, p. 63.
21 Rens et al. (eds), *Évasions*, pp. 54–59.
22 The converted liner HMT Ormonde had brought Allied troops to Algiers as part of Operation Torch.
23 Rens et al. (eds), *Évasions*, pp. 65–70.
24 MRAB, Fonds Georges Hautecler, 59/43, Rapports sur les évadés.
25 MRAB, Fonds Georges Hautecler, 59/43, Rapports sur les évadés.
26 MRAB, Fonds Georges Hautecler, 59/43, Rapports sur les évadés.

27 Cédric Leloup, 'Maintenir une hiérarchie des races ? La Belgique face à la question de l'africanisation des cadres de la Force publique du Congo belge (1908–1960)', in: *Journal of Belgian History*, XLV 2/3 (2015), pp. 46–79.

28 MRAB, Fonds Georges Hautecler, 59/43, Rapports sur les évadés.

29 See Nigel Thomas, *Foreign Volunteers of the Allied Forces, 1939–45,* (London: Osprey, 1991), p. 17. J. Lee Ready, *Forgotten Allies: The Military Contribution of the Colonies, Exiled Governments, and Lesser Powers to the Allied Victory in World War II.* Vol. I, (Jefferson NC: McFarland, 1985), p. 45.

7   Eastern Odysseys

Escape Through the Soviet Union and Eastern Europe

More remarkable than many of the other escape stories is the rare narrative of André Depienne, a Belgian soldier who travelled eastwards rather than westwards in the early years of the war, escaping his captors and making his way into the then-neutral Soviet Union.[1] Depienne, like so many of his comrades, had been taken to prisoner-of-war camps in Eastern Germany in the summer of 1940. He was put to work on a farm close to the border with the Soviet Union, where he seems to have been billeted rather than used as a day labourer. However, he was locked up next to the stables at night by the elderly guard that supervised him and deprived of his clothes.[2] The proximity of the Soviet frontier gave him the opportunity to attempt an escape. His story, told in the third person, was written by his English wife in the immediate post-war years and may be subject to some embellishment, but it nonetheless provides a wealth of detail on his experiences and highlights his thinking as he attempted to regain his freedom.

Depienne escaped from his farm on 11 April 1941, five weeks before the year of his captivity had ended.[3] The morning was warm and sunny and, when he went out into the fields he knew this was the day for which he had been waiting. If he did not succeed in his attempt it would be the worse for him but the risk must and should be taken. As he worked beside Marcel he glanced several times at his fellow prisoner, surprised by his own detachment and immovable calm.

"Marcel", he said at last, in a low voice "this is it. Today, I'm off!"

Marcel caught his breath, rigid with horror and incredulity.

"Good God man, don't do it!" he said urgently. "It's mad! Crazy! You'll be shot before you get ten yards!"

"Look at Hans," André responded, indicating their German guard. "He's come without his rifle for the first time since we got here. What do you think of that for a good omen? He can't stop me with a bullet in the back, at least, not in the first few minutes."

He paused, working steadily as Marcel continued to remonstrate, then looked obliquely at his companion.

"When they go in to eat I shall take my chance. Now, what about it? Are you coming? The weather's good. Everything's in our favour. Just say the word."

DOI: 10.4324/9780429027697-8

Marcel had no need to consider the question, his mind made up long before, and he bit his lip nervously as he stared round the field.

"I can't do it. I haven't the nerve. If you get away they might take it out on me. What about that?"

"They won't. They'll be too busy looking for me."

Marcel was silent, then he returned his companion's smile.

"I can't come with you but I wish you the best of luck. You'll need it."

"When you get back to our room I'd like you to destroy my identity card and any odd papers I've left behind. I can't take anything with me."

"I shall miss you," Marcel said glumly. "You help to keep things cheerful."

"You'll have Hanna all to yourself," André observed. "You always wanted her."

"She won't have me. I'm the wrong shape. I daresay she'll cry her eyes out when she knows you've gone, and the old woman, too."

"That won't last long," said André philosophically, and said no more, bending down to his task.[4]

These few sentences encapsulate the prisoners' differing views of captivity, the one plotting an escape for weeks and months before seeing an opportunity with an unarmed guard, the other too afraid of the consequences of fleeing and happier to stay put – although worried about possible reprisals from his comrade's actions. As a side issue, there is also the mention of André having had a relationship with Hanna – the young woman who worked on the farm – something that could carry severe penalties, both for the prisoner and for the woman concerned. As we have shown, Polish and later Soviet prisoners convicted of having relationships with German women were almost invariably executed, although the French and Belgians were better protected and could only be removed back to camps. Women could expect fines and sometimes terms of imprisonment from civil courts and *Volksgerichte* (people's tribunals) but were also sometimes subjected to ostracism and punishments from their own communities.

Every member of the household was out working in the fields, even the farmer himself giving some assistance on this occasion, and André was strained to breaking point as he awaited the master's signal to stop for the meal. At last the expected shout floated across the field and as he straightened himself Marcel peered once more into his face and winked, then turned to join the cavalcade to the house. The farmer was already well to the fore with his companions, Marcel strolling in the rear with the German guard whose hands were thrust comfortably into his pockets. André lingered behind pretending to occupy himself with the horses and his heart beat fast, but he did not feel afraid.

As his companions filed over the field he hid behind the animals, watching until he knew that it would be unsafe to count too long on remaining unseen then all at once he drew himself up, took a deep breath and began to run, concentrating with his entire heart and body on what he did, knowing that the next few moments would decide his ultimate destiny. In the strength and power of his limbs and in the quality of his endurance lay the fate which awaited him.

The farm was three miles from the Russian border and at times the fields in which the men worked were even closer, today was the nearest André had ever been – a distance of perhaps two and a half miles. He had been running for thirty seconds when a bellow arose from the guard who had missed him at last, and glancing back he saw that Hans had begun to give chase. [...]

He was also aware that not far distant were crowds of German troops. Five or six immense wooden observation posts had been erected in the vicinity during the past few weeks so that Russian movements on the other side of the border could be kept under surveillance, with German soldiers constantly on the watch with binoculars. André learned afterwards that all civilians had been evacuated from the district about fifteen days before war between Germany and Russia began. Had he been moved to some camp or farm miles from the Russian or any other border his plans for escape would have come to a different end.

Using every scrap of shelter he sped to the edge of the field, expecting to be picked off by troops within seconds of his departure, but the watchers were so absorbed by their interest in Russian territory that they did not scan the farmlands which lay at their feet. The going was rough, the guard elderly and out of training, but André on the other hand had a reasonable start and knew how to conserve his strength, gathering every ounce of energy in this desperate bid for liberty. The farmer and his employees were so far making no attempt to aid in the chase and this was to André's advantage. The first obstruction appeared, marking the end of German territory, a tangled, ingenious mass of barbed wire nearly five feet in height spreading to a depth of perhaps five yards. As he approached, his heart pounding, André knew that he must take it in his stride. There was no slowing down, no turning back, and the sound of a shot made it plain that soldiers or others had taken up the chase. Rushing straight at the obstacle he hurled himself on to the wires, crossing on hands and knees like a monkey dashing from branch to branch, leaping down to face the stretch of 'No-Man's-Land' and the formidable Russian barricades ahead.

Pausing for a split second he flashed a glance behind to see the guard labouring in vain pursuit, yelling futile commands at the prisoner who waved once in farewell before bounding onwards. André was sorry for Hans, who was a good fellow and who would be punished for losing one of his charges. The farmer also would be fined for the offence but the fugitive had no pity for his late master. André's hands were torn and bleeding, his clothes ripped by the barbs. Russian wires loomed ahead and flashed into his vision as he steeled himself for the task. Widespread at the base, he judged their height to be twenty feet, narrowing into the centre and again branching outwards, like an hourglass in which the sands of time were spent. He felt like a fly, minute, exposed and helpless, his flesh torn, his clothing now in shreds. He climbed, slipped, fell and remounted, moving with agonised speed, but in spite of this travail he did not feel the pain of his wounds, his whole being so consumed by burning resolve that injuries had no meaning.

After a maddening eternity of time he reached the summit of the wires and, crossing the top, he slipped and fell heavily into the barbs beneath. The sudden, sharp crack of a shot was followed instantaneously by others and galvanised by fear he tore himself free and jumped, falling to his knees as he hit the ground. Lifting his head he darted swift glances around him but saw no one and still on his knees zig-zagged over coarse grass on rutted, uneven terrain, fighting for breath. […]

Hours seemed to pass but it was a matter of seconds, and he drew alongside the blessed shelter of a wood. Springing to his feet he dashed at full speed for cover, but had scarcely drawn breath before he heard the thud of hooves. He had no time to hide, he climbed the nearest tree, hiding in the leaves. […] He did well because three powerful dogs were on his trail. Luckily, he was far away from their jaws. They would have mauled him. He was not reassured because the Germans had said that the prisoners of war who reached Russian territory were systematically shot. He spotted three horsemen carrying rifles on their backs and large capes blowing in the wind. They were wearing the Astrakan (karakul) hats of the Cossacks and the Poles. One of them was an officer. The three looked like Mongols and had slanted eyes. They reached the dogs at the foot of the tree and asked him to come down. Judging it wise to obey, André tried to go down but the dogs jumped up and André climbed back again. He indicated that he could not get down as long as the dogs were free. The Russians aimed their rifles at him, clearly signalling that they would fire if he didn't move. André continued to point at the dogs and finally the one who looked like their leader called back the dogs. He pulled a long whip out of his belt and used it on the dogs to control them. Finally convinced that the dogs would not intervene, André left his refuge and at that same moment felt the pain caused by the wounds of the barbed wire. He was pushed in front of the horses, hands behind his back and threatened by a spear. The Cossacks made him run but soon they realised that he could not keep up such a pace. They slowed their horses for a few kilometres. André walked, as in a dream, zigzagging across the ground that was filled with holes. He was about to collapse when he saw an ensemble of vast wooded barracks. Relieved, he entered the camp that was full of Russian soldiers.

His guards took him to a high wall inside the camp. His tiredness was momentarily forgotten and for a few seconds his whole body started to shake: "They are going to shoot me like a dog here," he thought, "without giving me the opportunity to explain myself." His apprehension increased when a group of soldiers armed with rifles came towards him, but they passed by without paying him the slightest attention. All these emotions weakened his resistance and he collapsed. When he woke up, in pain he tried to get up by leaning on the wall. The Russians fetched him and brought him inside the main building. He was given food and drink and a Russian soldier carelessly tended his wounds by spraying on an iodine solution. Next, he was interrogated by a few Russian officers who spoke a few words of French and

German. He could sense that the Russians found his story suspicious. They believed he might be a German spy who had constructed the perfect prisoner of war escape story. He was asked the same questions several times but was careful enough not to vary his answers.[5]

The first thing to note here is the heavily guarded frontier. Although Nazi Germany and the Soviet Union were still nominally at peace when Depienne made his escape, it was only a short time before the beginning of Operation Barbarossa. Yet even then, tensions were obviously very high and both sides had strengthened their borders, with increased manpower, patrols and barbed wire. Also relevant was the fear in his mind about being treated as a spy. While the Germans could tell the prisoners they would be shot by the Russians if they ventured into Soviet territory as a means of deterring escapes across the frontier, the truth was that the increasing tensions between the two powers in the spring of 1941 were influencing both sides. The Soviets were extremely wary of any and all people caught crossing their frontier, and any they caught were inevitably handed over to the security services for examination and interrogation.

He was taken by a soldier to a kind of cellar entered by means of a long flight of steps. It was not completely dark, and André noticed that, below the last step, the cell that the Russian wanted him to go in was filled with water. The soldier was resolved to make him descend to the bottom and to impress his wish on André he held a revolver against the small of his back. Andre turned and argued with him furiously but the Russian looked at him incuriously and continued to push him down. An officer, the one who understood a bit of French, was passing by and André screamed at him: "This imbecile wants me to sit in the water on the lowest step. Does he think I'm a blasted duck?" The officer smiled slightly and spoke to the soldier who ceased his apparent desire to drown the prisoner and permitted him to remain where he was. André stayed in this place for some hours sitting just above the water line, his guard squatting on the step above, revolver in hand. [...]

Then, he was taken in a closed truck to another building in what seemed to be a village, where the remnants of his clothing were searched by an ordinary soldier, but apart from the rabbit's foot which he still carried, his pockets were empty. The soldier disdainfully threw the rabbit's foot in a basket. As the soldier turned away, André bent down to tie his shoelaces and put his hand in the basket to recover his charm. The soldier saw this and with an expression of the utmost contempt and fury, flung the rabbit's foot back into the basket. This is how André lost the last thing connected to his past. He was then locked in a cell with a metallic door for the night. André was not alone in the cell. Small and dark, it contained four other tenants: three Lithuanian civilians and a Polish soldier. André could not converse with them and could barely see, although on the following day his eyes grew accustomed to the dimness that was relieved by a small window with iron bars. The Polish soldier lay in a corner and looked like he was dying. He did not move and was covered in hideous sores infested by maggots. A terrible smell came from his body. He was lying in his own faeces and had been given no care of any kind. After a night in this hell, André's face was swollen by flea bites which he believed came from this pitiful mass of humanity.

His morale was low and he believed he had reached rock bottom. When the sick man's food arrived at midday the others added it to their share, a bowl of thick soup and a slice of dark bread. In the evening, there was more bread, and water to drink. Once a day, the prisoners were made to leave the cellar and ascend a short flight of steps to an evil-smelling lavatory that consisted of a drain in the corner of a small room, from which arose a suffocating odour. There was neither soap nor towel and the men rinsed themselves under a cold tap low down in the wall. This daily visit was also made for the purpose of relieving nature and was compulsory, possibly in order to lessen the effluvia from the bucket in the cellar.

The Pole was not exempted from the visit to the toilet and the three Lithuanians carried him there before letting him fall heavily on the ground. He stays there, immobile, while his roommates go under the cold shower. The return was the same scenario, but the Lithuanians, exhausted, let him fall from the stairs and let him roll until he reached the cell. André is revolted by this but the men had no strength left to carry the sufferer and the man on the floor was long past caring. He was still breathing but would know no more of life.[6]

André's encounter with a Polish soldier and Lithuanian civilians in these Soviet gaols is unsurprising. Many Poles had tried to flee eastwards from the German occupation only to find themselves in the hands of the Red Army, which had occupied the other half of their country. By 1941, the USSR had also annexed the three Baltic states and treated their citizens with equal suspicion. Indeed, the Soviet takeovers in all these lands had led to the wholesale deportations of indigenous populations to labour camps in Siberia and elsewhere. It has been estimated that, in addition to the prisoners of war captured when Poland finally surrendered, the USSR removed around 1.75 million civilians from its occupied zone, and likewise removed any potentially 'subversive' elements from Latvia (35,000), Lithuania (75,000) and Estonia (60,000).[7]

On the fourth night, André was brought to an upper cell with six more Poles, including a boy of sixteen. They were civilians who had fled from German occupied Poland. They were polite and gentle, educated men. The young Pole spoke a bit of French and made André aware of their situation. One of the older men made a regular habit of urinating against the bars on the window and although he apologised to André he explained that he had to continue.

"He thinks the bars will begin to rot so that he can break out," the boy explained. "It's a bit of an obsession, but it keeps him happy." André was convinced that if the man remained in the cell for another twenty years the bars would be no less obdurate but this pitiful ray of hope was the one bright thought to which the prisoner could cling.

Shrieks and shouting were frequently heard from the adjoining cell housing a number of Polish women, the boy remarking that the Russian soldiers were probably interfering with them. "They're all young in there," he said with an air of weary resignation which would have sat ill on the shoulders of even older men. "My sister's one of them. She's seventeen."

"Is she all right?" André asked, and the lad shrugged his shoulders.

"I can't tell. I haven't been able to speak to her for weeks. I hope so, but what can I do?"

The next day, André met one of these women. He was ordered to leave the cell and his friend explained that he was being taken for a bath. André happily followed the guard, looking forward to the idea of a hot bath but to his disgust he was led to the same stinking lavatory [...] There was a steaming pail of hot water in the middle of the room and as André looked in vain for some sign of a bath he was astonished to see a young Polish girl entering the chamber. Without further discussion, the guard ordered them to undress. The girl was about nineteen and strikingly handsome, with elongated dark eyes and a mass of black hair, and understanding what was expected of her she began to cry.

André realised that she was not upset by the presence of the guard, she was used to such surveillance, but the knowledge that she was in the presence of a total stranger filled her with confusion. André saw that the soldier meant to be obeyed and explained that they had to hold each other and that he was going to pour hot water on them. André and the young girl were back-to-back, and the soldier began to spray hot water with a small bucket. The water was so hot that the young girl started to scream, and André jumped to his feet. The Russian soldier was amused by his joke and the screams of his victims. As they lacked soap, he ordered them to rub each other with their hands, then rinsed with icy water, laughing at the sight of them shaking. André picked up his shirt and gave it to the young Polish woman so she could dry herself. She thanked him in her language, but André did not understand what she said. When they were dressed, the Russian took them back to their respective cells. After a few days, André and many other prisoners were gathered in the courtyard and driven by truck to the train station in the village. They were all piled into a train to Kaunas. While boarding the train, André caught a glimpse of the young Polish woman he had met in such weird circumstances and smiled at her. She smiled back at him shyly. He never saw her again.[8]

The following day, they reached Kaunas. They were locked up in a very different prison from the one they had just left.[9] It was a vast building, very long with doors and bars everywhere. André was taken to a cell which already contained twenty men. The lighted corridor meant he could see his new companions through the open door and who immediately surrounded him and asked questions in several languages. Then the guards closed the doors and they were left in darkness. Someone gave André a mattress and a blanket and he lay happily in a corner of the cell. He had realised that his new friends were either Poles or Lithuanians and hoped to find someone who could speak French or English. In the morning, André saw that he was in a cell fifteen feet square with barred windows so high that he could not reach them. Most of his companions were political prisoners, elderly businessmen, in other words capitalist bourgeois who did not like the values of the communist regime. There were also three Polish soldiers who had escaped from German camps. Two were very young, the others were between 45 and 55. Much to André's delight, one of the Lithuanians spoke fluent English and one of the Poles had some knowledge of the French language and for the first time since his escape, his spirits rose as he could finally speak with other prisoners. The three of them conversed for a while. He tried without success to pronounce the Polish names of his new friends but resolved the issue by using the French equivalent: the Lithuanian was now Joseph and the Pole François.

Joseph was between 40 and 50 years old. Before having all his belongings confiscated by the Russians, he owned a prosperous flour mill. His wife and his child had also been in the prison for a year but he had not seen them since. He had not been brought before a tribunal. He told André that he expected to be sent to Siberia. He spoke very good English as he had lived in England in his youth. Like all the other prisoners, his face was very pale due to the lack of air and sun. His kind and friendly face sometimes betrayed this tragedy. He and André talked for a long time and the Belgian began to like his companion in captivity very much. This intelligent and cultivated man had been separated from those he loved and thrown into a prison in circumstances that might break many people. André sometimes felt a feeling of horror in this place and even regretted the German farm that he had seen before as a prison. Here, he might disappear without his relatives ever knowing it. The food in the prison was the same as the one where he had come from, with the difference that it was more plentiful and that he received two rations of bread: once in the morning and once in the evening. André did not suffer the hunger that he had on the German farm, but he was now incarcerated and did not have the open air to stimulate his appetite.

On the second day in his new cell, André saw a pile of bread loaves on the ground in a corner. As nobody paid any attention to them, he took the pieces and put them in his soup. His gesture went unnoticed but later there was a shout of surprise and strong protests. André looked with astonishment at his friend's sudden agitation.

"Dear friend," said Joseph in his precious English, "I am afraid you have just eaten our chess game."

"Oh God," said André, embarrassed. "I did not realise what they were for. I thought they were stale."

"Each of us contributed to create these chess pieces," continued Joseph, "But do not worry, we will make others."

"I will help with my next ration," said André, full of remorse.

So the next day, he gave his bread ration to replace the pieces he had eaten. The prisoners played chess often and watching them, André learned the game and its unexpected complications quickly. The thin straw mattresses were folded up in the daytime to make room. The prisoners walked in circles in the cell for hours, silently, like a clock, looking like caged animals in a zoo. There was nothing to read, the thing that André and a few other prisoners missed the most, no communication with the outside world which they could only presume existed as before. Their only hobbies were chess and the ever-lasting walk around the cell.

When André had entered the cell, he had noticed the inmates' tranquillity and their apprehension: they were obedient toward their guards and had no initial reaction to him. They had no idea who he was and André understood that they were doing their best to avoid any mutual suspicions or quarrels. Among themselves, they never talked about sexual matters or even about women as soldiers would do. He understood that their spirits were focused on very different matters.[10]

However, André had noticed in other camps in Germany that even weakness and hunger could not prevent this natural need. There was a system of communication between cells made of blows against the heating pipes using Morse code. The guards tolerated this activity that they perceived as innocent. André never saw the Russians being violent with prisoners. They were completely indifferent. They remained passive in the face of weakness and hunger and displayed typical oriental fatalism.

The great majority of the Soviet soldiers and NCOs, as well as some of the officers were from modest stock and ignored the existence of a free world outside the USSR. They had a childish sense of humour, adored horses, were playful, loud, and full of jokes. They could be heard in their rooms singing loudly and dancing energetically. The soldier who had poured hot water on André and the young Polish woman had not been malevolent. For him, this was just a funny joke. One of the prisoners spoke Russian. He tried several times to speak with the guards, but his conversations were invariably short and met with disinterest. When the other prisoners asked what the Russians had said, the translator shrugged his shoulders and said:

"What are they talking about? Well, the Moscow underground which, it seems, is made of solid marble."

"What do they think of us?" André asked one day.

"I think that the rest of the world does not exist for them. They do not know its existence. This is why one of them asked me if we lived in houses and if we had ever seen cars."

"Incredible," said André. "They think that we live like rabbits."

"Maybe," answered the other. "But I don't think they care in the slightest."[11]

Their incarceration became better with time. Once a week, they could go to the bath and had a new rough but clean shirt. Every hair on André's body was removed with clippers and, thanks to the weekly disinfecting bath, he never caught lice or parasites. Once a day, all the occupants of the cell were permitted to walk for half an hour in a small courtyard surrounded by high walls. The prisoners were forced to put their hands behind their backs and were not permitted to talk. They never saw the other prisoners from other cells. The prison housed many women and children and the little ones could often be heard crying. One day, while returning from a walk, André shouted as loud as he could: "Are there Frenchmen here?" His scream echoed off the walls. The guard arrived and thrust him back into his cell, and the next day his walk was cancelled but there was no further punishment.

One day, François, the Pole, was afflicted by a violent nosebleed lasting several hours. Doctors and nurses came to the cell to help him. This was much better than in the first prison where the unfortunate Polish prisoner had been left to die. He concluded that the Russians were less brutal than the Germans and were at least trying to keep their prisoners alive. But they had a goal: to use prisoners for work. Aged and handicapped people were unlikely to survive.

A few days later, François was brought in front of the tribunal. He had waited for this day for a long time and the long delays had been cruelly extended for those poor souls who had been their own masters: farmers, industrialists, businessmen, whose only crime was the love of free enterprise and independence. When François returned to his cell, he leaned against the door and looked at his friends without a word. They asked questions and he smiled.

"Do you know," he said at last, "I've just realised that today is my birthday."

"What did he say?" asked André. Joseph translated for him.

"What are they going to do with you?" asked André in French to François. "Will they send you away?"

"I am condemned to ten years in Siberia," François answered quietly.

All the prisoners had understood and were silent. François was a cultivated man, full of courage and months of boredom, anxiety and fear had not managed to destroy these qualities.

"I have waited for a long time for the moment to walk out of that door," He said. "Now the moment has come."

"But you dreamt of crossing it as a free man," said Joseph.

André felt the urgent need to hammer the door with his fists and scream against this inhumane doctrine which denied men their natural need for freedom, but he managed to control himself and sat silently. Joseph, without a word, stood up and gave François his last cigarette.[12]

Although there are no dates attached to the narrative, it can be assumed that Depienne spent no more than a few weeks in Kaunas before being moved again as this took place before the war in the East broke out on 22 June 1941. There were only a few prisoners of war who escaped from Germany into the Soviet Union and they were universally suspected as spies and handed over to the NKVD, which helps to explain why they ended up in a prison system where most of the inmates were civilians. Polish soldiers captured in the aftermath of the war of September–October 1939 had already been redeployed as labour in many parts of the country, and their officers had been interned and then exterminated between March and May 1940.[13]

> One morning, they came to fetch André for a short trip in a truck. He took advantage of a tear in the canvas to look outside. He saw horses and pitiful carts surrounded by peasants. All looked miserable and poor. The women all had scarves or handkerchiefs around their heads. He reached a big building full of soldiers and he was taken to one of the many offices in a corridor where he found a Russian officer. Sitting next to him, a young woman was working as a translator. André realised that she spoke excellent French. […][14]
> The interrogation was very much the same as the earlier ones. André tried to answer the same as before without giving away any further details. He was taken to a dining room where he received his best meal in a long time. He was given a thick rib well cooked, white bread, coffee, and a cake. As he wanted to take a knife to cut his meat, the Russian officer jumped in, took it from his hands and cut the meat in pieces. The translator looked confused. André smiled and asked if his strange domestic servant could cut smaller pieces. The young woman translated to the officer who did as he was told. After the end of this good meal, André was taken to the photographic room where they took his fingerprints. He was then brought back to his cell. During the evening's meal, André gave Joseph his soup and bread as well as a piece of cake that he had put in his pocket while the Russian officer was distracted. André was moved from Kaunas, without any explanation, in June 1941, only a few days before Hitler's attack on the USSR. He had an emotional farewell with Joseph. They kissed each other and did not hold back the tears. André never saw him again but could never forget his sad eyes and his kindness.[15]

André's next destination was some 300 kilometres from Moscow in a camp surrounded by high wooden fences permanently guarded by men and dogs. The main building appeared to have been a hunting lodge in the days of the Tsars, and a figure of Christ over the entrance had been partly smashed and disfigured by blows from a heavy instrument. Most of the prisoners in German captivity who had escaped by way of Russian territory were apparently gathered in this one camp, including some British servicemen. Inmates were allowed to send a few words home, although André learned later that his message never reached Belgium. Guards and their officers lived outside the camp and arrived daily for roll call but the atmosphere was 'not unhappy', the men mixing together and the French 'taking charge of the cuisine'.[16] Food was more plentiful and there were iron beds with mattresses. These was really necessary because, although the days were warm, the nights were already cold. Hygiene facilities were primitive with holes dug in the ground, but the prisoners were allowed a weekly visit to a bathhouse.[17] There was a distribution of sugar once a week, sometimes a bit of meat and usually a lot of fish.

André thought that it must have been a youth camp, because there were basketball and volleyball fields as well as a large recreation room in which there were guitars, mandolins and other instruments that the inmates were able to use. André loved sport and the prospect of training filled him with joy. His optimism and his love of life soon came to the fore. The Russians, both officers and soldiers, lived outside the camp and only came in for the roll call. Prisoners only received 10 roubles per month. This was not a lot because everything was expensive in the USSR. André bought a toothbrush and toothpaste at the canteen where, once a month, a woman sold toilet items, needles, pencils, etc. Unfortunately, she did not have cigarettes or chocolate. Every so often he was interrogated, sometimes daily. And it was always the same questions: they said he was a German spy and asked again and again his age, name, first name, date of birth, etc., where he had escaped from and why. To this last question, André was systematically furious and answered: "Because I was a prisoner of war and it is a duty for us to escape if possible." They either spoke French or were assisted by women [translators] who were usually friendly and kind. It was possible to speak with the Russians through the translators. It did not seem as if there was a barrier between the ranks: Russian officers and soldiers were brothers. One Russian in particular was very kind and mixed with the prisoners, laughing and playing with them. The prisoners considered him as another soldier and, while playing the *jeu des cavaliers*, hit his bottom as they were doing for the other players. But one day, he came wearing a Russian senior officer's uniform. The prisoners looked at him surprised and apprehensive. The Russian was also surprised and asked what the matter was.

"Have I offended you?" he asked. "You seem afraid of me."

This friendly behaviour reassured the prisoners and the cordial relations between them resumed.

Sometimes, prisoners talked to the translators, comparing their lives in their respective countries. These comparisons always saw the Russians on the losing side. One day, a female translator was so impressed that she broke down in tears. Their criticisms, to which she had no answer, upset her. A Russian captain came to ask why she was crying. The prisoners, really worried, apologised. The incident was forgotten and there was no punishment, but the prisoners swore to be more careful in future.[18]

There were Frenchmen in the camp who were tunnelling specialists. They met and decided to dig a path to freedom. For them it was a real passion. The tunnel started from a barrack and was progressing fast. It was a remarkable task done meticulously and buttressed like a mine. Among the British, there were only two Englishmen and they were, quite evidently, homosexuals. Tall, elegant, they walked arm-in-arm in the camp and kissed at every opportunity. The Russians noticed this and had them moved from the camp and settled in a little house. As for the tunnel, it was discovered before it was finished. It was assumed that the two Englishmen had denounced it to gain more freedoms. Those who dug the tunnel were not discovered and the Russians did not look for them. Many Russians, both soldiers and civilians, came each day to see the tunnel; it was a big attraction in the camp. They honestly admired the quality of the work and the ingenuity of its makers. There were no sanctions. Another of the British contingent, a thin and bearded Canadian sergeant, was particularly incensed by the shameful informing by the two Englishmen and said he was happy not to be with them in the camp.[19]

News from the front was not good and the Germans had progressed rapidly into Russian territory. There had been hostilities for a month when the prisoners were transferred to another camp.[20] After a day of walking while being watched by armed guards with dogs, they were loaded onto a cattle train. Hundreds of Poles from neighbouring camps were following the same route. During the night, the convoy passed through Moscow and the British were handed over to the British diplomats there. The other prisoners tore at the nailed boards at the windows that prevented them from seeing out and looking at the big unknown city, trying to see the Kremlin. Furious guards pushed back the curious with their rifle butts.

"Why do they not want us to look at the roofs of Moscow?" asked a Frenchman while shrugging his shoulders.

"Nobody knows," answered André. "It is one of their little mysteries."[21]

This move for the prisoners came about because of the rapidly changing military and international situation. The German attack on the USSR on 22 June 1941 had resulted in huge territorial gains for the Nazis and thrown Stalin into an unlikely alliance with the British, and this may explain why the small British contingent was handed over so rapidly to their diplomatic representatives in Moscow – only four weeks into the war. The other nationalities involved were probably viewed as less important politically as their states had already been overrun by the Germans, and the Soviets were doubtless keen to make sure they did not return to their homelands. Only when arrangements were made to evacuate them to the United Kingdom was their freedom guaranteed. The exceptions here were the Poles, who were now technically allies of the Soviet Union. Attempts by the Polish government-in-exile to remobilise them in the USSR under General Anders were subject to sustained animosity and obstruction from the Soviet authorities, not least because it would expose the absence of most of the Polish officers taken prisoner in 1939.[22]

Despite the changing international and military situation, André's captivity continued.

Other camps followed, with less food and comfort. It was the middle of summer and it was very warm. There were also a lot of mosquitoes. The guards wore protecting nets on their faces to shield themselves from these voracious beasts. The prisoners often received pieces of something looking like a catfish, an unknown species. Everybody hated it. Finally, the French discovered how to season it correctly and it became edible. They were camped next to a little river and, once a week, under supervision, they swam. Not far away, women, completely naked like the prisoners, were swimming in the same river. These women, young and old, came from a big collective farm nearby. Despite their calls, the prisoners did not pay much attention. Conditions were worsening. The war, welcomed at first, had brought only an aggravation of the situation. Morale at the camp was at its lowest. There were no games and no discussion. It was the lowest ebb: the monotony of a wasted life affected even the most optimistic. Not many were interested in looking at women but there was an exception: a middle-aged Frenchman, a big fellow, strong and focused on this inaccessible goal: to touch members of the opposite sex. He dreamt of it night and day and talked only of his good fortunes in the past and the ones to come. He reminded André of one of his companions in captivity in Germany who also had an immoderate taste for female company. Despite his natural optimism, André found that the time dragged. Only by studying his companions' morale did he survive this trial. He was surprised at the courage and enthusiasm displayed by some of the prisoners, something that no difficulty could deflate. He remembered his friends from the prison of Kaunas and pictured the beautiful sad eyes of Joseph. These memories, instead of making him feel better, contributed to his own low morale.

However, in the camp excitement grew as rumours of freedom began to circulate. It was said that negotiations about repatriations had started among the countries at war with Germany. One day, a French captain who had been dispatched to Moscow, came with the news that freedom was close. Hopes began to rise: the excitement in the camp became intolerable. André owned a small bag bought from a Frenchman for a few roubles which contained all his treasures (including his toothbrush and toothpaste). To pack his bag did not take long, but it made him feel as if freedom was getting closer. Finally, when the wave of optimism abated, anxieties reappeared until the distribution of new uniforms triggered a new wave of hope. However, these new clothes, lined with felt to keep out the cold, seemed to indicate a long stay in the USSR. André did not laugh or joke anymore. Like his companions, he wanted to leave. The excitement in the camp was intense. When the day came, darkness had already fallen. The joy of being free made them forget all the hours of despair that they had known in the Russian camps.[23]

The diplomatic negotiations to liberate the other Allied nationalities still held prisoner obviously took some time to complete. Leaving aside the problematic presence of the Poles, the Soviets were doubtless keen to get rid of their other escaped prisoners, but also anxious for them to take back as little information about the USSR as possible.

Locked inside closed trucks, they were nonetheless very concerned. Fortunately, the news that they would leave by train for Arkhangelsk eased their mind and they slept comfortably. They had received a small barrel of smoked fish to eat with bread and plenty of water. They received no food during their journey. The next day in the evening, they reached Arkhangelsk. They were put on a small Russian boat that was waiting for them. The boat was very dirty and the toilets miserable, but they did not care as they were happy to breathe the sea air. When André stepped onto the boat, his eyes were filled with tears. Suddenly, he felt a jolt and two arms wrapped round him. He turned and saw the familiar face of Jacques, whom he had known at Stalag I-A. He had just arrived with another group of prisoners and had immediately seen André. The two Belgians embraced emotionally.

"In the name of God!" Jacques exclaimed, when he had recovered his senses. "How happy am I to see you again. I had feared that you were gone forever."

They told each other of their escapes from Germany. Jacques had been sent to work in a farm which, like André's, was not very far from the border. When news of a Belgian prisoner escaping to the USSR had become known, Jacques had wondered if it was André. Anyway, he had decided on doing the same.

"What happened after we got separated?" asked André. "Were you in a good German farm?"

"It was not too bad," said Jacques. "The farmers were good to us and we had plenty of freedom. There were several women, Germans and Poles. One of the young Germans did not leave me alone at all. She was knitting socks for me and scarves for the winter as if I was in the army."

"And your fiancée in Belgium," asked André. "Have you forgotten her?"

"It is an old story," said Jacques. "It has been over for a long time. Let her go wherever she wants. Despite everything, it is not a bad memory, we had some good times."

He told of his own adventures that began seven days after André's escape. He hid in a train filled with supplies for the USSR without the Germans noticing. Toward the end of journey, he was starving and thirsty, at which point he was discovered by Russian soldiers at the border. He was the topic of an angry exchange between the Russians and the Germans on the train. The Germans wanted their prisoner back, but the Russians did not want to listen: Jacques had been discovered in Russian territory and was therefore their responsibility. The Germans were forced to back down. This was how Jacques came into the Russian camp system and was now on his way to Britain. He gave a big slap on André's back and looked at the grey sea while wetting his salted lips with his tongue.

"They say that we are to meet an English ship that will bring us to England," he said. "I hope it's true because I have a great desire to see it."

Their information was accurate and two hours later, they saw the English ship, which rapidly closed. The Russian guards were ordered inside the ship while their former prisoners, left on the deck, shouted and waved. The prisoners left the Russian ship as fast as possible and boarded the Royal Navy vessel.[24] It was as if the gates of paradise had opened, they were crazy with joy. The English sailors were surprised by their thin faces, pale with malnutrition, and heard of their adventures. They were served a plentiful meal. Some were so moved that they cried with joy.

"I was craving a strong coffee," said Jacques later. "But in the confusion I was served a cup of tea, which I usually cannot drink, and found it delicious."

When the fully loaded ship left for the high seas, many escapees suffered from seasickness and their first day of freedom was somewhat uncomfortable.

Their first destination was Spitzbergen, which had been occupied by the Russians and Norwegians working in the coal mines. The English ship was coming for them, as it had been decided to evacuate the island and destroy everything that could help the Germans. Those who wanted to disembark were allowed to do so but André did not go ashore. He was too sick for that. He stayed onboard, listening to the explosions caused by the English [demolition] teams. What happened there did not interest him; he looked intensely at the horizon, happy not to see the walls of the prison and the barbed wire. Jacques came back with a pair of Russian skis and a bottle of Russian perfume that he had found.

"What are you going to do with this in England?" asked André.

"I will sell it for a profit," answered Jacques. "As for the perfume, it is for the first young Englishwoman that I meet."

"You will first need to learn the language," said André.

"You think?" answered Jacques while laughing. "You forget the international language of the prisoner. So far, it has always helped me."

Summer was over and they reached the port of Glasgow [on 9 September 1941] during a sad and foggy autumn day without any incident, except for a mine that they saw not so far away.

The same evening, the non-British escapees left for the Patriotic School in London.[25]

This extensive narrative highlights the unusual trajectory of a small number of Western Allied servicemen who found refuge in the neutral USSR in the first phase of the war. Written in the post-war years, it may be subject to some Cold War bias but purports to be an accurate recollection of Depienne's escape and time in Soviet captivity. As it transpired, crossing the frontier was only the beginning of his problems as the fraught nature of the peace between the USSR and Germany in the months leading up to Operation Barbarossa meant that the Soviets were fixated on the escapees as possible German spies. Thus, the leitmotif of his captivity was of constant interrogations from the NKVD to make sure he was no more and no less than he claimed to be. His narrative also exposes the prisoner hierarchy imposed by the Soviets, with the French and Belgians being much better treated than the Poles, who were subjected to arbitrary arrest and deportations as Stalin's policies of political cleansing and mass forced population movements from eastern Poland and the Baltic States took hold. Once taken to the United Kingdom, it is perhaps ironic that his first experiences were of further interrogations, this time by MI5 at the Royal Patriotic School, where they also attempted to ensure that he was not a German agent.[26]

He and his comrade Jacques were possibly the only two Belgians to escape via the Soviet Union, but other countrymen did try travelling eastwards rather than westwards. In 1941, a French woman married to a Hungarian citizen, Mrs. Kapolnas, born Gabrielle Minam-Borier, a native of Lyon, set up a network in Budapest to provide relief for Belgian prisoners. Before Christmas, she had organised the transmission of 32,000 parcels with the help of the Red Cross. Soon the word spread among Belgians in the camps close to the border that Minam-Borier could help escaped prisoners. The first to try was Albert Leroy, who managed to reach Budapest in August 1942. Minam-Borier and the Belgian community in the city numbering around 120 people managed to host thirty-six of their compatriots. On 17 April 1944, the evasion network was denounced to the Gestapo, but Minam-Borier escaped unscathed. Arrested and on their way to Poland by train, the Belgians managed to escape once again by knocking out the guard, breaking the lock and then jumping from the train, an action which led to one of them being killed in the attempt. They returned to Budapest, where they were hidden by Minam-Borier with the complicity of several Hungarian families until the surrender of the capital city.[27]

The German occupation of Hungary in March 1944 had prompted several Belgians to leave the country for Romania. Mathieu Gretry, a fortress soldier from Soumagne who had been in Hungary since 10 October 1943, managed to reach the border on 7 August 1944. From there, he went to the Swiss Legation together with a friend named Henri Compain. Others, such as Armand Lobet, waited for the Russian capture of Budapest to head for Romania. Lobet walked to Monor and from there took a train to Arad. Once there, he boarded a train to Bucharest, where he presented himself at the French Legation. Both Lobet and another Belgian, Simon Bernard, explained that Romania was rumoured to be safer. At least six Belgians also fled Hungary for Slovakia and joined the French Legion of fighters in Slovakia in August 1944, a group of 250 partisans led by Captain Georges Barazer de Lannurien and made up mostly of escaped prisoners and STO (Service du Travail Obligatoire) workers that participated in the Slovak national uprising.[28]

The case of Renaat Van Den Berghe was even more unusual. He had been on a business trip in Hungary in April 1939 when he was arrested by the criminal police and accused of money laundering while trying to save money belonging to Hungarian Jews. Sentenced to a year and four months of hard labour, he was detained at the special prison of Szeged. Pardoned on 4 May 1940 and transferred to the freed prisoners' depot of Budapest, he was prevented by the Hungarians from returning to Belgium. On 14 June 1940, he boarded a train to Belgrade with a fake passport provided by the Belgian embassy. From there, he reached Athens and lived with the Belgian expatriates until Italy declared war on Greece. Having unsuccessfully tried to join the Greek army, he was able to enlist with the British forces in October 1940. In December 1940, he was evacuated to Egypt before being dispatched to the Commando Base Training Depot near Geneifa. Having completed his training, he was dispatched to the Long Range Desert Group. He fought against the Italians in the Western Desert of Libya and near Mersa Matruh, Sidi-Barrani, Sollum, etc. Promoted to the rank of lieutenant and sent to Cairo, Van Den Berghe left on 10 June for Port-Said and Haifa. He was captured at the end of June 1941 by men of the French Foreign Legion siding with Vichy in Lebanon and sent to a camp in Beirut. From there, Van Den Berghe travelled to Aleppo, Nerab, Athens and Toulon. Once in France, he was sent back to Beirut, where he was handed over to the British. The reason for his back and forth between France and Beirut or his release remained a mystery to him. After a few days, he was back in British ranks.[29]

Notes

1 André Depienne served in the Belgian Armed Forces and was taken prisoner in May 1940. After escaping from Germany via the Soviet Union, he arrived in Britain and worked for the Belgian government-in-exile. While in London, he married an English-woman, Amy Chelsom, in 1943 and decided to stay in the country after the war, becoming a naturalised British subject in 1949 and settling in Hertfordshire. He died, aged 89, in Brighton in 2008. The account of his experiences formed part of a longer and possibly embellished unpublished family history written by his wife and published in a local journal in 1952. It was later translated into French by Georges Hautecler, *Evasions réussies*, pp. 15–42. See also TNA, HO334/330/7845.

2 The authors are grateful to Mrs Lynda Depienne for the sight of her mother's manuscript and for permission to use it in tandem with the Hautecler version. Henceforward, Depienne Ms., here p. 95.

3 Hautecler, *Evasions réussies*, p. 15 suggests that German documentation gives his date of escape as 13 May 1941.

4 Depienne Ms., pp. 106–107.

5 Depienne Ms., pp. 110–113. Hautecler, Évasions réussies, pp. 20–21.

6 Depienne Ms., pp. 114–116. Hautecler, Évasions réussies, pp. 22–23.

7 Jan T. Gross, 'Sovietisation of Poland's Eastern Territories', in: Bernd Wegner (ed.), *From Peace to War: Germany, Soviet Russia and the World, 1939–1941*, (Providence RI: Berghahn, 1997), p. 77. Geoffrey Wallace, *Life and Death in Captivity: The Abuse of Prisoners in War*, (Ithaca NY: Cornell, 2015), p. 116. Moore, *Prisoners of War*, pp. 48–49.

8 Depienne Ms., pp. 117–118. Hautecler, *Évasions réussies*, pp. 23–24.

9 Although not specified, this may well have been the infamous 'Ninth Fort' in Kaunas, which was used by the NKVD for military and political prisoners for interrogation before execution or transfer to the Gulag.

10 Depienne Ms., pp. 121–122. Hautecler, *Évasions réussies*, pp. 26–27.

11 Hautecler, *Évasions réussies*, pp. 28–29.

12 Depienne Ms., pp. 123–125. Hautecler, *Évasions réussies*, pp. 30–31.

13 Moore, *Prisoners of War*, pp. 44–49.

14 Hautecler, *Évasions réussies*, p. 32.

15 Hautecler, *Évasions réussies*, p. 33.

16 Depienne Ms., p. 127.

17 Depienne Ms., pp. 126–127.

18 Hautecler, Évasions réussies, pp. 34–35.

19 Hautecler, Évasions réussies, pp. 35–36. Homosexuality does not often feature in prisoner-of-war narratives, but more recent academic research is beginning to uncover its forms and prevalence. See for example in relation to the British prisoners, Simon Mackenzie, *The Colditz Myth. The Real Story of POW Life in Nazi Germany*, (Oxford: Oxford University Press, 2004), pp. 211–213, 221–223. Clare Makepeace, *Captives of War: British Prisoners of War in the Second World War*, (Cambridge: Cambridge University Press, 2017), pp. 123–126, 226.

20 The Vologda region contained a whole series of camps that were used to house internees and prisoners of war. The Allied prisoners were collected there prior to their removal from the USSR at the end of June 1941.

21 Hautecler, *Évasions réussies*, pp. 36–37.
22 See, for example, Moore, *Prisoners of War*, pp. 50–53.
23 Hautecler, *Évasions réussies*, p. 37.
24 The ship was the RMS Empress of Canada, part of Operation Gauntlet, whose mission was to destroy the fuel stocks on Spitzbergen and evacuate the local population. RMS Empress of Canada arrived off Arkhangelsk on the night of 26–27 August and disembarked the Russian nationals from Barentsburg, before collecting 186 escapee 'French' soldiers who had been interned by the Russians. The ship returned to Spitzbergen to collect 800 Norwegian nationals before sailing back to the United Kingdom. The ship was subsequently sunk by an Italian submarine off the West African coast on 13 March 1943. See, Operation Gauntlet, https://www.canadiansoldiers.com/history/operations/operationgauntlet.htm [4 August 2023].
25 Hautecler, *Évasions réussies*, pp. 37–42. Like the escapers and evaders who came via the Iberian Peninsula, all non-British nationals arriving in the United Kingdom were first sent to the Royal Patriotic School in Wandsworth, London to be interrogated by MI5.
26 While in the United Kingdom, André Depienne married an Englishwoman, Amy Chelsom, in 1943 and decided to stay in the country after the war, becoming a naturalised British subject in 1949 and settling in Hertfordshire. He died, aged 89, in Brighton in 2008.
27 MRAB, Fonds Georges Hautecler, 59/43, Rapports sur les évadés. Minam-Borier was arrested at the end of the war and spent years in jail. She was able to move to Belgium, where she was helped by the State.
28 MRAB, Fonds Georges Hautecler, 59/43. This group was aided by the French mission in Budapest and was given a commission by Charles de Gaulle as a Free French unit on 9 December 1944, presumably to protect its members from reprisals as *francs-tireurs*.
29 Rens et al. (eds), Évasions, pp. 47–51.

8 The Price of Failure

Flight and Capture

Thus far, the focus has been almost exclusively on successful escapes and evasions, but it is also important to reflect on the failures and the very real risks that individuals took in order to free themselves from captivity. While not always known or understood at the time, the penalties for escape and evasion became increasingly draconian as the war progressed.

To begin with civilian evasions from Belgium after the occupation began, it is unclear how many Belgians attempted to leave the country after it had been occupied, although the overall numbers probably remained quite small. Nevertheless, there were important changes in the public mood. In 1940, when France had surrendered and the British Empire was the only remaining, but apparently powerless, belligerent, it seemed that the German victory had been overwhelming, but by the summer of 1942 the entry of both the Soviet Union and the United States into the war, coupled with the British military successes in North Africa, had changed the picture considerably. At home, economic conditions worsened during 1941 and into 1942 but pivotal was the German introduction of conscription for work in Germany for all men aged 18–50 and women 21–35 in the autumn of 1942. Announced suddenly by the *Militärverwaltung* (military administration) on 6 October, this had echoes in popular memory of the mass deportations that had taken place during the Great War, and more than any other factor 'mobilized popular hatred against the occupying forces and their Belgian allies'.[1] Most of this anger was manifest in increasing levels of public non-co-operation and opposition, and a commensurate increase in the numbers of *réfractaires*, and of men and women joining organised resistance groups.[2] While curbing the growth of internal resistance became a headache for the German security forces, stopping individuals leaving the country was also seen as a priority and helps explain the harsh treatment meted out to former soldiers and civilians for trying to leave Belgium and attempting to cross international frontiers. This reached its zenith when General Falkenhausen reportedly went as far as decreeing that anyone leaving Belgium with the intention of joining the Allies ran the risk of being sentenced to death.[3]

A few examples will have to suffice here. Fernand-Alexandre Duquenne was a 25-year-old who lived in Courcelles and had served in the Belgian Army in 1940 as a *sous-lieutenant* with the 1st Company of the 6th *Chasseurs à Pied*. He had still

DOI: 10.4324/9780429027697-9

been in the country when the surrender took place and had not attempted to flee but had also not apparently been interned. He fled towards France on 3 July 1942 but was arrested the following day at Montchanin, close to the line of demarcation between the occupied and Vichy zones of France. Like many other evaders and fugitives, he fell foul of the increased surveillance and security close to this internal border and spent several months in a variety of prisons (Chalon-sur-Saône, Dijon, Fort d'Hauteville) before being sent to KZ Dachau on 23 November 1942 where he survived until the end of the war, returning to Belgium only on 17 May 1945.[4]

Maurits Erauw was a career soldier from Bruges. Twenty years old when the war broke out, he had been undergoing pilot training at an aviation school in France when the surrender came. Ostensibly he was able to return home and only decided to try to join the Allied forces in late 1943. Leaving home on 7 September with Andre Firlefyn, the two men took an early train from Brussels to Paris and arrived that same afternoon. Checking in to the Hotel de Berne, they stayed until 11 September before taking a train to Bordeaux where they arrived the following morning. Setting off to reach Pau, they were apparently betrayed to the Gestapo at Arthez (Basses-Pyrénées) by a certain Clauwaerts and arrested. Taken to Germany, they spent the remaining eighteen months of the war as forced labourers, helping build V1 and V2 rockets before they escaped from an SS column on 30 April 1945 and reached the American lines four days later.[5] Erauw subsequently continued his career with the Belgian Air Force as a *sous-lieutenant*, but for reasons that are not entirely clear, he was initially refused a *Croix des Évadés* (Escapees' Cross) in spite of the fact that his comrade Firlefyn, whose trajectory was identical, had already received one. It was only granted after he specifically asked for his case to be re-examined.[6] There is no indication as to why he was so keen to receive the award, but his persistence appears to have paid off with a handwritten 'oui' appearing on his form and dated eleven days after his letter to the President of the Commission.

A similar fate befell Marcel Dupuis, a trader from Ronse/Renaix. Too young to have been in the armed forces (he was 16 years old at the time of the invasion), he had nonetheless fled southwards in 1940 and was in France on 28 May and had presumably returned home soon afterwards. He claimed to have been a member of a resistance organisation and had attempted to escape in January 1942, ostensibly to join the Allied cause. Caught near Bayonne trying to cross into Spain, he was held by the Germans at their Maison Blanche prison in Biarritz before being sent to Germany and condemned to three years forced labour by a *Volksgericht* in Breslau.[7] He subsequently spent a considerable portion of his sentence in KZ Gross-Rosen before the liberation.[8]

Others were even more unfortunate. Robert Thelen left his home in Eupen-Malmedy on 1 February 1943 with the intention of joining the Belgian forces in England. Around 23 February, he was arrested by the Spanish Civil Guard trying to cross the Pyrenean frontier and handed back to the Germans in France. He spent some time in the prison at Perpignan before being sent to KZ Mauthausen. His family received one communication from him there on 1 May 1944, but subsequently there was silence. One of his fellow inmates recalled him being allocated to an underground factory and it was reported by third parties that he had died from pneumonia.[9]

There were also some evaders who failed to survive the experience of being on the run. The 42-year-old Evariste Erculiste was older than most evaders and said farewell to his wife in La Bouverie on 2 February 1943 with the intention of reaching England. It is not clear if he travelled alone or as part of an organised group, but his journey to Spain took only seven days. Once there, his group was betrayed by the wife of a Civil Guard and the men were arrested and imprisoned at Figueras. According to his wife's later testimony, his poor treatment in prison, with insufficient food, no blankets and sleeping on concrete, meant that although he did manage to reach England in April of the same year and joined the Belgian forces there, he died some three months later.[10] Given that his story comes entirely from third-party testimony, there is no sure way to know if it was his treatment in Spain or some other medical condition that caused his untimely demise, but there is no doubt that the journey and long-term incarceration in inhospitable prisons could take their toll on even the fittest of men.

Rawa Ruska

At the beginning of 1942, Wehrmacht estimates suggested that there were up to 30,000 prisoners of war at large inside the Reich or in Reich-controlled areas, having either escaped from Oflags or Stalags or absconded from their places of work. This was perceived as a major internal security risk and prompted the RSHA to issue a circular 42/Sü/9 873, which threatened prisoners with removal from the protections of the Geneva Convention if they used civilian clothes and false documents to aid their enterprises. This was indeed the point where escaping was deemed 'no longer a sport'.[11]

In response to the increasing numbers of French and Belgian prisoners absconding or escaping from *Arbeitskommando* inside Germany and the manpower costs involved in recapturing them, the Wehrmacht finally lost patience and announced on 21 March 1942 that Stalag 325 at Rawa Ruska in Galicia would be used as a punishment camp for repeat offenders. A memoir from Lieutenant-Colonel H. Borck, the man in overall charge of these special camps, paints a chilling picture of their purpose:

> I was blamed for the unsanitary state of the buildings (of the stables), the lack of water, the excessive brutality. In times of war, only efficiency counts. Rawa Ruska will remain my work. I claim the credit for its creation and if I had had time to complete it no Frenchman would have come out alive. I had received secret orders from Himmler to annihilate all French terrorists. Galicia was to serve as a tomb for the bad seeds of the Stalags.[12]

This site had originally been a Russian cavalry barracks, but its 36 hectares had been adapted for use as a compound for Red Army prisoners taken during Operation Barbarossa. The first Western Europeans arrived there on 13 April 1942 from Stalag XII-A (Limburg) to find the camp being 'sanitised' by squads of young Jews and other deportees because the site had previously been used to imprison Red

Army prisoners who had suffered from typhus and then been worked to death or killed outright by the SS.[13]

A number of prisoners recorded their experiences of travelling to the camp. Roger Heine, who had escaped from Stalag XVII-B (Krems-Gneixendorf), was recaptured in Luxembourg after three days on the run. After a week at Stalag XII-D (Trier) and another at XII-A (Limburg), he was on the first convoy to Rawa Ruska that left in late March.

> Approximate duration: six days and six nights. I left handicapped at the beginning, like most of my comrades because I no longer owned anything and I had experienced 15 painful days before departure: minimum German diet, dungeon, vexations, shaving of all hair, beating... Usual transport in cattle cars, tightly packed, doors locked. Food at the outset: half a loaf of bread per person, 5 to 6 centimetres of sausage. I remember that a Flemish comrade, a career sergeant, ate the whole thing on the same day. We had not been warned that it was the ration for 6 days. Very painful journey: only one exit from the wagons during the journey, practically nothing to drink. A small tin can was used as a latrine. The contents, thrown through a small-screened skylight, partly came back to us inside the wagon. We were cold, especially at night (March), we were hungry, we were thirsty, and it stank. I preferred to stay constipated. It was not difficult.[14]

Paul Roser recounted his journey to the International Military Tribunal in January 1946.

> It was following another attempt to escape that I, with about two thousand other Frenchmen, was taken to Poland. I was at Limburg an der Lahn, Stalag 12A, where we were regrouped and placed in cars, railway cars. We were stripped of our clothes, of our shoes, and of all the food which some of us had been able to keep. We were placed in cars where the number varied from 53 to 56. The trip lasted six days. The cars were open generally for a few minutes in the course of a stop in the countryside. In six days we were given soup on two occasions only, once at Oppeln when the soup was not edible, and another time at Jaroslaw. We remained for thirty-six hours without anything to drink in the course of that trip, as we had no receptacles with us and it was impossible to get a supply of water.[15]

Léon Hertay, having arrived in Rawa Ruska in July 1942, noted that 'the trip to Galicia lasted 5 days. Meanwhile, we remained locked up, at 82 per wagon, in cattle cars, without food and water, urinating in a tin can'.

Gaston Soit had very similar experiences:

> I was part of a convoy from Arnoldsweiler to Rawa-Ruska, 1,500 French and Belgian prisoners of war recaptured after escape, suspected of escape, refusal of work, etc. The trip lasted 6 days. We were crammed at 60 or 45 per wagon,

depending on their capacity, nailed wagons, padlocked doors, no water, no food, no hygiene. We arrived in Rawa-Ruska in the first half of May. There were already Belgians in the camp at that time. The *homme de confiance* was Théo Arnould, who was part of the first convoy of Belgians, probably arrived at the end of March 1942.[16]

As did Roger d'Abrassart:

> We set off for the famous punishment camp of Rawa Ruska. Sixty men per wagon, 2,000 kilometres, seven days on the train. The dormers of the wagons are barricaded with barbed wire and very closely monitored. Despite this, the sentries discovered ornate holes in the wagons. They enter like furious lunatics and search everyone. Result: suppression of food and water for 2 days for the wagon and the threat of death for anyone found in possession of a knife. Four prisoners of war from the wagon will be shot if new holes are found. After a week by train: arrival in Rawa Ruska. Exhausted by thirst, cold, deprivation, we take possession of our new domain, a kingdom of fleas, lice and bedbugs.[17]

They had, in the testimony of one of the prisoners, 'arrived in another world', while another described it thus: 'For us it is the end of the world, we have just, it seems to us, completed our last journey. We just have to cross the border of the beyond'.[18] While the vast majority of the men sent to this camp were French nationals, there were also 311 Belgian soldiers and NCOs – all apparently recidivist escapers.[19]

A collective memoir of the camp describes it in more detail:

> The climate of the region is continental: cold in winter (five months of temperatures –25/–35 degrees and very hot in the summer. The camp is surrounded by numerous swamps and quagmires and infested by mosquitoes: typhus, typhoid, diphtheria, bacillary dysentery and choleric diarrhoea are endemic. On rainy days or when the snow melts, the camp was no more than a vast quagmire […].[20]

> The camp blocks were built on a sandy plain and the pathways between the blocks were not completed. There was a triple network of barbed wire surrounding the camp with watchtowers a short distance from each other, equipped with 2 searchlights and machine guns.[21]

Roger Heine, who arrived with the first cohort, described his arrival in the camp.

> The region of Rawa-Ruska looks a bit like the plain of Beverlo: In the middle of this plain, a very compact city, guarded by the military. There were 10,000 Jews of all nationalities there. All these Jews lived crammed together very miserably. All of them were skinny, pale, carried the Jewish star on their arms and watched us go by... Our camp was 1 kilometre from this city. To the north, to the south, everywhere sand, a little grass: landscape of desolation... We entered, in

an empty camp, we were the first. Not entirely, however, because the Germans had been kind enough to tell us that Russian prisoners had been there before and that very few had survived, typhus having destroyed most of them.[22]

Reports also claimed that the prisoners had to clean the camp themselves.

> The first thing they were forced to do after their arrival in the camp was to take the numerous bodies of the last Russian prisoners exterminated there outside the camp, under the eyes and blows of the SS stationed there.[23]
>
> Thus, as soon as they arrived in Rawa-Ruska, the men of the first convoy had to clear the premises of a pile of rubbish and in particular clothes soiled with blood. Afterwards, we learned that the Germans, in order to empty the camp for our benefit, had machine-gunned the Russian prisoners who had survived famine and exanthematic typhus.[24]
>
> In the buildings, there were bloody traces on the walls and floor that showed, if it were necessary, the cruelties suffered by our predecessors. The floor, the walls and the boards were infested by a multitude (millions) of fleas, lice: and bedbugs. There were no hygiene measures at all, not even disinfection, and of course, no heating.[25]

Accommodation was primitive. Roger Heine recalled that 'the accommodation consisted of 4 barracks [each of which] contained up to 600 men. We were stacked on the 3-storey low-flanks with about 35 to 40 centimetres for each of us', and Gaston Siot spoke of the first prisoners 'crammed into one of the blocks and stables. They had neither sleeping bags nor, until July 1942, blankets. Some slept on the clay'.[26]

The food provided by the camp authorities was insufficient in both quantity and quality. The daily 'soup' occasionally contained millet or cabbage leaves. Bread distribution was sporadic, and 1-kilo loaves had to be shared between thirty to thirty-five men, this meagre ration was sometimes supplemented by morsels of synthetic fats, margarine or rotten beets. In his memoirs of captivity, Francis Ambrière recounts the story of a carthorse that 'disappeared' and was butchered by the prisoners while its owner was absent.[27]

Léon Hertay described the first days and weeks:

> When, extraordinarily, we received a little tea or soup, our sabots or tiles lined with clay served as containers. We made soup with grass... After 5 to 6 weeks, we each had a tin can with a capacity of about one litre that served as a bowl... After 2 months of irregular supplies, we received a more consistent ration of about a litre of very clear soup, 3 potatoes and a piece of bread.[28]

Heine had much the same recollections:

> Menu of the day when the supplies have arrived. In the morning a ladle of juice; around 2pm, a ladle of hot water with millet, a seventh of bread, a

teaspoon of jam or a few grams of fat, two or three potatoes. Usually, the seventh of bread was replaced by a potato. Needless to say, no shortfalls were compensated. After a few days, it was impossible to find a nettle or chicory inside the camp.[29]

Another prisoner, Célestin Lavabre, a French inmate, went as far as to write the following:

> The daily food ration was more or less the same as the one served in concentration camps. It can be checked at the Auschwitz Museum (where the daily ration of a prisoner is on display) and even sometimes less, due to the isolated location of the camp and the difficulties of supplying it. At lunch, distribution of a litre of soup, very liquid, was received often only after a long queue, especially when the camp was overcrowded. This broth was prepared with millet, cabbage, leaves of all sorts, cereals and sometimes sauerkraut. Unfortunately, this was very acidic and almost unbearable. Stocked in barrels, there was not enough water to clean it and remove the salt. It was poured as such into the pots. It was a collective purge. The last ones had not been served before the first were already fighting for the toilets for an express evacuation. Of course, an already deficient digestive system took it hard, especially the intestine. [...] In the evening, the most substantial meal was served: bread. A rectangular loaf of two kilos supposed to be for six was shared in 8, 10, 12 rations... once even 30 portions![30]

Whereas in most Stalags, prisoners could rely on Red Cross or personal parcels to offset shortages in the camp food, these were deliberately withheld in Rawa Ruska. Heine recorded that he did not receive any ICRC or personal parcels while he was in the camp and explained what happened.

> Individual packages sent to prisoners by their families were stored until the end of June 1942. As a result, many foodstuffs were spoiled and became unfit for consumption. The German examiners could not hand over the cans to the prisoners. The latter were only entitled to their contents. The Germans took the opportunity to pour into the parcels the contents of all the canned goods of the package. This created an impossible mixture (for example, sardines and apricots etc.) but obliged the prisoners to eat the food immediately.[31]

While the food supply situation was undoubtedly precarious, it was the scarcity of water, and of drinkable water, that was critical. Hertay and Heine told very similar stories.

> For many months [there was only] a single tap, no bigger than a kitchen faucet, that was used to supply the whole camp with water (in July 1942, there were 15,000 of us). The water flowed only from 10am to 12 and from 2pm until 4pm. We lined up from 3am.

Every day, a feeble water tap gave us its benefits for an hour. Still, it was not necessary to be too far up the line to be able to enjoy it. At first, [...] I had a chance every 2 days, but when the camp size increased to 10,000, it was impossible. Only the less weakened were still trying their luck.[32]

To make matters worse, when the Germans discovered what they thought was an attempted escape, they cut off the water supply altogether for forty-eight hours. Conditions were designed to be harsh with primitive accommodation, minimal food and only one tap to serve as many as 15,000 inmates. This latter feature was supposedly explained by the presence of mass graves in the vicinity but also helped to explain Churchill's description as the 'camp of a drop of water and a slow death'.[33]

The lack of water to drink, let alone to wash, meant that hygiene conditions were perforce also desperate.

Thanks to the scarcity of water and our weakness, lice and fleas flourished in a terrifying way and became the worst of the camp's plagues. The buildings had [...] disinfection rooms but, due to the lack of water, they could not be used. The Germans, fearing that they themselves would be invaded by vermin or, worse, by a typhus epidemic, brought a shower facility, but its capacity was too small for the camp's large population [and] prisoners could not pass through regularly. The Germans also used a disinfection installation on the railway in order to disinfect the clothes.[34]

It became clear that the camp had not been disinfected after the Russians had been killed or evacuated and before the French and Belgians had arrived. The few medicines that could be found by French doctors on arrival in Rawa Ruska came from the Russians' stocks and included some aspirin pills and other medicaments, but nothing to combat typhus.[35] Overall, it was later estimated that conditions in the camp were so bad that each man lost between 15kg and 20kg in weight during his first month in the camp.[36]

The poor sanitary arrangements and almost non-existent medical facilities meant that the inmates were at the mercy of all manner of diseases. Many had also been robbed of their additional clothing when deported from the Reich, which made them susceptible to the vagaries of the climate. 'Almost all the men were barefoot in wooden clogs or clappers and were dressed in rags. They had no vessels to eat and drink, no utensils to help themselves, no spoons, no knives, no razors, no toiletries'.[37]

In mid-June, there were the first signs of changes in the camp. Its existence had been made known through a broadcast on the BBC and there was pressure to allow delegates of the ICRC access to the camp. The German authorities attempted to improve conditions in the camp, seemingly unwilling to admit to subjecting Western prisoners to the same appalling treatment afforded to Soviet captives. Nonetheless, despite the changes recorded by the inmates, such as the provisions of new blankets, the ICRC found a total of thirty-six violations of the Convention.[38]

1. Uninhabitable stables for prisoners; under no circumstances should they be used in winter since they have no light, heating, water, latrines and are full of vermin.
2. A block without electricity.
3. Sidewalls less comfortable than ordinary berths.
4. Lack of blankets.
5. Deplorable state of clothing, in the camp and in the (labour) detachments: lack of underwear, trousers, greatcoats, shoes.
6. Pullovers, body linen, personal shoes removed from German camps, without "receipts", therefore impossible to recover.
7. Insufficient food, according to the prisoners, mainly due to the fact that Red Cross consignments are rare; in particular insufficient food for the workers.
8. Bowls removed. A large number of prisoners do not know where to put their food.
9. Poor hygiene, premises not disinfected, vermin.
10. Rare, irregular showers.
11. Undrinkable water; a single hydrant for the whole camp. Which is clearly insufficient; water scarcity breeds vermin.
12. The soap given exclusively to the infirmary, to the kitchen and to the stores since 10 June 1942.
13. Too many members of the medical personnel idle in the camp.
14. The infirmary is deprived of light from 9.15pm, while the kitchen remains fully illuminated.
15. Precarious general state of health, given the insufficiency of food; cases of vitamin deficiency.
16. Impossible to X-ray the sick. Cases to be X-rayed have to wait a very long time to be seen.
17. Instruments available to doctors, non-existent; drugs rare.
18. Severe cases in Rawa Ruska Civil Hospital, despite good care, are not well fed at all.
19. Virtually non-existent dental service, the dentist has only a few instruments.
20. Contagious barracks too small.
21. The doctors would like to go out with the health personnel.
22. Searches imposed on doctors are carried out without regard to their rank.
23. The "DU" (*dienstunfähig*, unfit for service) stay in the camp without there being any question of repatriating them.
24. Physicians and health personnel received neither pay nor salary.
25. Detachments without priests.
26. Lack of games, sporting goods, musical instruments.

27. People from Lorraine and Alsace are not authorised to receive parcels from Lorraine or Alsace.
28. Certain items, such as shoes, sneakers, slippers, underwear, khaki shirts removed from individual packages.
29. Insufficient food in labour detachments.
30. Some NCOs should be in Frontstalag 169.
31. Salaries not yet distributed, nowhere. No money at camp.
32. Absence of canteen.
33. Numerous cases of brutality: the process of hitting recalcitrant prisoners with weapons is admitted by the Camp Commander.
34. The *homme de confiance* (French and Belgian) would like to visit the working detachments in the company of a chaplain, these detachments being lost far away and only in the hands of the sentries.
35. Finally, the prisoners tell us about the conditions in which they were assembled before being sent to Rawa Ruska, as well as the circumstances of their journeys: the assembly centres were: Düren, Ludwigsburg and Limburg. The prisoners were grouped together in small quarters, notably in barracks stables. They were authorised to leave these premises for a quarter of an hour only in the morning and in the evening, for two weeks. The toilets were overflowing; various acts of brutality, etc. During the trip, crammed in groups of 40 to 80 in the wagons, sometimes without eating for 36 hours, for 4 to 6 days, impossibility of sleeping in the wagons.
36. In conclusion, the French *homme de confiance* expresses the following wishes:

Before winter, prisoners falling into the following categories should be returned to Germany:

a) Prisoners who were sent to Rawa Ruska without any reason.
b) Medical personnel who came to Rawa Ruska only to accompany the convoys but who have been retained there.
c) North Africans, because of the climate.
d) Prisoners who escaped before 1 April 1942, the date fixed by the Oberkommando der Wehrmacht, it seems, for sending them to Rawa Ruska; the cases are numerous.
e) Prisoners who had only escaped once, since prisoners destined for Frontstalag 325 must be repeat offenders.[39]

By August 1942, there was a total cohort of 13,033 (overwhelmingly French) prisoners in the camp, a mixture of recaptured escapees, those who were suspected of treason (sabotage) or who had refused to work.[40] While it was noted that the variety of individual prisoners in the camp meant that there was no real overall solidarity, groups did form based on geographical origins, temperaments or social origins.

Four 'social classes' emerged; the 'aristocracy', the 'turbulent and dirty class of manual workers', the 'refractories' and the 'foreigners', the latter being those men who stayed only a few days before being allocated to an *Arbeitskommando*. There were also references to other 'mafias': the kitchen mafia, the police mafia, the theatre mafia, the infirmary mafia, the post office, the university mafia, the camp administration mafia. That said, the horrendous conditions did not stifle all cultural activities, and there were sporting events at weekends, a theatre, a library and even some news – gleaned by men from German newspapers while being taken to and from work.[41]

The regime in the camp remained unlike anything in a 'normal' prisoner of war camp. Prisoners were subjected to roll calls that lasted for hours, and to extensive searches of barracks that meant they might be outside for between six and seventeen hours – shirtless in summer and with only jackets in winter. As the kitchen staff were not exempt from searching, on those days the food was not prepared. In the event of an escape attempt, collective punishments were applied: mails and parcels were withheld, as was the distribution of water. Prisoners had to move in tight rows or carry heavy stones. During these exercises they were subjected to kicks or blows from rifle butts or bayonets. Nevertheless, Paul Roser claimed that there were more than 500 such attempts in the space of six months.[42]

It appears that the Belgians in the camp were visited only once by their own protecting agency, the DSLP – and then only by its head, Count Jacques t'Serclaes de Wommersom, who arrived on 7 October 1942. He reported that there were 117 of his countrymen in the camp, and a further forty-seven at *Arbeitskommando* Stryg and thirty-seven at Tarnopol. These included not only escapers and repeat escapers among the prisoners, but also some accused of thefts. The Belgian *homme de confiance* Arnould was quoted as saying that the diet had much improved and that the mails had returned to normal, i.e. each prisoner had two letters and three cards per month, as well as two labels to send to the families and which had to be affixed to the package intended for the prisoner. Parcel deliveries were also normal from the end of June 1942. That said, the report nonetheless commented on the unfinished nature of the camp and the shortages of water.[43] This may seem even more anodyne than the earlier Red Cross account of the camp but reflects the fact that all DSLP reports were heavily vetted by the Wehrmacht and other German authorities. Even then, t'Serclaes de Wommersom was clear that the conditions in Rawa Ruska were worse than anywhere else and bore no comparison with other prisoner-of-war camps.

As soon as he returned to Berlin, and in agreement with the ICRC, he demanded the evacuation of this camp. To some extent, he may have been pushing at an open door, as by this stage the Germans were trying to recover as much manpower as possible, so the French and Belgians were sent back to different Stalags in German territory. For their part, the Germans had inflicted a six-month punishment on the recidivist French and Belgian prisoners, but pragmatism now demanded they be returned to more productive work inside the Reich. Faced with the possibility of large-scale loss of life over the winter if the prisoners were kept in these conditions when temperatures might well be –20°C degrees, the Wehrmacht authorities decided on expediency rather than continuing the level of punishment envisaged at the outset.[44] The first transport left the camp on 6 October 1942 and a complete evacuation was decreed early in 1943, but some of the prisoners were sent to Lemberg, which became the central camp for Stalag 325, and non-commissioned officers who refused to work were sent to Stalag 369 (Kobierzyn).[45]

At the time of the ICRC visit in August 1942, only 3,243 French and 113 Belgians were actually present in the camp while the remainder had been sent out to *Arbeitskommando* in the region.[46] Conditions in the forty-one *Kommandos* attached to the camp were equally stringent. Tarnopol had been established in June 1942 and was described by one inmate as a 'real prison' in comparison with its base camp, where the men were continually searched and bullied and were constantly threatened with machine guns and revolvers.[47] In this *Kommando*, like many of the others attached to Rawa Ruska, the food provided was insufficient and men could be found eating grass in order to supplement whatever rations they were given.[48] The men were often employed in laying railway tracks under the supervision of Polish or Ukrainian policemen, with the latter reportedly surpassing their German masters in brutality and terror. At Lemberg the employment was in carrying out earthworks and levelling the runway of an airfield.[49]

The distribution of French and an indeterminate number of Belgian prisoners across the many *Arbeitskommando* also meant that they gained some first-hand experience of the exterminatory policies being carried out by the Nazis in Ukraine.[50] Rawa Ruska was not far from Belzec, and Jewish populations were cleared from many towns while the French and Belgian prisoners were there – for example in Tarnopol. The men also encountered Jews deported from other countries while working in labour detachments in the region. Thus, for example, Roger d'Abrassart recorded that the prisoners at Lemberg were 'very close to the Jews'.[51] Even more compelling was the story told to the DSLP representatives about events on 14 March 1943 near Kobierzyn.

> Following an attack on the military commander of Krakow, 5,000 Polish Jews from the ghetto were taken away in trucks and were driven along the road in front of the camp. This convoy, which included both women and children, was directed to a nearby quarry where the occupants of the trucks were apparently to be shot. Some tried to escape in front of the camp: pursued by motorcyclists, they were killed and women were also among the victims. The bodies were left on the ground for three hours. A German vehicle arrived and an officer finished off the wounded. The rest of the Jews in the convoy were shot. [...] The following day an order was issued forbidding the prisoners from talking about what they had seen.[52]

More testimonies were recorded after the war. A French prisoner interned at Rawa Ruska wrote the following:

> We all witnessed the massacre of Jews, especially during the 'Aktion'. At the front of the camp, we saw the killing of a Jewish child in the arms of his mother. The child was taken by an Ukrainian policeman by the feet and had

his skull crushed on the rocks. Then, they killed the mother on the body of her child. [...] The Ukrainians were terrorising French escapees and cruel punishment was promised to those who fell into their hands.[53]

Despite the dangers, escape attempts continued to be made from Rawa Ruska and the satellite camps, even though the chances of success were small. Perhaps the most spectacular success was that of the Frenchman Jean-Marc Frébour, who managed to reach Sweden by finding his way to a Baltic port and stealing a German military patrol boat, but in addition to the French escapers there were at least five Belgians who attempted to regain their freedom. Louis Karthaus escaped from the main camp on 14 July 1942 and found his way to Romania where he was interned, and Henri Dervaux had similar intentions on 1 September but, 'devoid of maps and a compass', he got lost in the Carpathian Mountains. Hungry and exhausted, he crossed the Hungarian border some thirteen days later.[54] Belgian escapees from satellite camps were less successful. Léon Leroy left the *Arbeitskommando* Trembowla on 20 July 1942 and set out for Romania but was captured by Ukrainian civilians as he attempted to swim across the Dniester river. They handed him over to the Ukrainian border guards who returned him to Rawa Ruska on 26 July. Likewise in October, Léon Beckers and Antoine Denoel absconded from *Arbeitskommando* 2026 (Demblin), but because they were in uniform they were rapidly arrested by the Ukrainian police and returned to the *Kommando*.[55] There were other French escapees who also managed to reach Romania or joined local partisan brigades, but those that were caught were treated like other civilians and transported to KZ Dachau or KZ Buchenwald.[56]

While Lemberg was one of the sub-camps, conditions had been somewhat better but still more severe than those in the camps inside the Reich. In March 1943, a DSLP visit discovered forty-four Belgians in the camp, housed in two rooms, alongside an estimated 2,000 Frenchmen. The kitchen and infirmary were reportedly suitable, although probably set up just for the visit, 'but the washing facilities had defeated any attempts to make them presentable'.[57] As in Rawa Ruska, the morale of the prisoners remained excellent. The recidivist escapers were all determined to try it again.[58] Six of them escaped a few days before the visit of the DSLP despite the reinforced surveillance: one guard for five prisoners. Those who escaped often found help and refuge among the Polish population. There is no indication of how many were successful, but there were reports of men making it back to Belgium, only to be later denounced and returned to captivity. To make escapes more difficult, the Germans wanted to put the Belgians in old blue French uniforms. The *homme de confiance* protested and, by citing the Geneva Convention, managed to have this decision revoked.[59] After being there for six months, the remaining corporals and soldiers were sent back to a *Kommando* in Germany. Non-commissioned officers, on the other hand, had to sign a commitment to work, but all refused. Sources suggest that the last Belgians were evacuated from the camp sometime in September 1943.[60]

When the main camp was closed in November 1942, many inmates were transferred back to various Stalags in Germany. This imperative had also prompted the

Germans to have NCOs included in the prisoner labour force. While not required to work under the terms of the Geneva Convention, pressure was increased from the winter of 1941, with those who refused being threatened with a 'special camp' at Kobierzyn in Poland. As we have seen, small numbers of Belgians were included among the francophone victims of this policy. While this was also intended as a punishment camp and the conditions were initially primitive and the food supply minimal, over time this was ameliorated to the point where the men had many of the activities common in other camps. With the Red Army advancing westwards, the camp was closed on 12 August 1944 and the remaining inmates transported to other Stalags inside the Reich, Block I to Sandbostel, Block II to Sagan and Block III to Markt Pongau.[61]

The Belgian escapees and refractories sent to the punishment camp at Rawa Ruska suffered the same privations as their more numerous French counterparts, with initial living conditions not markedly different from those of a concentration camp. However, the regime did improve over time once the camp's existence had become known to the wider world. This attempt at retaliation for the huge numbers of prisoner escapes from camps and *Arbeitskommando* inside the Reich somewhat backfired on the Germans as they were forced to ameliorate conditions – and ultimately sent most of the inmates back to 'normal' camps to augment labour requirements there. Hautecler also suggests that there was a further downside for the Germans in that by concentrating all the recaptured escapees and refractories in one camp they had increased the spirit of resistance which was then spread to other camps.[62]

Not all serial escapers were sent to Rawa Ruska. Denis Rolin was a sergeant-pilot in the Belgian Air Force in September 1939. In May 1940, he was shot down by a Messerschmitt and captured by the German army. Sent to Stalag II-C, he escaped from an *Arbeitskommando* at the beginning of 1942 and ended up in Berlin. There, he was caught by a guard in the train and sent back to Stalag II-C, where he was sentenced to ten days in a cell. In September 1942, he escaped again but was immediately caught and transferred to Bürg, a [punishment] *Strafkommando*. Again he attempted to go back to Belgium but was spotted by Hitlerjugend members and brought back. In September 1943, another escape saw him reach Berlin. However, in the German capital, his ginger-haired companion was spotted by a soldier who caught the pair saying *"Du bist ein Tommy!"* Rolin was sentenced to three months in a cell and transferred to yet another punishment *Kommando*. Life was hard:

A slice of bread per day, soup once per week, on Wednesday a light meal. Forbidden to read, a walk of half-an-hour per day, forbidden to talk, we are ten metres from one another. Being forbidden from reading is the most difficult. The friends in the prison who serve the soup asked if I needed anything. I answered that reading is essential, anything! The next time, they gave me a book *Assimil* to learn Spanish. The next day, I began my lessons. The guy in the next cell told me that I was rehearsing! In fact, I was dreaming in Spanish![63]

The stories of the evaders from Belgium show that there were inherent, and some-times fatal, risks involved. If not killed in the attempt, those captured seem to have been ultimately consigned to the concentration camp system, where survival was by no means guaranteed. Even those who made it over neutral frontiers could not be sure of safety, as border patrols and local authorities were permitted under in-ternational law to return illegal entrants. Thus in both Spain and Switzerland there are instances of French and Belgian fugitives being handed back to the Germans, although this became less commonplace as the tide of war turned against the Third Reich.

For the serial escapers among the prisoners of war, the price of being recaptured was initially a return to guarded camps and periods of solitary confinement. As the numbers of escapees continued to rise, especially as more and more men were allo-cated to *Arbeitskommando*, increasing amounts of German manpower, in the form of police, auxiliary police, border guards and other agencies, had to be deployed to track them down. This unwanted burden gave rise to the idea of a punishment camp whose known existence would supposedly act as a deterrent. Even if Rawa Ruska never achieved the murderous intent of its commanding officer, conditions there were very much worse than anything experienced in conventional Oflags, Stalags and *Arbeitskommando*. The testimonies indicate that conditions there, and in its satellite camps, were designed to be primitive and very different from the standard demanded by the Geneva Convention. That said, the experiment seems to have backfired. Knowledge of the camp seems to have made little or no difference to the number of escapes inside the Reich, and corralling recidivists in Rawa Ruska did not deter them from making further attempts. Moreover, when knowledge of the camp's existence reached the outside world and was ostensibly highlighted by no less a person than Winston Churchill, the Germans could only acquiesce to allowing visits by representatives of the ICRC and making at least token gestures towards improving conditions.

This failure to create an adequate deterrent and its exposure to the international community probably explains why most inmates were moved to other camps in Galicia or sent back to Germany. While most of the camp's inmates were French, at least 311 Belgians were held in the camp at one time or another. Most suffered severe privations and some certainly died as a result, but there were plenty who sur-vived to give testimony to their experiences. For both the Belgians and the French, Rawa Ruska became synonymous with German barbarity in the treatment of its prisoners of war.

Notes

1 Conway, *Collaboration in Belgium*, pp. 158, 164–166.
2 See, Pieter Lagrou, 'Belgium', in: Bob Moore (ed.), *Resistance in Western Europe,* (Ox-ford: Berg, 2000), pp. 27–63.
3 AGR, Ministère de Justice : dossiers relatifs à l'octroi de la Croix des Évadés, 1940–1945, file 1049, Note by Robert Gillon (President of the Senate), regarding the career of Officer Cadet Marcel Erdmer, 9 May 1944.

4   AGR, Ministère de Justice : dossiers relatifs à l'octroi de la Croix des Évadés, 1940–1945, file 1011.

5   AGR, Ministère de Justice : dossier relatifs à l'octroi de la Croix des Évadés, 1940–1945, file 1047. This was probably at Mittelwerk-Dora, not far from KZ Dachau.

6   AGR, Ministère de Justice : dossiers relatifs à l'octroi de la Croix des Évadés, 1940–1945, Erauw to President of the Commission on Croix des Évadés, 10 October 1948.

7   The Maison Blanche was located at 6, Allée Dominique Morin and was used to house suspected *passeurs* as well as fugitives of many nationalities attempting to cross into Spain.

8   AGR, Ministère de Justice : dossiers relatifs à l'octroi de la Croix des Évadés, 1940–1945, file 1013.

9   Archives de l'État à Liège, État-civil de l'arrondissement de Verviers, file 1921. This testimony was recorded after his family began legal proceedings to have him declared dead in August 1948.

10 AGR, Ministère de Justice : dossiers relatifs à l'octroi de la Croix des Évadés, 1940–1945, file 1048.

11 Luca Clément, *Rawa-Ruska, camp d'extermination à l'Est, préface du colonel Rémy*, (Marseille: Amicale des anciens de Rawa, 1983). Laurent Barcello, 'Itinéraires de "résistants-prisonniers" : ceux de Rawa-Ruska', in: Robert Vandenbussche (ed.), *L'Engagement dans la Résistance (France du Nord – Belgique)*, (Villeneuve d'Ascq: Publications de l'Institut de recherches historiques du Septentrion, 2003), p. 191.

12 *Le Prisonnier de guerre*, January 1974 cited in: Gillet, 'Histoire', RBHM, Vol. 28, No. 5, p. 364. Letter from Lieutenant-Colonel H. Borck to Procurer-General, Nuremberg, 25 September 1946 (five days after his sentencing), http://memoiredeguerre.free.fr/rawa/confession.htm [12 January 2023].

13 *L'Humanité*, 20 April 2012, claims that they were also involved in removing the bodies of dead Russians. Laurent Barcelo, 'Rawa-Ruska : Camp de la goutte d'eau et de la mort lente', in: *Guerres mondiales et conflits contemporains*, Nos. 202–3 (2001–2), pp. 155–164, suggests that 18,000 Red Army soldiers were killed or died there before April 1942, p. 156. Moore, *Prisoners of War*, pp. 83–84. On the precise date the camp opened see Hautecler, Évasions réussies, pp. 231–232.

14 MRAB, Fonds Georges Hautecler, 59/43, Rapports sur les évadés.

15 *Trial of German Major War Criminals: Proceedings of the International Military Tribunal Sitting at Nuremberg, Germany* (IMT), Vol. 5, p. 242. 29 January 1946.

16 MRAB, Fonds Georges Hautecler, 59/43, Rapports sur les évadés.

17 MRAB, Fonds Georges Hautecler, 59/43, Rapports sur les évadés.

18 Barcello, 'Itinéraires', p. 192 cites Roger Maire, *Ceux de Rawa-Ruska*, (Aude, 1995), p. 16, and Lucien Mertens and Jean Poindessault, *Rawa-Ruska, le camp de représailles des prisonniers de guerre évadés*, (Bagneux: Cep, 1945), p. 24.

19 MRAB, Fonds Georges Hautecler, 59/43, Rapports sur les évadés.

20 Maire, 'Ceux de Rawa-Ruska' cited in: Gillet, 'Histoire', p. 364.

21 MRAB, Fonds Georges Hautecler, 59/43, Rapports sur les évadés.

22 MRAB, Fonds Georges Hautecler, 59/43, Rapports sur les évadés.

23 'Ceux de Rawa Ruska' cited in: Gillet, 'Histoire', RBHM, Vol. 28, No. 5, pp. 364–365.

24 MRAB, Fonds Georges Hautecler, 59/43, Rapports sur les évadés.

25 'Ceux de Rawa Ruska' cited in: Gillet, 'Histoire', RBHM, Vol. 28, No. 5, pp. 364–365.

26 MRAB, Fonds Georges Hautecler, 59/43, Rapports sur les évadés.

27 Francis Ambrière, *The Long Holiday*, (Chicago: Ziff-Davies, 1948), p. 194. Ambrière was the pen name of Charles Letellier, who won the Prix Goncourt for this book and was later the editor of the *Guides Bleus*.

28 MRAB, Fonds Georges Hautecler, 59/43, Rapports sur les évadés.

29 MRAB, Fonds Georges Hautecler, 59/43, Rapports sur les évadés.

30 Célestin Lavabre, *Ceux de l'an 40*, (Rodez: Supervie, 1981), p. 214.

31 MRAB, Fonds Georges Hautecler, 59/43, Rapports sur les évadés.

32 MRAB, Fonds Georges Hautecler, 59/43, Rapports sur les évadés.
33 Barcelo, 'Rawa-Ruska'. Barcelo attributes the quotation to Churchill but without a precise reference. Elsewhere it is claimed that Churchill used the description in a BBC radio broadcast in 1942.
34 MRAB, Fonds Georges Hautecler, 59/43, Rapports sur les évadés.
35 MRAB, Fonds Georges Hautecler, 59/43, Rapports sur les évadés.
36 Lavabre, *Ceux de l'an 40*, p. 316.
37 Le Stalag 325 de Rawa, https://rawa-ruska-union-nationale.fr/index.php/histoire-memoire-5-description/ [11 March 2022].
38 Barcelo, 'Rawa-Ruska', pp. 159, 161.
39 La Croix-Rouge et Rawa-Ruska, https://rawa-ruska-union-nationale.fr/index.php/la-croix-rouge-et-rawa-ruska/ [11 March 2022].
40 *Pierre Gascar, Histoire de* la captivité des Français en Allemagne (1939–1945), (Paris: Gallimard, 1967), p. 40. Historique du camp de Rawa Ruska, http://www.rawa-ruska.net/historique-du-camp-de-rawa-ruska-1 [21 January 2019]. Moore, *Prisoners of War*, p. 83.
41 MRAB, Fonds Georges Hautecler, 59/43, Rapports sur les évadés.
42 MRAB, Fonds Georges Hautecler, 59/43, Rapports sur les évadés. IMT, Vol. 5, p. 242, 29 January 1946.
43 Gillet, 'Histoire', RBHM, Vol. 28, No. 5, p. 366.
44 Barcelo, 'Rawa-Ruska', p. 161.
45 Gillet, 'Histoire', RBHM, Vol. 28, No. 5, p. 367. MRAB, Fonds Georges Hautecler, 59/43, Rapports sur les évadés.
46 Durand, *La Captivité*, p. 175. Moore, *Prisoners of War*, p. 84.
47 Durand, *La Captivité*, p. 180.
48 Barcelo, 'Rawa-Ruska', p. 162.
49 MRAB, Fonds Georges Hautecler, 59/43, Rapports sur les évadés.
50 Gascar, *Histoire*, pp. 229–242.
51 MRAB, Fonds Georges Hautecler, 59/43, Rapports sur les évadés.
52 Gillet, 'Histoire', RBHM, Vol. 28, No. 5, p. 367.
53 Jérôme Guérin, *Rawa-Ruska : camp de représailles*, (Marseille: Oris, 1945), p. 81.
54 Hautecler, *Évasions réussies*, p. 244. The account gives the date of 13 September 1943, implying that he was on the run for more than a year, but this seems unlikely.
55 MRAB, Fonds Georges Hautecler, 59/43, Rapports sur les évadés.
56 Barcello, 'Itinéraires', p. 192.
57 Gillet, 'Histoire', RBHM, Vol. 28, No. 5, p. 367.
58 Gillet, 'Histoire', RBHM, Vol. 28, No. 5, p. 367.
59 Gillet, 'Histoire', RBHM, Vol. 28, No. 5, p. 367.
60 MRAB, Fonds Georges Hautecler, 59/43, Rapports sur les évadés.
61 Moore, *Prisoners of War*, p. 85. Le stalag 369 ou le camp de représailles de Kobierzyn, https://prisonniers-de-guerre.fr/le-stalag-369-ou-le-camp-de-represailles-de-kobierzyn/ [15 March 2022].
62 MRAB, Fonds Georges Hautecler, 59/43, Rapports sur les évadés.
63 Rens et al. (eds), *Évasions*, p. 228.

Epilogue
Memory and Recognition

An Association and Several Battles

When the First World War came to an end, the Belgian soldiers and civilians who had escaped the occupied territories or the German camps had no specific honour to display for their unique bravery. A civilian such as Herman Destexhe, who had crossed the Dutch border to enlist in the Belgian army, was rewarded with a war cross, a medal most often given on the frontline for bravery. While prestigious, this award did not reflect the fact that he had faced considerable dangers in crossing the electrified border fencing and escaped the vigilance of German patrols.[1] In fact, soldiers who had become prisoners of war were completely ignored by the Belgian government and there was no specific award or medal to mark their ordeal. Only Belgian civilians who met precise criteria were awarded the *Médaille du prisonnier politique 1914–1918*. Even then, only 5,000 were distributed despite the fact that more than 18,000 civilians had been deported to Germany.[2] The lack of interest displayed by the Belgian authorities did not prevent those who had escaped from German prisons to form an association in 1928. The *Union nationale des Évadés de Guerre (UNEG) – Nationaal Verbond der Oorlogsontvluchten* was founded as a local branch of the French association bearing the same name and grouped together all Belgian nationals without linguistic distinction. Its missions were described in the *Nation belge*:

> The association is forbidden from any political action. Its goal is to regroup all Belgians and allied subjects who answer the following criteria, to keep their spirit, to publish their bravery, to honour their memory, to help its members materially and morally, and to study the legal claims of those who have escaped during the war.[3]

Little is known of the association's activities, aside from the fact that to be a member it was a requirement to 'have escaped from Germany as a war prisoner or as a civilian having escaped the occupied territory in order to join the army'.[4] Its president was Colonel (later General) Jules Bastin, an officer wounded and captured on 16 August 1914 who had subsequently escaped and managed to reach the Belgian lines to carry on the fight against Germany.[5] Through the national press,

DOI: 10.4324/9780429027697-10

it was revealed that the association met on an annual basis in Brussels or Liège to discuss topics such as the creation of an Escapees' Cross.[6] It can be assumed that the war prisoners wanted to have their own award because the French had had a *Médaille des Évadés* since 1925, but the debate was never even mentioned in the press and the award never materialised. In the interwar period, there were so many competing war charities that most passed completely unnoticed, and the escapees as a group were very few in number.

The situation changed drastically during the later stages of the Second World War. On 25 February 1944, the Belgian Government of London decided to create the Escapees' Cross.[7] What had been a matter of debate for years in the interwar period became a reality overnight. Even then, it did not include First World War veterans but only to those who:

a) Had left the country occupied by the enemy,
b) Had during the war an attitude that demonstrated their patriotic feelings,

They also needed to meet one of the following criteria:

a) Membership of an espionage movement in occupied territories,
b) Had, for patriotic reasons, been in captivity for at least three months,
c) Had travelled illegally to fight for Belgium during the War.[8]

The law was poorly worded and was amended as early as 14 July 1944 to state that 'those who had faced grave danger by leaving a non-occupied region to carry on the fight against the enemy could also obtain the Escapees' Cross'.[9] During the conflict, this new medal was awarded primarily to Belgian soldiers and civilians serving in Britain, including numerous pilots serving in the Royal Air Force. Dozens were given posthumously to aviators or agents killed in action. Unsurprisingly, prisoners of war who had escaped from Germany or Poland and had gone home were unable to apply while Belgium remained occupied. At the end of the war, the Belgian newspapers announced that the Ministry of Justice would resume its work to reward those deserving the medal.[10] From 1945 to 1950, thousands of individuals contacted the Ministry in order to be granted the Escapees' Cross. Criteria were strictly reviewed by a specially created awarding panel and several requests were turned down. As successful applications usually required witnesses or German documents, these conditions were not always easy to fulfil since escaping was more than often done alone. On 22 December 1950, a ministerial decree was published to explain that by 'grave danger', the previous decree of 14 July 1944 meant:

a) Having left Dunkirk between 28 May and 2 June 1940,
b) Having left France before 1 November 1940,
c) Having left North Africa before 1 November 1940.[11]

At the end of 1951, the Ministry of Justice announced that it would soon cease to investigate new applications for the medal.[12] This announcement triggered a further influx of requests, but the Government issued a new law on 19 February 1954 which made it impossible to award the Escapees' Cross in the foreseeable future, and it seems that the last medals were awarded on 7 June 1954.[13] This distinction was one of the rarest ever created by the Belgian Kingdom. A total of 4,927 crosses were awarded between 1944 and 1954, making it a respected and coveted symbol, one systematically mentioned in an obituary or when worn at an official ceremony. However, the strict criteria and the limited timeframe to apply meant that numerous escapees were unable to get an award that they were undoubtedly entitled to.

The Escapees' Cross was not the only element of frustration among this group of veterans in post-war Belgium. Other distinctions were also supposed to be awarded to those who had successfully escaped from German camps or who had tried and failed. Officers who had managed to reach England or the Congo and who had subsequently fought for the Allied cause were entitled to the Knight's Cross of the Order of Leopold with palm and the War Cross with palm, while NCOs and soldiers were to receive the *décoration militaire de 2e classe (article 4)* and the War Cross with palm. The officers who had attempted to escape at least five times were also entitled to the Knight's Cross of the Order of Leopold, but NCOs and soldiers in the same situation were not entitled to any official recognition. This blatant form of

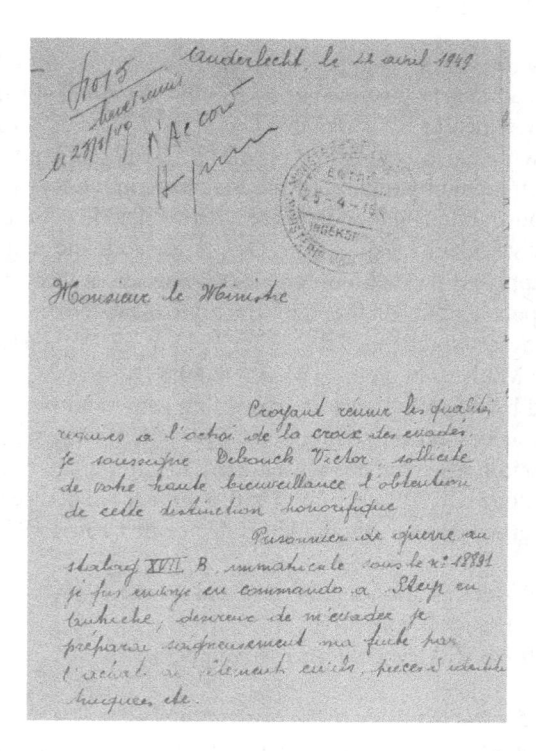

Figure 9.1 A request to obtain the Escapees' Cross (@Archives de l'État en Belgique)

discrimination was denounced by the *Fédération nationale des anciens prisonniers de guerre* in its newspaper *Le Prisonnier de guerre*:

> This proves that in the DN (National Defence), the escaped P.G. (war prisoners) were not appreciated. However, a few memories come to mind and we see the personal sacrifice of a few friends, such as lieutenant W. R., shot in cold blood in the barbed wire of his Oflag while escaping. Or soldier D... escaping at 5 in the morning on the bicycle of a German officer, sleeping that night at the kommando, and miraculously returning home without stopping, crossing the Rhine on a bridge at Koblenz, while the workers were going in the other direction. [...] Have we measured the risks taken for them and their families when the guards knew they would be sent to the eastern front? Have we seen at the M.D.N. (Ministry of National Defence) that poster stating 'to escape is no longer a sport' and which stated that they would be shot on sight?[14]

Meanwhile, the UNEG continued its mission. In 1940 and 1941, the escapees from the previous conflict had continued to gather illegally and had even provided services to the resistance. A parallel organisation, the *Amicale des Évadés de guerre de Belgique*, founded in 1943 in London, was merged at the end of the Second World War with the UNEG. A new generation of escapees was thus amalgamating with the veterans of 1914–1918, a positive outcome for the association, which became far more powerful than in the past, as highlighted by one of its board members:

> Several of us think that we need to take advantage of the fact that a big association, grouping the war escapees with those of 14–18 with the aim of maintaining a high patriotic spirit, which has always been the definition of those who did not want to passively accept enemy tyranny, is the way to work.[15]

The leadership was given to Robert Fourmanoit, who had escaped with the ship Atlas V from Liège to the Netherlands in January 1917. The post-war UNEG remained a local branch under the supervision of the French UNEG. Its president, Xavier Bracquart, reaffirmed the main mission:

> Born out of a long tradition of reciprocal esteem and mutual respect, confirmed by being constantly close in our efforts and thoughts, baptised by the terrible trials and the greatest sacrifices of the two wars, the brotherly friendship which unify the Belgian and French escapees has matured during its long development and has acquired strength that only confraternity in combat and the same ideal of liberty in honour and duty can give.[16]

In 1947, the UNEG launched a campaign to request the creation of an official *Statut de l'Évadé*, a form of recognition allowing those who had escaped the occupied territories or the German camps to be formally acknowledged by Belgium. The Government was wary of such demands as it opened the door for financial compensations, something that was perceived as a dangerous path to follow because, at the time, most escapees were still young men and the State might have to pay pensions for decades to come.[17] UNEG argued that several of its members had been refused the Escapees' Cross or had waited too long to apply and that another form of recognition was fundamental. The organisation also brought forward the fact that political prisoners were not included in the criteria for the Escapees' Cross, a cruel mistake considering that it was far more difficult to escape from concentration camps than a Stalag or an Oflag.[18] For decades, the UNEG fought this battle. A first proposal was made by senators Jean Allard, René George and Robert De Man on 6 March 1951 and was passed on 19 December 1951 but was stalled at the *Chambre des Représentants* by the Minister of National Defence, who claimed that the project would cost 35,000,000 francs.[19] This remained the situation until 1975, when a concerted campaign launched jointly by patriotic associations, former *réfractaire* workers, the civilian victims and the war veterans finally paid off. On 11 March 1975, the title of évadé de la guerre de 1940–1945 was created by royal decree and and would be considered if the applicant had:

> ... in the six months after the end of the evasion, resumed a patriotic activity recognized by a national status, or having fought in an allied army. This delay is extended for the duration of a hospitalisation if the person has been wounded during his captivity or escape.[20]

A board of three former escapees was formed to examine applications, which were then officially agreed by the Ministry of National Defence.[21] As expected, requests for financial benefits were immediately introduced by those formally recognised as escapees. In 1975, a fund of 150,000,000 francs was allocated to those who had contributed to the war effort, and a further 300,000,000 francs were also to be distributed in subsequent years. Of course, the money was supposed to be divided between various categories of war victims and veterans, and not just escaped soldiers and civilians. In 1976, it was suggested that a lump sum could be offered to former escapees, of whom 3,000 were then still alive.[22]

This new status had the potential to help a specific category of escapees who had been thus far excluded from consideration. After the war, 300 men who had successfully fled German prisons and had lived underground without taking part in the resistance had been denied both the prisoner's and the combatant's pensions.[23] The UNEG also saw in the reforms of 1975 the opportunity to request the resurrection of a committee with the power to award the Escapees' Cross to those who had been ignored between 1944 and 1955 but had been recognised as évadés by the recent *Statut*. This effort failed and the holders of the *statut de l'évadé* were to wait another twenty-six years, until 2001, before having the chance to apply for the distinction. The association also argued in favour of its First World War veterans and requested the *Croix des Évadés* for them. Despite this demand, the Escapees' Cross was never awarded for attempted escapes in the First World War.[24]

The deaths of the last First World War escapees in the 1970s and the retirement of most Second World War veterans during the next decade meant that the profile of the UNEG changed drastically. In the 1980s, 2,500 people had at one point been registered as members of the UNEG but several had since passed away.[25] This diminishing power did not prevent the UNEG from fighting other battles. Helped by the *Conseil supérieur des invalides de guerre, anciens combattants et victimes de guerre*, founded in 1981, they carried on the fight for medals and distinctions.[26] Surprisingly, the law of 19 February 1954 closing the applications for the Escapees' Cross was superseded by a new law voted on 19 April 2001.[27] The then Minister of Defence André Flahaut had finally addressed the demands made by the *Conseil supérieur des invalides de guerre, anciens combattants et victimes de guerre*, but if a few more medals were awarded, it was too late for many others. By 2001, only 427 members were still registered with the UNEG.[28] Nevertheless, another fight was finally won in 2005 when the same *Conseil supérieur des invalides de guerre, anciens combattants et victimes de guerre* convinced the Defence Minister to modify the royal decree of 11 March 1975 on the *statut des évadés* and awarded the War Cross 1940–1945 with palm, the Resistance Medal and the Military Decoration first class to the escapees of 1940–1945 who had fought in Britain, Congo, in an allied army or in the resistance for at least a year.[29] However, by then only a handful of escapees were still alive.

Remembering

The UNEG was not only an association aimed at defending veterans' rights. It also fought several battles to promote the memory of its members and to create a cultural bond between former escapees and the broader society. A newspaper named *L'Évadé* was founded in January 1949. J. Denoel, a member of the board and a First World War veteran, wrote in the first issue the following statement:

> Our association was born after the war of 14–18 as the expression of the need to be united and to defend an ideal that had kept us alive and had made us act, something that the mercantile spirit of the interwar period had threatened. [...] With the help of all the escapees, the elders from 14–18 and the new ones of 40–45, our Association has resumed its activity, has raised its flag. We will carry on, as we did in the past, to make great the idea that made us act, the idea for which we happily sacrificed so much. We can say without modesty that among the best of the country's servants, we were the best. Maybe this could give us rights, it is certain that it gave us duties.[30]

The determination shown here was clear but from the start the newspaper was under threat from the costs of production. On several occasions, the paper asked its readers to support the publication by sending 25 francs or by finding sponsors:

> Try to find sponsors and if you have a business, ask for our advertising cost by writing to the management of the newspaper at 56 rue Victor Lefèvre in Brussels and sign a contract. Without the subscriptions paid by members of

the UNEG, the newspaper cannot survive. Support us so we can stay free of any outside influence! Help us![31]

Despite this desperate call, the association failed in its mission to keep the newspaper alive for more than a few years. *L'Évadé* ceased to exist sometime during the 1950s after only a few issues.[32]

UNEG organised a yearly meeting from the end of the Second World War until the beginning of the 2000s, and cooperation with the French and international escapees' associations was also very important. The UNEG archives clearly show that the Belgians travelled not only to France but also to the Netherlands to present their activities and share old memories. On various occasions, speeches highlighting friendship were read at public events, such as this one by Xavier Bracquart, president of the French UNEG:

> [...] In captivity, where the fortunes of war had thrown them, these Belgian and French soldiers, driven by the same courage and the same patriotism, refused spontaneously to believe that their duty had ended. Putting in common their intelligence, the same spirit of enterprise and an equal taste for risk, they managed to get free of their chains and recover their freedom, prepare and plan the most dangerous escapes, driven by the burning desire to resume their place in the fight.

In 1970, they also worked with the Belgian army to create a sporting event named *Challenge de l'évadé* (the escapee's challenge), a competition held once a year in a different part of the country.[33] This physically demanding challenge, 42 kilometres on foot, was repeatedly won by elite units of the Para-Commando. By the 1980s, it was held bi-annually and survived until 2012, when it took place for the twentieth time.[34]

The creation of a newspaper named *Dedalos* in 1985 as a spiritual successor to the ephemeral *L'Évadé*, which had disappeared in the 1950s, proved that the UNEG was still a dynamic association. The first three issues of this new publication were sent for free to the 2,282 people who held the status of évadé and were still alive, a way to reach those who were not members of the UNEG. Subsequently it was decided by the board that the fourth *Dedalos* would be posted to paying members only.[35] Its content was mostly made up of stories of daring escapes, summaries of the board's annual meeting, book reviews and obituaries. The question of a national monument was also debated by its editors. As early as 12 July 1945, a first memorial had been inaugurated in Gibraltar bearing the following inscription:

> This stone is dedicated by Belgium to the fortress and garrison of Gibraltar in deep acknowledgement for the warm understanding with which during the years 1940–1944, it welcomed Belgium from occupied Europe on road to serve the allied fight for freedom.[36]

Figure 9.2 The Escapees' monument today in Brussels (Private collection of the author)

Elsewhere inside Belgium there were, here and there, plaques to commemorate in-dividual actions but nothing in the capital city.[37] As time took its toll on its member-ship, UNEG felt the need to press for a new national monument. This took the form of a giant V representing victory breaking the chains of submission and bearing the crown of heroism, and was finally accepted by the authorities and inaugurated in Uc-cle on 20 September 2001 by Princess Astrid and the Minister of National Defence.[38]

The editors of *Dedalos* celebrated both this new monument and the revisions made to the award of the Escapees' Cross that had occurred in the same year, but henceforward it and UNEG were destined to decline as their membership dwin-dled. While it is uncertain exactly when *Dedalos* ceased publication, the last copies conserved at CegeSoma come from 2008, and the archival record suggests that UNEG was probably disbanded during or soon after 2009.

Notes

1 MRAB, Personal file of Herman Destexhe.
2 Andre Borné, *Distinctions honorifiques de la Belgique : 1830–1985*, (Brussels: Creadif, 1985), p. 417.
3 *La Nation belge*, 3 October 1928.

4 *La Libre Belgique*, 22 May 1937.
5 CEGES/SOMA, Archives de l'UNEG, Report on the association's history, 1970.
6 *Le Vingtième Siècle*, 2 March 1937.
7 *Le Moniteur belge*, 25 March 1944.
8 Borné, *Distinctions honorifiques de la Belgique*, p. 440.
9 *Le Moniteur belge*, 21 August 1944.
10 *Le Soir*, 9 November 1945.
11 Borné, *Distinctions honorifiques de la Belgique*, p. 442.
12 *Le Soir*, 11 October 1951.
13 *Le Soir*, 17 July 1953.
14 *Le Prisonnier de guerre*, March 1971.
15 CEGES/SOMA, Archives de l'UNEG, Report to Colonel Kestens, 7 November 1949.
16 CEGES/SOMA, Archives de l'UNEG, Report on the association's history, 1970.
17 CEGES/SOMA, Archives de l'UNEG, Report on the association's history, 1970.
18 CEGES/SOMA, Archives de l'UNEG, Report on the Statut de l'évadé, 1976.
19 *L'Évadé*, November 1952.
20 CEGES/SOMA, Archives de l'UNEG, Report on the Statut de l'évadé, 1975.
21 CEGES/SOMA, Archives de l'UNEG, Report on the *rente de l'évadé*, 1978.
22 CEGES/SOMA, Archives de l'UNEG, Report on the *rente de l'évadé*, 1976.
23 CEGES/SOMA, Archives de l'UNEG, Report on the *Statut*, 1976.
24 CEGES/SOMA, Archives de l'UNEG, Report on the Statut, not dated.
25 CEGES/SOMA, Archives de l'UNEG, Report on the Union, 1982.
26 *Le Moniteur belge*, 8 September 1981.
27 *Le Moniteur belge*, 1 June 2001.
28 *La Libre Belgique*, 5 September 2001.
29 *Le Moniteur belge*, 21 February 2005.
30 *L'Évadé*, January 1949.
31 *L'Évadé*, December 1950.
32 The latest found in the archives was n° 14 issued in November 1955.
33 CEGES/SOMA, Archives de l'UNEG, Report on the escapee's challenge, 1977.
34 *La Dernière Heure*, 19 avril 2012.
35 CEGES/SOMA, Archives de l'UNEG, Board report, 1985.
36 Rens et al. (eds), Évasions, p. 11.
37 There is still for example a marble plaque remembering the daring escape of three resistant fighters from the Citadel of Liège.
38 *La Libre Belgique*, 6 September 2001.

Bibliography

Primary sources

Archives

Belgium

Archives de l'État en Belgique, CEGES/SOMA (CEGES/SOMA),
  Archives de l'Union nationale des Évadés de Guerre (UNEG).
  Manuscript of Edouard Cuvelier, Villégiature en Espagne.
Archives de l'État à Liège (AEL), État-civil de Verviers, dossiers de soldats allemands décédés et de civils tués durant le conflit.
Archives Générales du Royaume (AGR), Ministre de la justice : dossiers relatifs à l'octroi de la Croix des Évadés, 1940–1945.
Musée Royal de l'Armée belge (MRAB),
  Fonds Georges Hautecler.
  Soldiers' files, Herman Destexhe.

Britain

House of Commons Debate 04 June 1940, vol. 361, cc. 789.
House of Lords by Viscount Caldecote, House of Lords, Debate 04 June 1940, vol. 116, cc. 455–462.
The National Archives,
  208/3675/5.
  HO334/330/7845.
  KV2/1720.
  KV2/3854.
  KV2/53.
  PCOM9/940.
  PCOM9/1044.
  WO203/3676.
  WO208/3675/5.
  WO208/3676.
The private papers of André Depienne, in the care of Lynda Depienne.

Newspapers

Boston Globe, 15 April 2004.
La Dernière Heure, 19 April 2012.
L'Évadé, January 1949, March 1950, December 1950, November 1952.
L'Humanité, 20 April 2012.
Le Journal des combattants, 5 June 1966.
London Gazette, 10 March 1953.
Meldungen aus dem Reich, No. 27, 11 December 1939; No. 44, 24 January 1940; No. 47, 31 January 1940.
Mensuel de l'Amicale des Anciens Prisonniers de Guerre de Stalag XIIIB (Weiden), n° 203, 1970; n° 251, 1975; n° 301, 1979; n° 317, 1980.
La Libre Belgique, 22 May 1937, 5 September 2001, 6 September 2001.
Le Moniteur belge, 25 March 1944, 21 August 1944, 8 September 1981, 1 June 2001, 21 February 2005.
La Nation belge, 3 October 1928.
Le Prisonnier de guerre, March 1971, January 1974.
Le Soir, 9 November 1945, 11 October 1951, 17 July 1953.
The Times, 24 June 1944.
Le Vingtième Siècle, 2 March 1937.

Internet

Les amis de la section Marine du Musée royal de l'Armée et d'Histoire militaire, http://www.marine-mra-klm.be/georges_ragaert__dsc__1920___2008__848.htm [17 January 2019].
La Croix-Rouge et Rawa-Ruska, https://rawa-ruska-union-nationale.fr/index.php/la-croix-rouge-et-rawa-ruska/ [11 March 2022].
Historique du camp de Rawa Ruska, http://www.rawa-ruska.net/historique-du-camp-de-rawa-ruska-1 [21 January 2019].
Letter from Lieutenant-Colonel H. Borck to Procurer-General, Nuremberg, 25 September 1946, http://memoiredeguerre.free.fr/rawa/confession.htm [12 January 2023].
Operation Gauntlet, https://www.canadiansoldiers.com/history/operations/operationgauntlet.htm [4 August 2023].
Le récit de Jacques Wanty, http://www.francaislibres.net/pages/page.php?id=236 [24 January 2023].
The Royal Navy "Section Belge", http://www.be4046.eu/RNSB.htm [17 January 2019].
Le Stalag 325 de Rawa, https://rawa-ruska-union-nationale.fr/index.php/histoire-memoire-5-description/ [11 March 2022].
Le stalag 369 ou le camp de représailles de Kobierzyn, https://prisonniers-de-guerre.fr/le-stalag-369-ou-le-camp-de-represailles-de-kobierzyn/ [15 March 2022].
Testimony of Georges Rovillard, Forchies-la-Marche, 22 August 2011, http://nouvellesduprogres.skynetblogs.be/archive/2011/12/09/sur-les-prisonniers-de-guerre-1940-1945-de-forchies.html [6 August 2015].
Unnamed testimony, 28 December 2014, http://gege6220.skyrock.com/451931930-Les-prisonniers-de-guerre-belges.html [6 August 2015].
Les Vieilles Tiges, Roger Malengrau, http://www.vieillestiges.be/nl/bio/16; Henry Gonay, http://www.vieillestiges.be/nl/bio/13; Paul J.N. Evard, http://www.vieillestiges.be/nl/bio/11 [all 18 January 2019].

Printed

Doc Adam, *S'évader mort ou vif*, (Brussels : Collet, 1986).

Francis Ambrière, *The Long Holiday*, (Chicago: Ziff-Davies, 1948).

René Autphenne, *Les Chasseurs ardennais à Bodange,* (Bruxelles: Office du Livre, n.d.).

Belgian Ministry of Foreign Affairs (BMFA), *Belgium: The Official Account of What Happened, 1939–1940*, (London: Evans Brothers, 1941).

Vic Bodson, *La Croix des évadés*, (Harlue: De la terre à la plume, 1987).

Charles Burdick and Hans-Adolf Jacobsen (eds), *The Halder War Diary 1939–1942*, (London: Greenhill, 1988).

Luca Clément, *Rawa-Ruska, camp d'extermination à l'Est, préface du colonel Rémy*, (Marseille: Amicale des anciens de Rawa, 1983).

Willy Coppens de Houthulst, *Hélices en croix*, (Genève: Éditions du Rhône, 1945).

David Dilks (ed.), *The Diaries of Sir Alexander Cadogan, 1938–1945*, (London: Cassell, 1971).

Jérôme Guérin, *Rawa-Ruska : camp de représailles*, (Marseille: Oris, 1945).

Hague Convention (1907) V. Convention Respecting the Rights and Duties of Neutral Powers and Persons in Case of War on Land.

Roger Jacquemin, *Le chemin de Londres : une évasion vécue*, (Brussels: La Renaissance du Livre, 1945).

Marcel Jullian, *H.M.S. Fidelity : bateau mystère; souvenirs recueillis auprès de Pat O'Leary*, (Paris: Amiot-Dumont, 1956).

Pierre Kalmar and Alphonse Fouilhoux, *Lettres à ma mère*, (Le Mont-Doré: Crébu Nigo, 2012).

Célestin Lavabre, *Ceux de l'an 40*, (Rodez: Subervie, 1981).

Louis Legrand, *Destin d'un homme*, (Brussels: L'Avenir).

Roger Maire, *Ceux de Rawa-Ruska*, (Aude, 1995).

Jean-Baptiste Piron, *Souvenirs 1913–1945*, (Brussels: La Renaissance du Livre, 1969).

Étienne Plissart, *Souvenirs de guerre*, (2001).

Jean Poindessault, *Rawa-Ruska, le camp de représailles des prisonniers de guerre évadés*, (Bagneux: Cep, 1945).

Gustave Rens, Guy Weber and Willy Deheusch (eds), *Évasions de guerre, 1940–1945*, (Braine l'Alleud: Éditions J.-M. Collet, 1995).

SD-Berichte zu Inlandsfragen, 10 June 1943, (Blaue Serie: Volkstum und Volksgesundheit).

Harry Spiller, *Prisoners of Nazis: Accounts of American POWs in World War II*, (Jefferson NC and London: McFarland).

Trial of German Major War Criminals: Proceedings of the International Military Tribunal Sitting at Nuremberg, Germany (IMT), Vol. 5, p. 242. 29 January 1946.

Jacques Wanty, *Combattre avec la Brigade Piron*, (Bruxelles: Collet, 1985).

Bernard Wilkin (ed.), *Correspondance du brigadier Armand Ghiot : prisonnier de guerre belge au Stalag IIb (1940–1945)*, (Brussels: Archives Générales du Royaume, 2018).

Secondary sources

Internet

Tom Simoens, 'Belgian Soldiers', in: Ute Daniel, Peter Gatrell, Oliver Janz, Heather Jones, Jennifer Keene, Alan Kramer and Bill Nasson (eds), *1914–1918 International Encyclopedia Online.* https://encyclopedia.1914-1918-online.net/article/belgian_soldiers [1 August 2023].

Theses

Guillaume Avalosse, Les activités de la Sûreté de l'État belge dans la péninsule ibérique, 1940–1944, (Master's Thesis, Louvain-la-Neuve University, 2022).

Léa Buchkremer, L'engagement féminin dans la Croix-Rouge de Belgique pendant la Seconde Guerre mondiale (1939–1945) : une réelle contribution à l'émancipation? (Master's Thesis, University of Louvain, 2021).

Joline Maenhout, Een Concentratiekamp op het Politiek Schaakbord van Franco, (Master's Thesis, Universiteit Gent, 2019).

Michael Wiesner, "Wer die Macht hat, hat Recht". De Belgische krijgsgevangenen in Duitsland en de Conventie van Genève, 1940–1945, (Licentiate Thesis, KU Leuven, 2005).

Articles

Roger Absalom, 'Allied Escapers and the Contadini in Occupied Italy, (1943–5)', in: *Journal of Modern Italian Studies*, Vol. 10, No. 4 (2005), pp. 413–425.

Roger Absalom, 'Hiding History: The Allies, the Resistance and Others in Occupied Italy 1943–1945', in: *Historical Journal*, Vol. 38, No. 1 (1995), pp. 111–131.

Robert W. Allen Jr., 'Britain Revives the Belgian Army, 1940–45', in: *Journal of Strategic Studies*, Vol. 21, No. 4 (1998), pp. 78–96.

Laurent Barcelo, 'Rawa-Ruska : camp de la goutte d'eau et de la mort lente', in: *Guerres mondiales et conflits contemporains*, Nos. 202–3 (2001–2), pp. 155–164.

Eddy de Bruyne, 'Le recrutement dans les stalags et des oflags en faveur de la Légion Wallonie', in: *Histomag*, No. 92, July–October (2015), pp. 62–90.

Jonas Campion, 'Être gendarme en Belgique occupée. Droits et devoirs d'une profession au regard de la répression pénale d'après-guerre (1944–1950)', in: *Journal of Belgian History*, No. 24 (2011), pp. 187–208.

Simon Catros and Bernard Wilkin, 'Sur les chemins de l'exode : les réfugiés belges dans l'Eure, 1940', in: *Histoire, économie & société : époques moderne et contemporaine*, 41st year, n° 1 (2022), pp. 57–73.

Matilde Eiroa and Concha Pallarés, 'Uncertain Fates: Allied Soldiers at the Miranda De Ebro Concentration Camp', in: *The Historian*, Vol. 76, No. 1 (2014), pp. 26–49.

Jean Fosty, 'Les Réseaux belges de France. Essai sur l'Histoire de Services de Renseignements et d'Action belges de France durant la Seconde Guerre mondiale', in: *Cahiers d'histoire de la Seconde Guerre Mondiale*, Vol. 2 (1972), pp. 79–111.

Alberto Franco (trans. Janet Reynolds), 'Victor Reynolds: Our Man in Estremoz', in: *British Historical Society of Portugal: Annual Report and Review*, Vol. 31 (2004), pp. 12–21.

Jay Howard Geller, 'The Role of Military Administration in German-occupied Belgium, 1940–1944', in: *Journal of Military History*, Vol. 63, No. 1 (1999), pp. 99–125.

E. Gillet, 'Histoire des sous-officiers et soldats belges prisonniers de guerre, 1940–1945', in: *Revue belge d'histoire militaire*, Vol. 27, No. 3 (1987), pp. 229–245.

E. Gillet, 'Histoire des sous-officiers et soldats belges prisonniers de guerre, 1940–1945', in: *Revue belge d'histoire militaire*, Vol. 27, No. 5 (1987), pp. 355–379.

E. Gillet, 'Histoire des sous-officiers et soldats belges prisonniers de guerre, 1940–1945', in: *Revue belge d'histoire militaire*, Vol. 28, No. 1 (1989), pp. 45–78.

E. Gillet, 'Histoire des sous-officiers et soldats belges prisonniers de guerre, 1940–1945', in: *Revue belge d'histoire militaire*, Vol. 28, No. 2 (1989), pp. 123–166.

E. Gillet, 'Histoire des sous-officiers et soldats belges prisonniers de guerre, 1940–1945', in: *Revue belge d'histoire militaire*, Vol. 28, No. 3 (1989), pp. 217–254.

E. Gillet, 'Histoire des sous-officiers et soldats belges prisonniers de guerre, 1940–1945', in: *Revue belge d'histoire militaire*, Vol. 28, No. 4 (1989), pp. 299–335.

E. Gillet, 'Histoire des sous-officiers et soldats belges prisonniers de guerre, 1940–1945', in: *Revue belge d'histoire militaire*, Vol. 28, No. 5 (1990), pp. 351–382.

Georges Hautecler, 'Statistiques au sujet des évasions réussies de prisonniers de guerre belges en 1940–1945', in: *Revue belge d'histoire militaire*, Vol. 19, No. 8 (1972).

Louis-Armand Héraut, 'Miranda de Ebro. État sanitaire du camp de concentration à l'automne 1943', in: *Histoire des Sciences Médicales*, Vol. 42, No. 2 (2008), pp. 210–213.

Sir Brian Horrocks, 'The Comet Line', in: *The Listener*, 14 January 1960, pp. 61–64.

Cédric Leloup, 'Maintenir une hiérarchie des races? La Belgique face à la question de l'africanisation des cadres de la Force publique du Congo belge (1908–1960)', in: *Journal of Belgian History*, XLV 2/3 (2015), pp. 46–79.

Alexis Neviaski, '1919–1939 : le recrutement des légionnaires allemands', in: *Guerres mondiales et conflits contemporains*, n° 1 (2010), pp. 39–61.

Prosper Vandenbroucke, 'La route de Londres', in: *HISTOMAG 39–45*, No. 65, May–June (2010), pp. 42–49.

Jean-Marc Vanderlinden, 'La réinsertion socio-professionnelle des anciens de la « Légion Wallonie ». Première approche', in: *Journal of Belgian History*, Vol. 1 (1991), pp. 203–222.

Jean-François Verbruggen, 'Le Grand Quartier Général belge et la bataille de la Lys (15–28 mai 1940)', in: *Revue du Nord*, No. 209 (1971), pp. 239–245.

Luc De Vos and Hans Keymeulen, 'Een definitieve afrekening met de 80%-mythe?' Het Belgisch Leger (1914–1918) en de sociale en numerieke taalverhoudingen onder de gesneuvelden van lagere rang', in: *Belgisch Tijdschrift voor Militaire Geschiedenis*, XXVII/8, December (1988), pp. 81–104; XXVIII/1, March (1989), pp. 589–612 and XXVIII/2, June (1989), pp. 1–37.

Bruno de Wever, 'Militaire collaboratie in België tijdens de Tweede Wereldoorlog', in: *Bijdragen en mededelingen betreffende de geschiedenis der Nederlanden*, Vol. 118, No. 1 (2003), pp. 22–40.

Book chapters

Michael Amara, 'Les grands défis de la propaganda belge durant la Première Guerre mondiale', in: Bénédicte Rochet and Axel Tixhon (eds), *La Petite Belgique dans la Grande Guerre : une icône, des images*, (Namur: Presses universitaires de Namur, 2012), pp. 21–35.

Michael Amara, 'Le retour en Belgique en 1918–1919', in: Pierre Lierneux and Natasja Peeters (eds), *Au-delà de la Grande Guerre : la Belgique 1918–1928*, (Tielt: Racine, 2018), pp. 55–60.

Laurent Barcello, 'Itinéraires de "résistants-prisonniers" : ceux de Rawa-Ruska', in: Robert Vandenbussche (ed.), *L'Engagement dans la Résistance (France du Nord – Belgique)*, (Villeneuve d'Ascq: Publications de l'Institut de recherches historiques du Septentrion, 2003), pp. 189–199.

A.J. Beirens, 'Vissen in bezette wateren', in: *Vlucht naar Penzance*, (Puurs: Uninbook, 2010).

Alain Colignon, 'Belgium: Fragile Neutrality, Solid Neutralism', in: Neville Wylie (ed.), *European Neutrals and Non-Belligerents during the Second World War*, (Cambridge: Cambridge University Press, 2002), pp. 97–117.

Jean-Pierre Decock, 'Ivan du Monceau de Bergendal', in: *De Vieilles Tiges van de Belgische luchtvaart. Gedenkboek van de Belgische luchtvaart.*

Jan T. Gross, 'Sovietisation of Poland's Eastern Territories', in: Bernd Wegner (ed.), *From Peace to War: Germany, Soviet Russia and the World, 1939–1941*, (Providence RI: Berghahn, 1997), pp. 63–78.

Pieter Lagrou, 'Belgium', in: Bob Moore (ed.), *Resistance in Western Europe*, (Oxford: Berg, 2000), pp. 27–63.

Benoît Majerus and Xavier Rousseaux, 'The World Wars and Their Impact on the Belgian Police System', in: Cyrille Fijnault (ed.), *The Impact of World War II on Policing in North West Europe*, (Leuven: Leuven University Press, 2004), pp. 43–90.

Rüdiger Overmans, 'Die Kriegsgefangenenpolitik des deutschen Reiches 1939 bis 1945', in: Jörg Echternkamp (ed.), *Das Deutsche Reich und der Zweite Weltkrieg Vol.9/2 Die Deutsche Kriegsgesellschaft 1939–1945: Ausbeutung, Deutungen, Ausgrenzung*, (München: Deutsche Verlags-Anstalt, 2005), pp. 729–875.

Rémy Porte, 'Armée belge', in: François Cochet and Rémy Porte (eds), *Dictionnaire de la Grande Guerre 1914–1918*, (Paris: Robert Laffont, 2008), p. 124.

Sophie de Schaepdrijver, 'Occupation, Propaganda and the Idea of Belgium', in: Aviel Roshwald and Richard Stites (eds), *European Culture in the Great War*, (Cambridge: Cambridge University Press, 1999), pp. 267–294.

Michael Smith, 'Britain and Belgium in the Nineteen Thirties', in: *Belgique 1940 : une société en crise, un pays en guerre*, (Brussels: Centre de Recherches et d'Études Historiques de la Seconde Guerre Mondiale, 1993), pp. 85–111.

Kenneth Steuer, 'German Propaganda and POWs during World War 1', in: Troy Paddock (ed.), *Propaganda and World War One*, (Leiden/Boston: Brill, 2011), pp. 155–180.

Luc de Vos, 'The Reconstruction of Belgian Military Forces in Britain, 1940–1945', in: Martin Conway and José Gotovitch (eds), *Europe in Exile. European Exile Communities in Britain, 1940–45*, (Oxford: Berghahn, 2001), pp. 81–90.

Maurice de Wilde, 'De Belgische Krijgsgevangenen', in Paul Louyet (ed.), *België in the Tweede Wereldoorlog. Vol. 3 De Nieuwe Orde*, (Kapellen: DNB/Peckmans, 1982), p. 102.

Books

Maartje Abbenhuis, *The Art of Staying Neutral: The Netherlands in the First World War, 1914–1918*, (Amsterdam: Amsterdam University Press, 2006).

Robert W. Allen, *Churchill's Guests: Britain and the Belgian Exiles during World War II*, (Westport CT: Praeger, 2003).

Claire Andrieu, *When Men Fell from the Sky. Civilians and Downed Airmen in Second World War Europe*, (Cambridge: Cambridge University Press, 2023).

Jean-Jacques Becker, *Dictionnaire de la Grande Guerre*, (France: André Versailles, 2008).

Luis Bernardo y Garcia, *Miranda de Ebro ou l'internement des Belges en Espagne au cours de la Seconde Guerre mondiale*, (Brussels: CEGES/SOMA, 1995).

Reinhold Billstein, Karola Fings, Anita Kugler and Nicholas Lewis, *Working for the Enemy: Ford, the General Motors, and Forced Labor in Germany*, (New York: Berghahn Books, 2004).

Georges Blond, *Histoire de la Légion étrangère 1831–1931*, (Paris: France Loisirs, 1981).

Herman Bodson, *Agent for the Resistance. A Belgian Saboteur in World War II*, (College Station TX: Texas A&M University Press, 1994).

Brian Bond, *France and Belgium, 1939–1940*, (London: Davis Poynter, 1975).

Andre Borné, *Distinctions honorifiques de la Belgique : 1830–1985*, (Brussels: Creadif, 1985).

Vincent Brome, *The Way Back*, (London: Cassell, 1957).

Donald Caskie, *The Tartan Pimpernel*, (London: Oldbourne, 1957).

Jean-Claude Catherine, *La captivité des prisonniers de guerre : histoire, art et mémoire 1939–1945*, (Rennes: Presses universitaires de Rennes, 2015).

Martin Conway, *Collaboration in Belgium. Léon Degrelle and the Rexist Movement, 1940–1944*, (New Haven CT: Yale, 1993).

Karolien Cool, *Het Leven van de Vlaamse krijgsgevangenen in Duitsland in de Eerste Wereldoorlog*, (Brussels: Algemeen Rijksarchief, 2002).

Albert Crahay, *L'Armée belge entre les deux guerres*, (Brussels: Louis Musin, 1978).

Frank Decat, *De Belgen in Engeland 40/45: de Belgian strijdkrachten in Groot-Brittannië tijdens WOII*, (Tielt: Lannoo, 2007).

Robert Devleeshouwer, *Les Belges et le danger de guerre*, (Louvain/Paris: Nauwelaerts, 1958).

Clayton Donnell, *Breaking the Fortress Line 1914*, (Barnsley: Pen and Sword, 2013).

Michel Dumoulin, *L'entrée dans le XXe siècle. Nouvelle histoire de Belgique*, (Brussels: Le Cri, 2010).

Yves Durand, *La Captivité. Histoire des prisonniers de guerre français 1939–1945*, (Paris: FNCPG, 1980).

Yves Durand, *Nouvel ordre européen nazi (1938–1945)*, (Paris: Complexe, 1990).

Lionel F. Ellis, *The War in France and Flanders 1939–1940*, (London: HMSO, 1953).

Jonathan Epstein, *Belgium's Dilemma: The Formation of the Belgian Defense Policy, 1932–1940*, (Leiden: Brill, 2014).

Edmond de Fabribeckers, *La campagne de l'Armée belge en 1940*, (Brussels: Rossel, 1978).

M.R.D. Foot and J.M. Langley, *MI9 Escape and Evasion 1939–1945*, (London: Bodley Head, 1979).

W. Gardner (ed.), *The Evacuation from Dunkirk: 'Operation Dynamo', 26 May–June 1940*, (London: Frank Cass, 2000).

Pierre Gascar, *Histoire de la captivité des Français en Allemagne (1939–1945)*, (Paris: Gallimard, 1967).

Johnny Geldof, *Royal Navy Section Belge in Focus 1940–1945*, (Heule: Verraes, 2002).

Robert Gellately, *The Gestapo and German Society: Enforcing Racial Policy, 1933–1945*, (Oxford: Clarendon, 1990).

Georges Hautecler, *Évasions réussies*, (Liège: Soledi, 1966).

Georges Hautecler, *Het Gevecht te Bodange, 10 mei 1940*, (Brussels: Ministerie van Landsverdediging, Generale Staf-Landmacht, Algemene Directie Inlichtingen, Cijferschrift en Geschiedenis, Krijgskundige Sectie, 1955).

Uli Herbert, *Hitler's Foreign Workers: Enforced Foreign Labour under the Third Reich*, (Cambridge: Cambridge University Press, 1997).

Histoire de l'armée belge : tome 2 de 1920 à nos jours, (Brussels: Centre de documentation historique des forces armées, 1988).

Jean Jamart, *L'armée belge de France en 1940*, (Bastogne: Schmitz, 1994).

Roger Keyes, *Outrageous Fortune: The Tragedy of Leopold III of the Belgians 1901–1941*, (London: Secker and Warburg, 1984).

Megan Koreman, *The Escape Line: How the Ordinary Heroes of Dutch-Paris Resisted the Nazi Occupation of Western Europe*, (Oxford: Oxford University Press, 2018).

E.H. Kossmann, *The Low Countries 1780–1940*, (Oxford: Clarendon, 1978).

Peter Longerich (ed.), *Akten der Partei-Kanzlei der NSDAP. Rekonstruktion eines verlorengegangenen Bestandes. Regesten*, Vol. 4, (Munich: K.G. Saur und R. Oldenbourg, 1992).

Simon Mackenzie, *The Colditz Myth. The Real Story of POW Life in Nazi Germany*, (Oxford: Oxford University Press, 2004).

Clare Makepeace, *Captives of War: British Prisoners of War in the Second World War*, (Cambridge: Cambridge University Press, 2017).

Edward Marriott, *Claude and Madeleine: A True Story of War, Espionage and Passion*, (London: Picador, 2005).

Lucien Mertens and Jean Poindessault, *Rawa-Ruska, le camp de représailles des prisonniers de guerre évadés*, (Bagneux: Cep, 1945).

Bob Moore, *Prisoners of War: Europe 1939–1956*, (Oxford: Oxford University Press, 2022).

Meg Ostrum, *The Surgeon and the Shepherd: Two Resistance Heroes in Vichy France*, (Lincoln NE: University of Nebraska Press, 2004).

Reinhard Otto, *Wehrmacht, Gestapo und sowjetische Kriegsgefangene im deutschen Reichsgebiet 1941/42*, (München: Oldenbourg, 1998).

Raoul Van Overstraeten, *Albert I – Léopold III : vingt ans de politique militaire belge 1920–1940*, (Bruges: Desclée de Brouwer, 1948).

Henri Pirenne, *La Belgique et la Guerre mondiale*, (Paris: Publications de la Dotation Carnegie pour la Paix Internationale, Section d'Économie et d'Histoire, 1928).

Graham Pitchfork (ed.), *Escape from Germany. True Stories of Escapes in WWII*, (London: National Archives, 2009).

J. Lee Ready, *Forgotten Allies: The Military Contribution of the Colonies, Exiled Governments, and Lesser Powers to the Allied Victory in World War II. Vol. I*, (Jefferson NC: McFarland, 1985).

Brooks Richards, *Secret Flotillas, Volume 2, Clandestine Sea Operations in the Mediterranean, North Africa and the Adriatic, 1940–1944*, (London: Frank Cass, 2004).

Margaret L. Rossiter, *Women in the Resistance*, (New York: Prager, 1986).

Sophie de Schaepdrijver, *La Belgique et la Première Guerre mondiale*, (Brussels: Peter Lang, 2006).

Rolf Schwarz and Gerhard Hoch (eds), *Verschleppt und Sklavenarbeit. Kriegsgefangene und Zwangsarbeiter in Schleswig-Holstein*, (Bremen: Geffken, 1985).

Gisela Schwarze, *Gefangen in Münster: Kriegsgefangene, Zwangsarbeiter, Zwangsarbeiterinnen 1939 bis 1945*, (Essen: Klartext, 1999).

C(ornelis) Smit, *Nederland in de Eerste Wereldoorlog (1899–1919), Tweede Deel: 1914–1917*, (Groningen: Wolters Noordhoff, 1972).

Jill Stephenson, *Hitler's Home Front: Württemberg under the Nazis*, (London: Bloomsbury Academic, 2006).

Hew Strachan, *The First World War: Volume I: To Arms*, (Oxford: Oxford University Press, 2001).

Fabien Théofilakis, *Les prisonniers de guerre français en 40*, (Paris: Fayard, 2022).

Nigel Thomas, *Foreign Volunteers of the Allied Forces, 1939–45*, (London: Osprey, 1991).

Jean Vanwelkenhuyzen, *Neutralité armée. La politique militaire de la Belgique pendant la 'Drôle de guerre'*, (Brussels: Renaissance du Livre, 1979).

Jean Vanwelkenhuyzen and Jacques Dumont, *1940 : le grand exode*, (Brussels: RTBF éditions, 1983).

Jan Velaerts and Herman van Goethals, *Leopold III: de koning, het land, de oorlog*, (Tielt: Lannoo, 2001).

Wilfried Wagner, *Belgien in der deutschen Politik während des Zweiten Weltkrieges*, (Boppard am Rhein: Boldt Verlag, 1974).

Geoffrey Wallace, *Life and Death in Captivity: The Abuse of Prisoners in War*, (Ithaca NY: Cornell, 2015).

Werner Warmbrunn, *The German Occupation of Belgium 1940–1944*, (New York: Peter Lang, 1993).

Guy Weber, *Les Belges et la Légion étrangère*, (Brussels: Louis Musin, 1984).

Nigel West, *MI5: British Security Service Operations, 1909–1945*, (New York: Stein and Day, 1982).

Bernard Wilkin, *Aerial Propaganda and the Wartime Occupation of France, 1914–1918*, (London: Routledge, 2017).

Els Witte and Jan Craeybeckx, *La Belgique politique de 1830 à nos jours : les tensions d'une démocratie bourgeoise*, (Antwerp: Labor–Nathan, 1985).

Jacques Wullus-Rudiger, *La Belgique et la crise européenne, 1914–1945. Vol. II : 1940–1945*, (Paris: Berger-Levrault, 1945).

Jacques Wullus-Rudiger, *La Défense de la Belgique en 1940*, (Villeneuve-sur-Lot: Alfred Bador, 1940).

Neville Wyle (ed.), *European Neutrals and Non-Belligerents during the Second World War*, (Cambridge: Cambridge University Press, 2002).

Neville Wylie, *Britain, Switzerland and the Second World War*, (Oxford: Oxford University Press, 2003).

Bruno Yammine, *Fake News in oorlogstijd. Duitse mediamanipulatie en de Flamenpolitik (1914–1915)*, (Leuven: Leuven University Press, 2021).

Index

Printed in the USA
CPSIA information can be obtained
at www.ICGtesting.com
LVHW011836041124
795688LV00004B/561

9 780367 136420